PENGUIN BOOKS

IROQUOIS DIPLOMACY ON THE
EARLY AMERICAN FRONTIER

Timothy J. Shannon is professor of history at Gettysburg College. He is the author of *Indians and the Colonists at the Crossroads of Empire*, as well as numerous scholarly articles.

IROQUOIS
DIPLOMACY
ON THE
EARLY
AMERICAN FRONTIER

TIMOTHY J. SHANNON

THE PENGUIN LIBRARY
OF AMERICAN INDIAN HISTORY

PENGUIN BOOKS

PENGUIN BOOKS

Published by the Penguin Group

Penguin Group (USA) Inc., 375 Hudson Street, New York, New York 10014, U.S.A.

Penguin Group (Canada), 90 Eglinton Avenue East, Suite 700, Toronto,
Ontario, Canada M4P 2Y3 (a division of Pearson Penguin Canada Inc.)

Penguin Books Ltd, 80 Strand, London WC2R 0RL, England

Penguin Ireland, 25 St Stephen's Green, Dublin 2, Ireland (a division of Penguin Books Ltd)

Penguin Group (Australia), 250 Camberwell Road, Camberwell,
Victoria 3124, Australia (a division of Pearson Australia Group Pty Ltd)

Penguin Books India Pvt Ltd, 11 Community Centre,
Panchsheel Park, New Delhi – 110 017, India

Penguin Group (NZ), 67 Apollo Drive, Rosedale, North Shore 0632,
New Zealand (a division of Pearson New Zealand Ltd)

Penguin Books (South Africa) (Pty) Ltd, 24 Sturdee Avenue,
Rosebank, Johannesburg 2196, South Africa

Penguin Books Ltd, Registered Offices: 80 Strand, London WC2R 0RL, England

First published in the United States of America by Viking Penguin,
a member of Penguin Group (USA) Inc. 2008
Published in Penguin Books 2009

1   3   5   7   9   10   8   6   4   2

THE LIBRARY OF CONGRESS HAS CATALOGED THE HARDCOVER EDITION AS FOLLOWS:
Shannon, Timothy J. (Timothy John), 1964–
Iroquois diplomacy on the early American frontier / Timothy J. Shannon.
p. cm.—(The Penguin library of American Indian history)
Includes bibliographical references and index.
ISBN 978-0-670-01897-0 (hc.)
ISBN 978-0-14-311529-8 (pbk.)
1. Iroquois Indians—Kings and rulers.   2. Iroquois Indians—Government relations.   3. Iroquois
Indians—Politics and government.   4. Diplomacy—United States.   I. Title.
E99.I7S447 2007
973.04'97—dc22   2007040434

Printed in the United States of America
Set in Granjon
Designed by Katy Riegel

For Caroline, Daniel, and Elizabeth

CONTENTS

IROQUOIS DIPLOMACY
ON THE EARLY AMERICAN
FRONTIER

PROLOGUE

FOUR KINGS AND A QUEEN

IN THE SPRING of 1710, four Indians from the Mohawk Valley arrived in London for an audience with Queen Anne. Colonel Francis Nicholson and Colonel Peter Schuyler, the colonial administrators who sponsored this trip, hoped to impress their Indian guests with the riches of Britain's capital city. Having weathered the upheavals of civil war, plague, and fire during the seventeenth century, London in 1710 was well prepared for the visit. The great symbol of the city's rebirth, St. Paul's Cathedral, towered over the skyline, while smaller churches also designed by Sir Christopher Wren anchored neighborhoods rebuilt in a neo-classical style to evoke the glories of ancient Rome. Everywhere one looked, the streets were crowded with people buying and selling goods from all over the world, while in counting houses and coffee houses, bankers and merchants cut the deals that made them rich. What Indian from the backwaters of New York, a colony that was itself on the fringe of the civilized world, could help but be impressed by the sights, sounds, and smells of a city on the cusp of world power?

A funny thing happened on the way to see the queen. The "four Indian kings," as the local press called them, became celebrities. Londoners, not the Indians, were the smitten ones. In addition to being wined and dined by leading officials of church and state, the Indian kings toured London's sights, drawing admiring crowds wherever they went: the Tower of London, St. Paul's, theaters, and cockfights. Like other foreign dignitaries, they observed the lunatics confined at Bethlehem (Bedlam) Hospital and offered alms to the poor at the city's workhouses. Theater owners published advance notices of the Indian kings' attendance at their shows, hoping their popularity would boost their crowds. On one such occasion, unruly spectators in the gallery refused to let a performance of *Macbeth* proceed until they had a better view of the four Indian kings seated in a front box. Actors calmed the crowd by placing chairs on the stage and having the guests of honor moved there. Londoners with a few pence to spare could purchase ballads, chapbooks, and engravings in the city's print shops and bookstalls detailing the Indian kings' adventures. Three artists painted their portraits, one working at the behest of the queen. By any measure, plebian or patrician, the four Indian kings had taken London by storm.[1]

We know very little about the personal backgrounds of the four Indian kings. Their sponsors, Nicholson and Schuyler, were colonial military adventurers trying to launch an expedition against French Canada. In New York, one of their chief concerns was recruiting warriors from the five Iroquois nations to assist them. The Iroquois (from east to west, the Mohawks, Oneidas, Onondagas, Cayugas, and Senecas) controlled the territory between Albany and Canada, and Nicholson and Schuyler could not expect to move an army through there without Iroquois cooperation. Plans for such an expedition had fizzled a year earlier because naval support promised by the queen's ministers had failed to materialize. Ever resourceful, Nicholson and Schuyler believed that a carefully planned visit to the royal court by a party of allied Iroquois just might convince the queen to endorse another expedition planned for the 1711 campaign season, while also impressing the Iroquois with Britain's military power and wealth.

Nicholson and Schuyler had initially planned to recruit one chief from each of the five Iroquois nations for their mission. Instead, they ended up with a much less representative sample. Three were Mohawks, the Iroquois nation closest to Albany and the one most closely allied with the British. Tee Yee Neen Ho Ga Row, also known by his Christian name Hendrick, was styled by Nicholson and Schuyler the "Emperour of the Six Nations." So Ga Yean Qua Rah Tow, also known as Brant, was identified as "King of the Maquas" (Mohawks). Oh Nee Yeath Tow No Riow, also known as John, was identified as "King of Ganajoh Hore" (Canajoharie, a Mohawk town). The fourth Indian king was not even an Iroquois. E Tow Oh Kaom, also known as Nicholas and identified by Nicholson and Schuyler as the "King of the River Indians," came from a community of Indians who lived in the northern Hudson Valley.

Of the four, we know the most about Hendrick. He was about fifty years old in 1710, and an influential figure among the Protestant Mohawks who lived near Albany. Brant and John were also Christians, but they did not appear to have any particular political authority or influence among their people. Nicholas was a war chief among the River Indians, who were mostly Mahicans pushed east of the Hudson by the Mohawks in the seventeenth century. His Christian name indicates religious conversion, but the lack of any documentation to this effect in local sources suggests that Nicholson and Schuyler may have arranged his conversion as last-minute window-dressing for his audience with the queen. Hendrick's grand title, "Emperour of the Six Nations," rings a bit hollow for a fellow who had no apparent reputation beyond the lower Mohawk Valley (the "Six" presumably refers to the five Iroquois nations plus the River Indians represented by Nicholas). Likewise, the claim of the other three to the title of "king" appears to have begun and ended with the publicity accorded to them by Nicholson and Schuyler. Whatever power these four individuals may have held over Iroquois other than their immediate neighbors remains unclear; all that we can say definitively about them is that they were four British-allied Indians with at least nominal Christian identities. One observer in New York stated bluntly that Hendrick could not "command ten Men," and that "the other three were no Sachems."[2] Had Nicholson and Schuyler been more practiced in honesty than spin, they might have billed their Indian travelers as "one local chief and his improvised entourage."[3]

There are many ways to interpret the visit of the four Indian kings to London. Anyone familiar with the habit Europeans made of turning pliable Indians into "chiefs" so that they could sign away land in fraudulent treaties might view this episode as tragedy, just another chapter in a centuries-long swindle of continental dimensions. It is worth noting, however, that the four Indian kings did not sign a treaty or sell any land while in London. Others might be inclined to describe the four Indian kings' trip as comedy, a reality-show reversal of Shakespeare's *The Tempest*, in which Indians rather than Europeans found themselves shipwrecked in a strange, magical place inhabited by inscrutable natives. London's satirists saw it as such and used the occasion to pen critiques of English manners and customs by assuming the perspective of these beleaguered and bemused foreign visitors. At least one contemporary writer preferred the conventions of romance. He composed a ballad in which one of the Indian kings fell in love with an English maiden he met in St. James's Park.[4]

Literary representations aside, the four Indian kings' visit to London was first and foremost an exercise in diplomacy. Hendrick and his compatriots were received in the royal court as foreign heads of state, and they had meetings with such prominent officials as the captain-general of the British army, the lords commissioners of the Admiralty, the Board of Trade (an advisory body on colonial administration), and the bishop of London. Observers described the Indian kings' conduct and appearance in these encounters with the same deferential superlatives typically bestowed on foreign nobility, praising their graceful carriage, quiet gravitas, and generosity toward the poor.

What purpose then did this embassy have? The motives of its chief orchestrators, Nicholson and Schuyler, were clear enough. They wanted the Indian kings and queen to impress each other, so that each side would be more willing to support their scheme for conquering Canada. One has to admire their gumption, for their plan could have backfired in all sorts of ways. What if the queen had refused an audience with these uninvited visitors? What if the Indians had proven to be less than majestic in their comportment? What if a skeptical minister in the queen's court had asked the Indians to present their credentials, as any other foreign diplomat was expected to do? In any such instance, the four kings held by Nicholson and Schuyler might have been easily exposed as a bluff.

Determining what the four Indians wanted to get out of this embassy is much harder to do. Were they dupes or partners in Nicholson's and Schuyler's poker game? The Indian kings left no record of their own purposes or impressions from their trip. One died shortly after returning to America, and two slipped quietly back into anonymity. Only Hendrick remained a significant figure in New York's Indian affairs, but if he ever offered commentary on his experiences in London, it has not survived.[5]

The only portal we have into the Indians' perspective on their trip is the speech they delivered to Queen Anne at St. James's Palace. Even this source is problematic. It was read by Major David Pigeon, an aide to Nicholson and Schuyler, while the Indians stood by in silent testimony (none of them spoke English; Abraham Schuyler, cousin to Peter, acted as their interpreter). The speech was short, and much of it reflected Nicholson's and

Peter Schuyler's agenda, asking for the queen's help in making war against "her Enemies the *French*." Some elements of the speech, however, suggest the Indians' input. The Iroquoian metaphors of taking up the hatchet and hanging up the kettle are used to describe preparing for war, and at the end of the speech, the Indians presented the queen with "Belts of *Wampum*," the traditional device used by the Iroquois to punctuate diplomatic speeches. Most significantly, the Indian kings requested that the queen send a missionary to live among them, lest their people be seduced by French priests into leaving their homes to live among other Iroquois who had converted to Catholicism and resettled in Canada.[6]

This request for a missionary would certainly have received Nicholson's and Schuyler's approval, but it is also reasonable to assume that the four Indian kings considered this the primary objective of their embassy. In the late seventeenth century, French Jesuits had converted a considerable number of Mohawks and moved them to communities around Montreal. This out-migration of kin and neighbors threatened the security and stability of those Mohawks who remained in their homelands. A Protestant missionary, sponsored by the queen herself, would be a powerful agent on their behalf, someone with the material resources and spiritual commitment necessary to counter the lure of the Jesuits and to help those Indians who remained in the Mohawk Valley. Queen Anne took their wishes seriously. She referred them to the Society for the Propagation of the Gospel (SPG), the missionary arm of the Anglican Church, which appropriated funding to pay for two missionaries and chapels among the Iroquois. The SPG also presented each king with a Bible and copy of the Book of Common Prayer. Queen Anne chipped in with two sets of silver communion plates. These handsome gifts marked the start of a relationship between the Mohawks and the SPG that would continue for several generations. In the years ahead, Anglican missionaries would assist the Mohawks in their material needs during times of want and serve as important inter-mediaries between them and the Crown's American officials.[7]

At the conclusion of the Indian kings' royal audience, Queen Anne also ordered that £200 be spent on presents for them. When the Indians departed for home several weeks later, this generous grant had been converted into goods Indians typically acquired from the North American fur trade: bolts of cloth, gunpowder and lead for ammunition, knives and kettles, scissors, razors, combs, mirrors, necklaces, and other jewelry and novelties. Each king also received a personal present that included a hat, trunk, gun, sword, pistols, and a variety of other incidentals, including a picture of the queen (no mention made of autographs) and a "Magick Lanthorn with Pictures."[8]

A magic lantern? This item was a plaything of the wealthy in the early eighteenth century, a sort of primordial television that projected images from hand-painted glass plates onto a wall or screen. We do not know whether the Indian kings ever made use of their magic lanterns for this purpose, but they were a fitting souvenir of their trip, which had been an exercise in the manipulation of appearances from start to finish. Four anonymous Indians had crossed the ocean to be feted as kings before the queen and her subjects. They came with only the clothes on their backs but left like movie stars on Oscars night, lugging gift bags overstuffed with swag. Nicholson and Schuyler may have been engaged in an elaborate bluff, but the four Indian kings played the winning hand.

Iroquois peoples can be found today on *reserves* in the provinces of Quebec and Ontario in Canada and on reservations in New York, Wisconsin, and Oklahoma in the United States. Many other Iroquois choose to live and work among non-Indians in the cities, suburbs, and rural towns of North America. In this respect, twenty-first-century Iroquois are no different from other modern Native Americans, whose lives reflect the cultural, political, and economic legacies of five hundred years of exchange and conflict with

Europeans. Some Iroquois today practice the Catholic or Protestant faiths their ancestors first encountered in the colonial era, while others follow the spiritual beliefs and traditions of their non-Christian ancestors. Some speak a native tongue as their first or second language, while others know only English or French. Centuries of political and military conflict have led to the dispersal and displacement of many Iroquois from their ancestors' homelands, but they have maintained their cultural identity despite the best efforts of governments, churches, and schools run by non-Indians to eradicate it. Like other Native Americans, modern Iroquois peoples live with one foot firmly in the past, committed to preserving their unique culture and history, and the other in the present, doing the best they can to make their way in a world that has often insisted that they cease being Indian if they want to survive.

Despite their continued vitality in the modern world, mention of the Iroquois among non-Indians today will most likely call to mind the image of a fierce warrior from the colonial era. The usual story goes something like this: When confronted by grasping colonizers and meddling missionaries, the Iroquois fought back. Other Indians may have made peace with the invaders, selling their land for beads and broken promises, sending their children off to missionary schools run by their new overlords, but the Iroquois stood firm. They had conquered an empire of their own in wars with other northeastern Indians, and as long as they remained united, they kept their French and British rivals at bay. Internal divisions finally divided the Iroquois League during the Revolutionary War, enabling the Continental Army to invade their homelands and disperse the fractured remnants of their once-mighty confederacy to reservations in New York and Canada.[9]

This image of the Iroquois has a very distinguished lineage. Its roots can be traced to impressions of the Iroquois recorded by French missionaries and British colonial officials during the colonial era. In the nineteenth century, writers and scholars such as Francis Parkman, James Fenimore Cooper, and Lewis Henry

Morgan assigned the Iroquois a central role in American history and literature and depicted them as first-rate statesmen as well as warriors. Other Indians may have fought bravely against the European invaders, but only the Iroquois created a confederacy that was capable of withstanding the juggernaut of colonization for so long. That it was a doomed effort made it no less noble. Nineteenth-century Americans never doubted that divine providence had ordained the conquest and subjugation of the continent's indigenous peoples, but they saw in the Iroquois a political genius that was uniquely American. This powerful Indian confederacy met defeat only when it was confronted by another homegrown American union, one made up of liberty-loving colonists intent on throwing off the yoke of British monarchy. The United States was the phoenix that arose out of the destruction of the Iroquois, another fruit born of the American wilderness, arrayed in all the blessings of Christian civilization but without the Old World's corruption or inequality.[10]

The misguided notion that the Iroquois somehow served as midwives to the birth of the United States has come into full flower within the last generation or so. In 1987, the United States Senate passed a resolution acknowledging "the contribution of the Iroquois Confederacy of Nations to the development of the United States Constitution." In this same spirit of recognition, some writers have described the Iroquois as "forgotten founders" whose indigenous forms of government provided a model for democracy and federal union from which the more famous Founding Fathers, especially Benjamin Franklin and Thomas Jefferson, borrowed freely. In this story, the Iroquois warrior puts down his hatchet and picks up his wampum belt, so that he can pass along ancient native wisdom on freedom and liberty to the new nation.[11]

It is not easy to fit the four Indian kings who visited Queen Anne in 1710 into either of these commonly held perceptions of the Iroquois. The four kings did not arrive in London as warriors painted for the warpath. They did not throw the scalps of their enemies at the queen's feet. Nor did they offer any tutorials to the queen and her ministers on how to set up a confederation of self-governing republics in America where all could live in liberty and equality. Rather, their English counterparts called them "kings," and they were happy to be treated as such.[12]

Diplomacy, unlike warfare, is about getting something you want from someone else by convincing them that they are benefiting from the bargain. The four Indian kings went to London to see what the queen might be able to do for them in exchange for what they might offer her. This negotiation followed its own intercultural logic. It was draped in the ceremony of the royal court, but it also involved Native American customs, such as the exchange of wampum and gift giving. All participants spoke in high-minded language about friendship and alliance, but an air of deception and manipulation hung about the proceedings. Each side was willing to pretend to be something it was not in order to advance its ends. Queen Anne and her ministers pretended to be interested in the fate of a distant colony few of them could have placed on a map, the four kings pretended to be loving and dedicated allies, and Nicholson and Schuyler pretended to each side that they could command the resources necessary to conquer Canada.

It was all a bit suspect, but only if our perception of Indians is limited to stereotypes of bloodthirsty warriors and grandfatherly wise men. The eighteenth-century Iroquois were neither mercenary killing machines nor idealistic forest-dwelling democrats. They were flesh-and-blood participants in a scramble for dominion in North America, and diplomacy was their tool of choice. Their negotiations with Indian and European counterparts involved occasional subterfuge, obfuscation, and exaggeration of the sort witnessed in London in 1710, but negotiation on the colonial frontier also demanded flexibility and innovation, the ability to create and maintain peace with others who rarely shared your interests or perspectives. This is the story of the Iroquois in early America that deserves to be told.

1

PEACE IN THE BALANCE

IN JULY 1743, four visitors arrived to a fine welcome at the town of Onondaga, the geographic and ceremonial center of the Iroquois League. Their arrival was expected, for the travelers had sent messengers ahead as they traveled northward through the Susquehanna Valley. At each Indian town along the route, residents came out to greet them—old and young, men and women—singing songs, beating drums, and offering lodgings and meals. Children climbed onto rooftops to get a better look at them. All this fanfare culminated with their arrival at Onondaga, where the local chiefs greeted the travelers with "a grave cheerful complaisance, according to their custom," provided them with comfortable lodgings and an ample meal, and then shared a pipe of good tobacco with them.

The chiefs already knew two of the visitors. Conrad Weiser was a colonial Indian agent who had lived among the Mohawks as a child before moving to southern Pennsylvania. On this trip he was working for the governor of Virginia, who wanted to restore peace after some Iroquois and settlers had clashed on the frontier of his colony. Weiser was accompanied by Shickellamy, an Oneida chief who lived in the Susquehanna Valley and knew the route between Pennsylvania and Onondaga well. The other two members of the party were strangers. John Bartram was a Philadelphia botanist, and Lewis Evans a Welsh cartographer who had recently immigrated to America. Both men had come along at Weiser's invitation so that they could get a better look at the country of the Iroquois.

Bartram recorded in his journal the many new experiences he had on this trip. He described the food he ate, the houses he slept in, and the strange sights and sounds that surrounded him. All the smoking, drinking, and dining gave him a quick intimacy with his hosts, but he still encountered customs and behavior that he could not begin to comprehend. Luckily, Weiser and Shickellamy were there to assist him. After bedding down for their first night in Onondaga, the visitors were awakened by a masked Indian dancer who shook a rattle and "made a hideous noise." A panicked Bartram called out to Weiser for an explanation, but his answer came from Shickellamy, who told him to "lye still *John.*" This reply left Bartram even more startled, for although he had already spent plenty of time on the road with Shickellamy, he had never heard him "speak so much plain *English* before."[1] What else was his Indian companion not telling him?

Over the next several days, Bartram and Evans pursued their scientific interests while Weiser and Shickellamy attended to their own business. The chiefs dispatched messengers, and gradually representatives from other nations in the confederacy trickled into Onondaga. Weiser spent several days in private meetings with chiefs he already knew well, hoping they would smooth his way once their formal council began. Weiser was an old hand at conducting such diplomacy, but he still felt it necessary to enlist Indian partners who could tell him "how to speak to everything when the Council should be met." Each passing day brought more smoking, eating, and drinking, until finally, ten days after Weiser's arrival, the chiefs said they were ready to hear him. He made his speech on behalf of the Virginians, offering to renew peace and promising a substantial present of trade goods. At key points Weiser punctuated his speech by passing across the council fire strings and belts of wampum, beads manufactured from marine shells. The chiefs responded in kind and professed their renewed friendship for the Virginians. Weiser's embassy wrapped up "according to the Ancient Custom" of his hosts, with a "Song of Friendship and Joy" sung by the chiefs and well-wishing for their guests. Weiser and his companions left town with their missions accomplished, their bellies full, and their horses weighed down with provisions for "the Road homeward."[2]

The journals of Weiser and Bartram from this trip are filled with valuable eyewitness accounts of Iroquois politics and culture, but like so many sources used by historians, they also raise more questions than they answer. Encountering the Iroquois for the first time, Bartram filled his pages with wonderful anecdotes about their hospitality, work routines, and ceremonies, but he made no attempt to describe their culture in a systematic way. Weiser, the seasoned Indian agent, provided a detailed record of his private and public negotiations, but he felt no need to elaborate on matters already familiar to him, such as how the Iroquois built their homes, wore their clothes, or made their livings. Neither of these observers tackled the big questions that historians ask about the Iroquois: How did their confederacy originate, what purposes did it serve, and how did they keep it together?

To answer these questions, we must rely on a variety of evidence, much of it as fragmentary and impressionistic as the journals left by Bartram and Weiser. Other colonial Europeans—travelers, traders, missionaries, captives—left written descriptions of the Iroquois, each with its own distinctive perspective and bias. Archaeological evidence offers clues about Iroquois life before and after European contact, but material objects cannot reconstruct a culture in its entirety. Oral traditions open another perspective on Iroquois history, revealing how the Iroquois explained their place within the natural and spiritual worlds. The work of anthropologists and linguists, who began studying the Iroquois in earnest in the mid-nineteenth century, provides yet another vantage point, but such information reflects Iroquois life and culture at the time it was collected and cannot be relied on to reveal what came before it. In short, all of these sources are valuable but imperfect; they cannot answer all of our questions definitively. To a certain degree, we are like Bartram during that first night in Onondaga, calling out in the darkness for an explanation of something we barely comprehend.

THE TURTLE'S BACK

At the time of their contact with Europeans, the Iroquois inhabited a region south of Lake Ontario that stretched across modern upstate New York from Albany to Buffalo (see map). From east to west, the Mohawks, Oneidas, Onondagas, Cayugas, and Senecas recognized a cultural kinship with each other and maintained peace amongst themselves. They spoke different but related languages, all derived from what linguists call the Iroquoian stock. There were other Iroquoian-speaking peoples in eastern North America, but that linguistic similarity did not make them a part of the distinctive political union that encompassed these five groups and eventually a sixth, the Tuscaroras, who migrated from North Carolina into Iroquoia in the early eighteenth century.

Iroquoia was a region of rich and diverse resources. Major waterways connected it to the eastern seaboard as well as the continent's interior. The Mohawk River flowed eastward to the Hudson, a river that along with Lake Champlain formed a wide north-to-south corridor between modern Montreal and New York City. In the west, the Allegheny River flowed out of Seneca country toward modern Pittsburgh, where it joined with the Monongahela to form the Ohio, the Mississippi's major eastern tributary. Lakes Erie and Ontario provided the Iroquois with access to the vast northern waterways of the Great Lakes, and the Susquehanna River flowed out of southern Iroquoia into Chesapeake Bay.

Winter acts like a bad guest in this region, arriving early and staying late, but the temperate summers make for bountiful growing seasons. The surrounding woodlands provided fuel for heating and cooking as well as plenty of animals to hunt for meat and pelts. Fishing and seasonal gathering of fruit, nuts, roots, and sap from maple trees rounded out a diverse and healthy diet.

Based on analysis of pottery and other man-made objects, archaeologists believe that the Iroquois emerged from the Owasco people, a cultural group that inhabited the region south of Lake Ontario from approximately AD 900 to AD 1350. The formation of a distinctive Iroquois culture was a gradual process that occurred as successive generations adapted to their environment, asserted control over their borders, and developed a common identity.[3] That identity included a shared sense of the past, and the Iroquois told a creation story to explain where they came from. According to it, the world began in this manner:

When the earth was only a limitless sea, there lived in the Sky-World a pregnant woman who craved odd things to eat. She sent her husband out one day to find her new delicacies by digging about the roots of the Great Tree, the sacred center of the Sky-World. The husband's digging opened up a hole in the floor of the Sky-World, exposing another world below of limitless sea and sky. Fearful, he backed away, but his curious wife moved closer for a better look, until she slipped into the hole (in some versions of the story, her husband pushes her). Grasping at the roots of the Great Tree for a hold, she fell into the world below.

The birds of the sky saw her coming. They rescued her by flying together and forming a net to break her fall. One of their number flew down to the creatures of the sea to ask for their help, and a turtle allowed her to land on his back. A muskrat brought a bit of dirt up from the

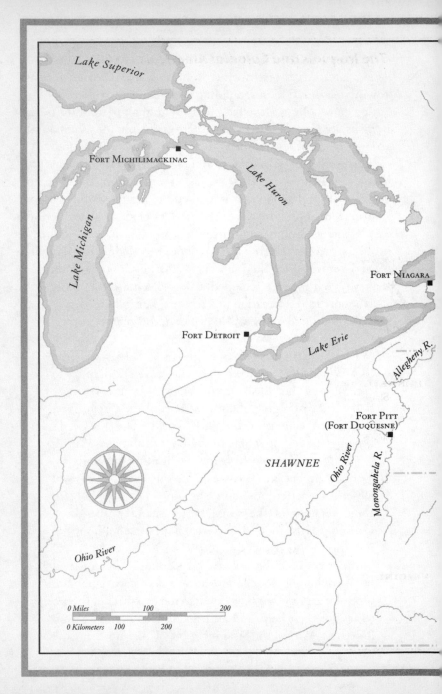

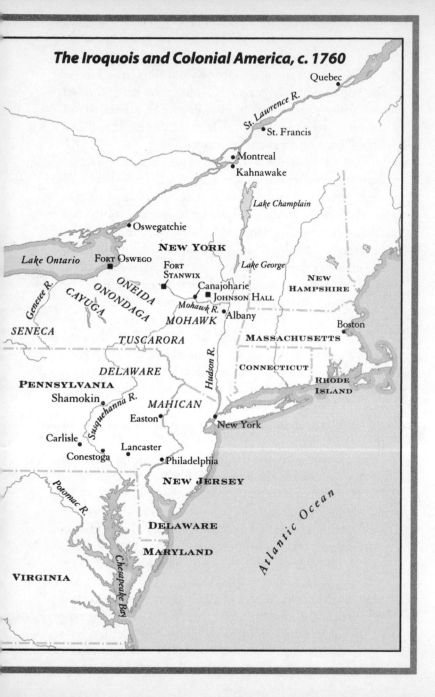

The Iroquois and Colonial America, c. 1760

Quebec

St. Lawrence R.

St. Francis

Montreal

Kahnawake

Lake Champlain

Oswegatchie

NEW YORK

Lake Ontario

FORT OSWEGO

FORT STANWIX

Lake George

NEW HAMPSHIRE

Genesee R.

ONEIDA

ONONDAGA

CAYUGA

Canajoharie

JOHNSON HALL

Mohawk R.

Albany

SENECA

MOHAWK

Boston

TUSCARORA

MASSACHUSETTS

DELAWARE

CONNECTICUT

Hudson R.

PENNSYLVANIA

RHODE ISLAND

Shamokin

Susquehanna R.

MAHICAN

Easton

New York

Carlisle

Lancaster

Conestoga

Philadelphia

NEW JERSEY

Potomac R.

DELAWARE

MARYLAND

Atlantic Ocean

VIRGINIA

Chesapeake Bay

ocean floor, which the woman augmented with the bits of earth and roots she had grabbed from the Great Tree as she fell. From this meager beginning the earth formed and plants grew to sustain the woman. She gave birth to a daughter, who assisted her in tending this earth until she herself became pregnant with twins.

While still in the womb, the twins fought. The right-handed twin was born normally, but the left-handed twin moved upward rather than downward in his mother's body, coming out of her armpit and killing her in the process. The twins buried her body, and from her head grew corn, beans, and squash, the "three sisters" of Iroquois horticulture. From her heart grew tobacco, used in Iroquois healing and sacred ceremonies. The twins shared in their mother's and grandmother's generative powers, but they also checked each other's efforts in a constant contest for dominance. The right-handed twin made deer and squirrels, but the left-handed twin made mountain lions and weasels. Likewise, the right-handed twin's fruit trees and berries were countered by the left-handed twin's briars and poison ivy. The rivers that the right-handed twin made straight and free of obstacles were turned crooked and full of rapids by his brother. The twins also made humans, forming them out of clay and baking them in a fire, like pottery.

Through their many battles the twins remained evenly matched, until one day the right-handed brother finally triumphed and killed the left-handed one. His act of fratricide angered his grandmother, the Sky-Woman, and he killed her as well, throwing her head into the sky, where it became the moon. He then went to live in the Sky-World as the Master of Life, where he continues to watch over the humans he created and to enjoy the scent of the tobacco they burn in his honor. His brother, who some call Flint, also remains attentive to human affairs. He rules the realm of night, and warfare and human suffering please him.[4]

Elements of this story resonate throughout Iroquois culture. The primary roles of Sky-Woman and her daughter in the earth's creation reflect the considerable authority and respect women commanded in Iroquois society as the heads of families and the growers of the crops that were the mainstays of the Iroquois diet. This creation story is also indicative of Iroquois perceptions of human-animal relations. Several creatures played important roles in saving Sky-Woman after her fall, and while the right-handed and left-handed twins created animals, they did not give humans lordship over them. On the contrary, humans were only one piece in this creation, not its crowning achievement. Even the story's parallels to the Book of Genesis—the tree, the "fallen" woman, the sons who personify good and evil—suggest how contact with colonial missionaries may have affected the Iroquoian worldview.

The story of Sky-Woman also holds important insights for understanding the origins and purposes of Iroquois diplomacy. The most significant elements in this regard are its themes of balance and reciprocity. In the biblical version of creation, the absence of evil from the world before Eve's sin makes it a perfect place. It is only after Eve has eaten the forbidden fruit that this paradise is irretrievably lost and suffering is introduced to humankind. In the Iroquoian creation story, perfection rests not in the absence of evil, but in its balance with good. As embodied in the right-handed and left-handed twins, these two forces exist side by side in the World on the Turtle's Back. The twins' acts of creation are complementary, and the world grows because of their rivalry with each other. To the Iroquois, relations with others—whether kin or outsiders—were likewise a perpetual give-and-take aimed at sustaining peace and prosperity.

Iroquois Family and Community

That balancing act began within the most immediate human relationships in Iroquois communities and then fanned outward. At
the start of the colonial era, the Iroquois inhabited a string of about
ten towns and numerous smaller hamlets along an east-to-west axis
from the Hudson River to the Genesee Valley. Populations within
these communities ranged widely, from 100 to 200 for the hamlets
to 1,000 to 2,000 for the larger towns, which were typically built on
hilltops and surrounded by palisades of wooden posts sunk verti-
cally into the ground. Not surprisingly, Europeans took to calling
these impressively fortified Iroquois towns "castles." Within the
palisades, the Iroquois lived in longhouses, long rectangular struc-
tures made from saplings and tree bark that housed several related
families. An average longhouse was about one hundred feet in
length and twenty feet in width, with a central aisle dotted by four
or five hearths, each one serving the heating and cooking needs of
two families who made their lodgings on opposite sides of the
aisle.[5] The physical closeness of individuals living within a longhouse encouraged the communal pursuit of such tasks as cooking
and child-rearing, and it also placed a premium on conflict avoid-
ance and consensus-building in social interactions. This communal ethic extended to the world outside the longhouse. Men and
women cooperated in their different types of work: the men in
hunting and fishing, the women in planting and tending the fields
beyond the palisades. Related families also traveled and worked together in annual commutes to fishing and hunting camps, where
they took advantage of seasonal bounties in natural resources.[6]

Our modern tendency is to think of Indians as identifying
themselves according to membership in a "tribe," but this problematic term did not gain currency until the nineteenth century, and
even then, it was used more often by non-Indians than by Indians
themselves. Colonial observers recognized Indians as belonging to
"nations," groups of people who shared the same language, cultural

practices, and territory.[7] This designation made sense when the Iroquois dealt with outsiders, but in their day-to-day affairs, more immediate ties of kinship shaped their identity and interaction with others.

Like many other Native Americans in eastern North America, the Iroquois organized themselves into extended families and clans. The families that shared a longhouse were related to one another through a common maternal ancestor. Their lineage was part of a larger clan, whose membership was also determined matrilineally, children deriving their affiliation from their mother rather than their father. Iroquois clans had animal totems—the bear, wolf, and turtle being the most common—and the image of this totem, worn as jewelry, carved or painted on a longhouse, or drawn with quill and ink on a treaty document, announced a person's or group's clan affiliation. Clans played such a powerful role in Iroquois identity that an incest taboo existed against marrying within your clan, even if the potential mate was from another community. Regardless of biological or physical distance, another clan member was still a brother or sister.[8] Within and between their communities, the Iroquois divided their clans into moieties, complementary opposites that owed reciprocal social and ceremonial obligations to each other. This was another common practice among eastern Indians, who used it to create webs of social interdependence between people that extended well beyond their immediate families.

The Iroquois practiced their most important forms of government at the local level. Each community was autonomous, relying on councils made up of clan elders—some of whom held their position by virtue of hereditary status, others by virtue of accomplishment and reputation—to make decisions and settle disputes that concerned the whole. A seventeenth-century French captive among the Oneidas described how such councils worked:

> He then, or she, who has some propositions to make begins by assembling the elders of his or her family

[meaning clan], and if it is something that concerns the warriors, one or two captains of this same family are summoned to be witnesses to the thing being proposed. Each one there gives his opinion in a very serious manner, after which they agree upon the procedure. That being finished, an elder appointed by them goes to invite the other families, I mean the elders and war chiefs, supposing that the thing requires it. In this way, all these formalities are done in a very similar manner. . . . If in the decision they judge it appropriate to give notice of it to the other villages . . . they appoint one or two of the principal men of each family to go and explain their plans to their allies.[9]

As this description indicates, lineage played a central role in group decision-making, and as this process spiraled outward, clan affiliations provided the means for communicating with and including others. Such deliberations were time-consuming, but also remarkably effective at creating consensus without resorting to coercion.

Iroquois notions of reciprocity also shaped their relations with outsiders. From an Iroquoian perspective, the outside world could be divided into two groups: those with whom you traded and those with whom you warred, or as an Iroquois speaker put it at an Albany treaty council in 1735, *"Trade and Peace we take to be one thing."*[10] Before the arrival of Europeans, the Iroquois traded and warred with other native peoples in eastern North America. Archaeological evidence indicates that the Iroquois acquired a variety of objects and materials from long-distance trading partners, including marine shell beads from coastal New England, soft copper from the Upper Great Lakes, and pipestone from the upper Mississippi Valley. However, there is not any corresponding evidence for large-scale trade in what might be called the necessities of life: food, clothing, tools, or weapons. Before contact with Europeans, the Iroquois supplied these material wants through their own labor and local resources.

The small quantities of the shell beads, copper, pipestone, and other nonindigenous goods found at Iroquois sites suggest that such items were probably acquired as diplomatic presents exchanged with outsiders. Gifts given in diplomatic encounters established mutual obligations between the giver and recipient in much the same way that the clan and moiety system created those bonds within a nation.[11] Harmen Meyndertsz van den Bogaert, a Dutch trader who visited Iroquoia in 1634–35 to counter competition from the French, learned this lesson quickly when a Mohawk chief "came to ask me what we were doing in his country and what we brought him for gifts." The Dutchman replied "that we brought him nothing, but that we just came for a visit." The chief called the Dutch scoundrels, "worth nothing because we brought him no gifts," and praised the French who had "traded with them here with six men and had given them good gifts."[12]

Diplomacy with outsiders, then, was an extension of the same principles that governed social relations within Iroquois families and communities. Each side engaged in councils with the other to maintain peace between them. Such negotiations brought tangible benefits to both sides, such as safe passage through the homelands of a neighboring people or alliance against a common enemy. Reciprocal acts of gift exchange in these diplomatic encounters, although they involved only small quantities of goods, were nevertheless central to their success, for the objects involved gave tangible form to the emotions and relationships expressed in the negotiations: friendship, esteem, alliance. Just as the maintenance of healthy social relations within an Iroquois community required constant attention to communal obligations, so too did keeping the peace with outsiders depend on regular participation in diplomacy and gift exchanges.

The Roots of Diplomacy: The Iroquois League

When referring to themselves collectively, the peoples who formed the Iroquois League called themselves the *Haudenosaunee*, the People of the Longhouse. That name reflected the geographic dimensions of their homelands, stretching in a long rectangular corridor south of Lake Ontario. The Onondagas were known as the "firekeepers" of the League, because of their location at the geographic center of Iroquoia. The Senecas were known as the "keepers of the western door" and the Mohawks as the "keepers of the eastern door."[13] Just as life within an Iroquois longhouse required cooperation among families who shared resources, labor, and living space, so too did keeping the peace within the Iroquois League require maintaining a delicate balance between individual autonomy and communal obligation. The League commanded no temporal institutions or resources to achieve its ends, no armies, courts, or taxes. To make it work, the Iroquois applied the same tools that they used to cultivate peace and prosperity within their communities. Lineages and clans were the sinews that tied people together, moieties allowed for the proper observation of rituals that preserved peace and well-being, and the exchange of sacred objects created a web of mutual obligations.

The diplomatic customs the Iroquois used to deal with Europeans derived from their own experience in constructing and maintaining their confederacy with each other. Perhaps the most common misconception about the Iroquois League is that it functioned as a sort of federal government for its member nations in a manner that anticipated modern American federalism's use of representative government, deliberative lawmaking, and majority rule. Such observations have been the foundation of the so-called Iroquois Influence Thesis, the notion that American democratic institutions and ideals bear a distinct but overlooked Iroquois imprint. However appealing that connection may be, few colonial Americans had even the vaguest sense of how the Iroquois League operated, and its kinship-based organization had no correlation whatsoever to the constitutional principles and mechanics embraced by the Founding Fathers.[14]

Scholars have long debated the origins of the Iroquois League.

As early as the mid-seventeenth century, colonial observers were aware of the cooperative relationship between the Mohawks, Oneidas, Onondagas, Cayugas, and Senecas, but they had no precise idea of when it began or how it worked. The earliest extant account of the League's origin is a brief passage recorded by a German missionary in the 1740s, but no colonial observer, even one as familiar with the Iroquois as Conrad Weiser, ever attempted to explain the intramural operations of the League. It was not until the mid-nineteenth century that anthropologists undertook the first scholarly study of the League's ceremonial and political dimensions, relying on field notes, oral traditions, and interviews they collected among contemporary Iroquois peoples. It is an obvious point, but one nonetheless worth remembering: Like any aspect of Iroquois culture, the League changed over time as it responded to specific historical circumstances. We cannot assume that the depiction of the League compiled by anthropologists during the reservation era accurately represents how it worked in the precontact or colonial periods.

Archaeologists generally agree that the League originated sometime between 1450 and 1600. Iroquoian cultural patterns were not firmly established in modern central New York until about 1300, and for much of the following century, Iroquois communities were small, dispersed, and sparsely fortified. During the sixteenth century, town sites began to cluster in ways that resembled the territorial borders of the nations that would eventually make up the League. This period also witnessed a shift toward more densely populated and heavily fortified hilltop towns, suggesting a time of insecurity and violence. Human remains from these sites show evidence of ritual torture, execution, and cannibalism, supporting the conclusion that the fifteenth century was a time of endemic warfare between neighboring peoples in Iroquoia.[15]

Iroquois oral tradition tells what happened next. According to the founding myth of the Iroquois League, a virgin Huron woman living north of Iroquoia gave birth to a son. In a dream, she learned he was destined to be a prophet, so she named him Deganawidah, the Peacemaker. As he grew, Deganawidah's eloquence was evident to all, yet his people failed to heed his message. He left his homeland for Iroquoia, where he found the people torn apart by war. Deganawidah traveled about, preaching his message of peace. His most important convert was Hiawatha, an Onondaga who had killed and eaten many of his enemies but whose grief over the loss of his own daughters left him inconsolable. Deganawidah restored Hiawatha's well-being by giving him three strings of beads while reciting words of condolence. One string dried Hiawatha's tears so that he might see clearly again. Another cleared his throat, so that he could speak, and the last opened his ears, so that he could hear. Deganawidah taught the sacred words and use of the sacred beads to Hiawatha, who used them to spread the prophet's message of peace. His greatest triumph came when an Onondaga sorcerer named Tadadaho, a man so full of hate that it had twisted his body and turned his hair into a tangled mass of snakes, finally accepted the prophet's message. Hiawatha used the sacred beads and words to straighten Tadadaho's body and to comb the snakes out of his hair. Subsequently, Hiawatha and Tadadaho worked together to found the Iroquois League so that the peace secured by Deganawidah's message and gifts might be preserved among the Iroquois forever.[16]

The condolence ritual described in the Deganawidah Epic became the ceremonial centerpiece of the Iroquois League. Each year, a Grand Council of Iroquois chiefs met to recommit themselves to the preservation of the peace and unity first secured by Deganawidah, Hiawatha, and Tadadaho. They divided themselves into two moieties—the "older brothers" (Mohawks, Onondagas, Senecas) and "younger brothers" (Oneidas and Cayugas)—and re-enacted the League's founding by exchanging the sacred beads and reciting the sacred words Deganawidah had taught to Hiawatha.

In the historical era, it became customary to refer to the men who made up the Grand Council as sachems. Their work was mostly ceremonial, and their seat on the Grand Council did not necessarily give them command or influence over the daily politics and leadership of their local communities. Rather, a sachem owed his seat on the Grand Council to his birth and place within his lineage. When a sachem died, the elder women of the lineage he represented chose his successor from among the adult men in their families.[17] Tradition dictated that they select someone skilled in the art of consensus-building: a good speaker and listener, with a slow temper and a thick skin. These were all traits that favored older, experienced men already possessing reputations for influence and eloquence, but the most important factor was making sure the lineage retained its intergenerational prominence by continuing to send a representative to the Grand Council.[18] There were fifty seats on the Grand Council. They were not divided equally or proportionately among the League's nations, and some clans and lineages were not represented at all. This disregard for equal representation did not bother the Iroquois because they did not conceive of the Grand Council as a democratic institution designed to govern individuals. Instead, it functioned according to the same bedrock principle that united Iroquois communities: Political unity arose from kinship, binding people together across space and through time.

One of the most important ceremonial functions of the Grand Council occurred when one of its members died and it became necessary to raise up a new sachem in his place. The formal condolence ritual was an elaborate affair that could take several days. It started with a rite of greeting "at the woods' edge" as visiting participants arrived at their hosts' town for the council. After all the chiefs were gathered, they divided into two sides: "the clear-minded" recited the sacred words and presented the sacred beads to "the bereaved," to take away their grief. When properly recited and punctuated by the passage of beads from speaker to listener, the sacred words wiped away the tears from the eyes of the bereaved and opened their ears and throats, brought light to end their darkness, and covered the graves of the deceased. Once the bereaved were able to see, hear, and speak clearly again, the rite of condolence passed into one of "requickening," in which a new sachem took the name of the deceased and his place on the Grand Council. Singing, smoking, and feasting accompanied all of this ritual, providing long intervals for participants to rest, renew, and reacquaint themselves, and to restore good feelings wherever antagonisms or difficulties may have arisen since they last met. Condolence and requickening were the one-two punch of the Iroquois League's ceremonialism, the method by which one generation preserved the peace and passed it along to the next.[19]

Nineteenth-century anthropologists wrote the earliest descriptions of the Deganawidah Epic and the Grand Council. By that time, the Iroquois had been dispossessed of their original homelands and dispersed to reservations and *reserves* in the United States and Canada. No such accounts of the League's operation predate 1800, and therefore, we simply cannot know how well those nineteenth-century sources reflect the reality of the Iroquois League in the colonial era. Nonetheless, we can draw some reasonable conclusions from the fragmentary evidence available, such as Bartram's and Weiser's journals from their visit to Onondaga in 1743.

Onondaga was more than just the geographic center of Iroquoia; it was the ceremonial and political center of the League, the place where chiefs from its member nations regularly converged to discuss their affairs. When Weiser was sent by the governor of Virginia to negotiate with the Iroquois, he knew Onondaga was the place he needed to go. The process he described for conducting this business shared many elements with the condolence and requickening rituals as observed by anthropologists a century later. Weiser and his party received an elaborate welcome at Onondaga and witnessed a great deal of singing, smoking, and feasting related to their visit. More significantly, Weiser and Bartram recorded eyewitness accounts of the formal deliberations of an Iroquois council in Onondaga that seemed to mimic the Deganawidah Epic. According to Weiser, the council began with the Onondagas retelling "the beginning of the Union of the five Nations" and invoking the protection of their forefathers' spirits. One of their chiefs presented a string of wampum beads "to wipe off the Sweat from their [the assembled deputies' and messengers'] Bodies" and to give thanks for their safe passage through the Woods.

In his description of the same opening council, Bartram described three speakers. The first two "walked backward and forward in the common passage" of the longhouse, speaking "with a slow even pace and much composure and gravity in their countenance." The third speaker remained seated in the middle, and exhorted his listeners to cultivate "indissoluble amity and unanimity" in the spirit of the "perfect union" forged by their forefathers. All of this, Bartram wrote, was done according to "their antient custom." The council continued over the next several days, with Weiser making his speech to the assembled chiefs and receiving their answer. Speakers on both sides punctuated their words by passing strings and belts of beads, which were then hung on a pole across the interior of the longhouse to serve as a running archive of their negotiations. Women appeared at intervals with steaming kettles and bowls of food for the speakers and their audiences.[20]

The scenes recorded by Weiser and Bartram raise all sorts of intriguing questions about how the Iroquois League operated internally and with outsiders in the colonial era. What relation did the group of chiefs who assembled in Onondaga to hear Weiser's speech bear to the Grand Council of the League? Was Weiser speaking to hereditary sachems selected by clan mothers, an ad hoc collection of chiefs assembled by the messengers sent out after his arrival in Onondaga, or some combination of both? Did the Grand Council serve as a single Iroquois voice for conducting affairs with outsiders, or did it limit itself to only the intramural ceremonies of condolence and requickening associated with preserving the Iroquois League? We cannot definitively answer these questions because observers such as Weiser and Bartram did not exhibit any familiarity with the Grand Council or its role within the League.[21]

While sources such as these leave much unexplained about how the Iroquois League operated, they do reveal a strong correlation between the ritual structure of the League in the nineteenth century and the methods the Iroquois used to conduct diplomacy during the colonial era. The rituals witnessed by Weiser and Bartram in 1743 shared the same cultural DNA as the condolence and requickening rites the Iroquois were still practicing a century later: Participants greeted each other, assumed complementary roles, made speeches and exchanged beads across a council fire, and feasted with each other until their business was done and their peace renewed.

THE SEVENTEENTH-CENTURY WARS OF THE IROQUOIS

Contact with Europeans brought a wave of convulsive changes to Iroquois society, but it did not alter the fundamental ways in which they defined themselves or their relations with others. Warfare and diplomacy remained complementary methods for dealing with the outside world, and kinship remained the primary means of creating and extending ties between peoples. In a world torn apart by epidemic disease, violence, and economic competition, the balance necessary for sustaining peace and prosperity became difficult to maintain. For much of the seventeenth century, the Iroquois struggled to right a world gone wrong.

Although Bartram enjoyed a peaceful trip to Onondaga in 1743, he described the Iroquois as "the most warlike people in *N. America*" and claimed that their "uninterrupted state of war" with colonists and other Indians had "made them the dread of people above 1000 miles distant."[22] This reputation for martial fierceness had its roots in the so-called Beaver Wars that followed Iroquois contact with French and Dutch traders. European trade goods trickled into Iroquoia during the late sixteenth century, but not in quantities sufficient to transform their material culture or economic production. Glass beads and European metal wares probably first reached the Iroquois in much the same manner as exotic goods of Native American manufacture, by way of diplomatic encounters with other Indians. It was not until the Dutch set up shop at Fort Orange (modern Albany) in the upper Hudson Valley and the French at Quebec in the St. Lawrence Valley that Iroquois communities gained reliable access to European trade goods. The Mohawks, at the eastern door of the Longhouse, were the most immediately and profoundly affected by this exchange. They brought furs to Fort Orange and traded them for arms and ammunition, kettles, iron axes and knives, woven cloth, glass beads, liquor, and a host of novelties, such as mirrors, mouth harps, and clay pipes.

Some European goods rapidly replaced their native equivalents. Iron axes, knives, and scissors were sharper and lighter than cutting and striking tools made from stone. European trade goods also provided new raw materials for objects of Iroquois manufacture. Scrap metal from kettles and trade axes, for example, could be reworked as arrowheads, jewelry, and edged tools. The production of some native goods declined because it was cheaper to acquire their substitutes from the fur trade. Beaver pelts and deerskins that would have been turned into native clothing were more profitably traded for European-made woolens that became the new staple of native dress. Native ceramics also declined as Indians adopted copper and brass kettles for cooking and storing food.[23] When Dutch trader Harmen Bogaert visited Iroquoia in 1634, many of the Indians he encountered had never laid eyes on a European before. They crowded his party wherever they went and even "pushed one another into the fire in order to see us." Yet, those same Indians already had a surprising amount of European iron goods in their homes, including chains, bolts, hoops, and spikes. One longhouse even had European-style plank wood doors hung on iron hinges. Bogaert noted that the Mohawk term for the Dutch was "*kristoni asseroni,*" literally meaning "I am a metal-maker" or "axe-maker."[24]

While the acquisition of furs fit readily into pre-existing patterns in the gender division of labor—men hunted and women processed the pelts—it gradually redirected labor away from traditional economic activities toward production for the transatlantic marketplace. As animal populations declined, men spent longer periods away on the hunt, and transporting furs to Quebec and Fort Orange became part of the seasonal economic cycle. The fur trade introduced the Iroquois to long-distance commercial exchange, and with it came dependence on Europeans for the new necessaries of life: cloth, metal wares, and arms and ammunition.[25]

Labeling the wars the Iroquois fought against other native peoples during this era as the "Beaver Wars" is misleading, because the name suggests a purposeful effort by the Iroquois to improve their position vis-à-vis their neighbors in the fur trade.[26] Ascribing such economic motives to the Iroquois is tricky business. Their League was not a centralized government charged with devising and enforcing a uniform economic or foreign relations policy. On the contrary, Iroquois warfare—like most other aspects of Iroquois culture—had its causes in interpersonal relations at the family and community level. Young men went to war as a rite of passage to prove themselves as warriors and to gain reputation among their peers. Families supplied war parties and encouraged them to bring back captives who could be adopted to replace lost kin. Iroquois warfare in the seventeenth century was certainly affected by the fur trade, but its spiraling violence and geographic reach owed at least as much to the traditional purpose it served in helping Iroquois communities replenish populations ravaged by disease, internal strife, and out-migration.

Iroquois war parties usually formed at the instigation of

family members grieving the loss of a loved one. If traditional mourning practices failed to assuage grief, the next step was to acquire captives who might take the place of the deceased. Clan matrons played a central role in such "mourning wars" by goading the men of their families into taking up arms and by supplying them with the necessary provisions. The war party, which would attract other young men anxious for the opportunity to prove themselves, would seek out traditional enemies and try to secure as many prisoners as possible while incurring minimal casualties themselves. Such objectives encouraged the warriors to practice what Europeans called the "skulking way of war," surprise raids and ambushes followed by rapid retreats before a superior force could be organized for a reprisal.[27]

Captives faced a harrowing journey to their captors' home. If wounds or fatigue prevented them from keeping pace, they were dispatched with a blow to the head and their scalp taken as a war trophy. Tortures might also occur en route, such as having a thumb cut off, fingernails torn out, or the tips of fingers burned or crushed, all extremely painful but nonfatal ways of limiting a captive's ability to handle a weapon or attempt an escape. If members of the war party were particularly aggrieved, perhaps over the loss of one of their own in battle, they might torture and execute some of their captives even before returning home.

Successful war parties sent runners ahead to inform their kin of their impending return. The community turned out to greet the warriors and captives, forcing the latter to "run the gauntlet" between two rows of villagers who delivered blows with fists and clubs along with taunts and jeers. The captives were then typically stripped naked and forced to stand for more physical and verbal torments on a public scaffold or platform. While the entire community took the opportunity to hurl insults at the captives, poke them with firebrands, or force them to hold hot coals or ashes, chiefs and clan elders apportioned them among different families, leaving each to decide the fate of its new charge. Young children and women were likely to be adopted and "raised up" in the place of deceased loved ones, but adult men faced the strong likelihood of being marked for adoption of a different sort. Their captors designated a day for their execution and allowed them to hold their death feast, at which the captives recited or sang of their prowess, bravery, and triumphs in battle. Afterward, they would be tied to a stake and tortured to death over many hours. Torture began at the extremities of body: the burning of feet, dismemberment of ears and fingers, flesh sliced off legs or arms. A brave warrior was expected to suffer these pains stoically, and while still capable of speech, to urge his executioners to do their worst. After he succumbed, his tormentors scalped his corpse and dismembered and cooked it for communal consumption. In this manner, the spirit and bravery the captive had exhibited in death was absorbed into the community.[28]

Europeans who witnessed Iroquois warfare and the treatment of captives did not hesitate to condemn both practices as savage. The common complaint of missionaries and colonial officials was that Indians made war for sport, and thus failed to pursue more civilized objectives such as the conquest of new territory or peoples. While these same observers noted that the Iroquois could be exceptionally tender to captives they chose to adopt, they were shocked by the torture and cannibalism endured by those marked for death, and attributed both to a primitive bloodlust lurking in the pagan souls of the Iroquois. The Iroquois, of course, saw it differently. To them, warfare was a natural and necessary activity for keeping the community strong. It offered a means of assuaging the grief of the inconsolable and of venting rage and taking vengeance outside the community. It also restored life to the community by bringing in captives who could be assimilated in place of lost kin. War was a partner to diplomacy in dealing with outsiders. Whereas the latter relied on peaceful and voluntary exchange to bring the resources of others into the community, war employed violence to the same end.

When the microbes brought to North America by Europeans reached Iroquoia in the 1630s, the mourning war provided a framework for dealing with the consequences. The full impact of smallpox, measles, and other communicable diseases on Indian populations is notoriously hard to calculate, but historians estimate that over the course of the seventeenth century, the entire Iroquois population was probably halved from about twenty thousand to ten thousand by this onslaught. Furthermore, not all of the Iroquois nations were affected equally. The Senecas, at the western door of the Longhouse, fared much better than any other Iroquois nation, while the Mohawks, who were in close contact with the French and Dutch, suffered a loss of about 75 percent.[29] This demographic crisis, unfolding at the same time as the immersion of the Iroquois in the fur trade, put a tremendous pressure on Iroquois communities to replenish their populations. In the middle decades of the seventeenth century, their traditional mourning wars blended together into an escalating pattern of conflict with enemies on all sides.

The Iroquois directed the bulk of their martial energies against French-allied Indians in the St. Lawrence River Valley and the Great Lakes region. The French fur trade, anchored in Montreal after that city's founding in 1642, attracted flotillas of canoes laden with beaver and other animal pelts every trading season. French Jesuit missionaries in pursuit of Indian converts opened diplomatic and commercial ties with distant western nations. During the 1630s, their greatest success was among the Hurons, a confederacy of Iroquoian-speaking Indians who lived in modern Ontario astride trade routes to the western Great Lakes.[30] The Iroquois warred against the Hurons in the 1640s with a ferocity that earned them the enmity of the Jesuits and a lasting reputation for cruelty in the pages of the *Jesuit Relations*, the annals of the Jesuit enterprise in North America. The Jesuits also chronicled Iroquois wars in the 1650s against other Iroquoian-speaking nations in the vicinity of Lakes Erie and Ontario: the Wenros, Eries, Petuns, and Neutrals. To the north, the Mohawks attacked Algonquins, Montaignais, and other St. Lawrence Valley Indians as they plied the trade routes between Lake Ontario and Montreal. They also fought a series of wars with their eastward neighbors the Mahicans, so that the Mohawks could have unfettered access to the Dutch at Fort Orange.[31]

The Iroquois adopted their vanquished foes in vast numbers to make up for their losses from smallpox and other diseases. By one estimate, they took about six thousand captives during the seventeenth century.[32] Jesuit missionaries, when they finally gained entry to Iroquois communities in the 1650s and 1660s, were heartened to find so many Hurons and other Canadian Indians living among them. According to one such report, adopted Hurons, Petuns, Neutrals, Eries, Algonquins, Montaignais, and Mahicans formed "without doubt the largest and best part of the Iroquois."[33] Adopted captives made up two-thirds of one populous Mohawk town.[34] Similar languages and cultural patterns made the Hurons and other nations of the Ontario region prime candidates for Iroquois adoption. Algonquian-speakers like the Mahicans, Algonquins, and Montaignais may have had a more difficult time, but the Mohawks' losses from epidemics encouraged a similar pattern of forced assimilation.

Protracted warfare proved to be unsustainable for the Iroquois. The dispersal and adoption of immediate neighbors sent Iroquois warriors farther afield on their mourning wars in the latter seventeenth century. Attacks on the Susquehannocks, an Iroquoian-speaking nation in the lower Susquehanna Valley, devolved into a stalemate of raids and reprisals during the 1670s. Likewise, efforts to subdue the Illinois, Foxes, Ottawas, Miamis, and other Indians from the western Great Lakes and upper Mississippi Valley were inconclusive and costly. Most important, the Iroquois had incurred the wrath of the French colonizers of Canada. Several Jesuits met their martyrdom at Iroquois hands, and Iroquois warriors had dealt a fatal blow to the once-promising Huron missions. French traders and merchants suffered considerable disruption in their business, and inhabitants of New France lived under a pervasive sense of insecurity. An army of French soldiers invaded Mohawk country twice in 1666, the first time nearly freezing to death, but the second time burning the crops and homes of three Mohawk towns abandoned in advance of the soldiers' arrival.[35]

French firepower forced the Iroquois to be more accommodating to their colonial neighbors to the north. As part of peace negotiations after the 1666 campaign, the Iroquois nations agreed to receive Jesuit missionaries. The arrival of these agents added to the factionalism within communities already stressed by the rapid adoption of so many strangers and the turmoil of recurrent epidemics. The Jesuits urged their converts to shun traditional ceremonies and practices they deemed pagan and barbaric. Whenever they succeeded in winning a convert of stature, such as the Onondaga chief Garakontíe, they also won a valuable political ally whose influence could tilt an entire lineage or town toward New France. To avoid backsliding by their converts and the hostility of traditionalists, Jesuits encouraged their spiritual charges to resettle on *reserves,* Indian mission communities established near Montreal, Quebec, and along the northern shore of Lake Ontario. After relations between the Iroquois and French soured in the latter 1670s, this out-migration increased markedly. Individual converts may have made the journey out of spiritual desire, but the bonds of kinship also led others to make the move into Canada. By 1700, about one thousand Iroquois were living in the Canadian *reserves*, including the majority of Mohawks.[36]

War, like any other human activity, is governed by culturally sanctioned rules and customs intended to make it useful to the people who practice it. Iroquois warfare, rooted in the logic and imperatives of the mourning war, served an important purpose in preserving the social and demographic health of Iroquois communities. During the profound disruptions of the seventeenth century, however, it also had a destructive and wasting impact on Iroquois communities. Warriors spent time away from economically productive pursuits necessary to feed their families. Constant warfare accumulated casualties, even if the Iroquois were skilled in the methods of surprise attacks and rapid retreats. Warfare also cultivated enemies and made borders insecure. Lives already exposed to disease, competition for resources, and social fragmentation were left even more precarious when armies destroyed crops and homes. If the Iroquois were going to survive and adapt to their new colonial neighbors, they needed to restore the balance between war and diplomacy.

ORIGINS OF THE COVENANT CHAIN

In July 1654, a Mohawk war chief appeared in Quebec to engage in treaty negotiations. The French already knew him as the leader of a Mohawk raid in 1650 on Trois-Rivières, a colonial settlement about halfway between Quebec and Montreal, and as a peace emissary from the Iroquois and Dutch at Fort Orange earlier in 1654. They called him the Flemish Bastard, and while that name no doubt derived from his parentage—he was the son of a Mohawk mother and Dutch father—it is not hard to imagine that it may also have reflected a certain frustration the French had in dealing with him.[37]

The Mohawks had been New France's most intransigent foe among the Iroquois. Even when the Flemish Bastard carried letters from Fort Orange testifying to the Mohawks' readiness for peace and made good on promises to return hostages, the French were still not sure if they could trust him. In council, he delivered a stinging speech, marked by "cleverness and intelligence," chastising the French for sending a Jesuit missionary to Onondaga before doing likewise for the Mohawks. Making reference to the Mohawks' role within the Iroquois League as the keepers of the eastern door, he asked, "Ought not one to enter a house by the door, and not by the chimney or roof of the cabin, unless he be a thief, and wish to take the inmates by surprise? We, the five Iroquois Nations, compose but one cabin; we maintain but one fire; and we have, from time immemorial, dwelt under one and the same roof. Well, then, will you not enter the cabin by the door, which is at the ground floor of the house?"[38]

Offering that kind of verbal drubbing to the French was a provocative act, but the Flemish Bastard lived up to his name, making no apologies for previous hostilities between the Mohawks and New France. For the next thirty years, he continued to play the dual role of warrior and diplomat, sometimes marshaling forces against New France and other times brokering peace with them. At some point, he apparently converted to Catholicism and joined those Iroquois who resettled in the *reserves* near Montreal and Quebec, for he last appears in the documentary record as a leader among Christian Indians allied with a French army that invaded Seneca country in 1687. When some of his fellow converts wavered in attacking the Senecas, the Flemish Bastard reportedly rallied them to the French commander with the cry, "Come, you are lusty Men, let us goe with him."[39] Perhaps by that time, the Senecas were calling him the French Bastard.

The career of the Flemish Bastard embodied many of the changes and choices faced by the Iroquois in the latter seventeenth century. The Flemish Bastard's biracial background was a product of the economic partnership the Mohawk had forged with the Dutch, a partnership that was complicated by the arrival of the English when they conquered the colony of New Netherland in 1664. The Flemish Bastard's speech, in which he likened the Iroquois to a single longhouse, is the first evidence we have of an Iroquois diplomat using that metaphor to impress upon outsiders the strength and unity of the Iroquois League. Yet, the speech's jealous assertion of the Mohawks' precedence over the Onondagas also tells us something about divisions within the League. Those divisions were exacerbated by the defection of Christian Iroquois to Canada, and then brought home again by the devastating violence of renewed warfare with New France in the 1680s and 1690s. By the end of the seventeenth century, the Iroquois were still a divided people, trying to preserve their League from the pressures unleashed on it by European colonization.

When the Flemish Bastard appeared in Quebec as a diplomat, he was working in conjunction with the Dutch at Fort Orange. Dutch colonists had their share of hostilities with Indians in the Hudson Valley, but they enjoyed peaceful relations with the Iroquois. Dutch traders tended to stay put at Fort Orange, content to have furs brought to them rather than venturing into Indian country as French traders did. Nor did the Dutch devote much energy or resources to missionary work among the Indians. The Flemish Bastard's birth notwithstanding, they tended to keep the Iroquois at arm's length, defining their relationship as a commercial one between traders and customers.[40] One French captive who had been adopted by the Mohawks declined the opportunity to be ransomed by the Dutch, citing his regard for his new family and his disdain for "those beere-bellies" living at Fort Orange, an opinion probably learned from his captors.[41]

Despite such mutual aversion, the Dutch and Iroquois hammered out a system of diplomacy that combined the former's concern for the bottom line with the latter's cultural precedents for mediating peace and friendship. In a story retold at treaty conferences throughout the colonial era, the Iroquois explained the origins of this relationship:

> One day, the Dutch arrived in Iroquois country on a ship, bringing with them hatchets, knives, guns, and other trade goods. They gave these things to the Iroquois, who found them useful and decided to tie the Dutch ship to a tree. They anchored the other end of the rope in Onondaga, at the seat of the Iroquois League. They then sat on the rope, so that if the ship were ever in trouble, they would know and come immediately to its assistance.

As the years passed, the Iroquois provided land for the
Dutch to settle on and invited them to "enter into League
and Covenant with us, and to become one People with
us." Their union having grown stronger, the Iroquois
and Dutch replaced the rope with an iron chain. When
the English came and saw "what great Friendship sub-
sisted between us and the *Dutch,*" they, too, sought to enter into covenant with the Iroquois. Knowing that an
iron chain would rust and break, the English replaced it
with a silver one and agreed to keep it bright and clean so
that it would endure forever.[42]

While the Dutch were inclined to see their relationship
with the Iroquois strictly in commercial terms, the Iroquois
perspective, as reflected in this origins story, does not distinguish
between trade and alliance. Exchange occurs, but not in a mone-
tary sense. Rather, the Dutch give trade goods to the Iroquois, who
offer in return land and security. This exchange forges a stronger
bond between the parties, represented by the progression from
rope to iron chain to silver chain, creating a covenant of mutual
obligations and benefits that needed to be "brightened" regularly.
    The method of that brightening became formalized in the lat-
ter half of the seventeenth century, as Dutch rule in New Netherland gave way to English rule in New York. The fur-trading
community at Fort Orange, renamed Albany after the English conquest, became the council fire for the Covenant Chain. The city's
magistrates, who remained overwhelmingly Dutch, convened periodic treaty conferences there with the Iroquois. When the English
governor of New York attended these meetings, he became the presiding officer. Treaty conferences typically opened with a version of
the Iroquois condolence ceremony. Each side took a turn as the
"clear-minded" moiety, giving three strings of the marine shell
beads known as wampum to the other side to assuage their grief and
clear their eyes, ears, and throat, so that they might see, hear, and

speak clearly again. The bulk of the proceedings were then given over to speeches, as each side presented and responded to grievances and requests concerning trade, land, and alliance.[43]

Just as they did in the condolence ceremony, speakers punctuated their remarks in treaty negotiations by passing wampum strings and belts across the council fire. As Bartram and Weiser witnessed at Onondaga in 1743, these strings and belts were displayed on a rack or pole during the proceedings to provide a visual record of what was being said. White wampum beads symbolized peace, friendship, and well-being. Purple beads, referred to as black by their users, symbolized mourning, war, and disruption in the natural order of things. The contrast between these two types of beads made it possible to weave designs into belts, which the orator could then interpret for his audience. Typically, the designs found on wampum belts featured geometric or anthropomorphic designs, such as parallel lines, linked diamonds or squares, or human figures holding hands. The size of the belt indicated the importance of the point it accompanied relative to others made in that same speech or council. Once accepted by the other side, the belt became part of the official record of the council, an artifact that would be saved and used at subsequent meetings to recall what had transpired there.[44]

When all points had been answered to everyone's satisfaction, each side exchanged presents and professions of friendship before parting. In a manner similar to the use of titles on the League's Grand Council, Iroquois participants in the Covenant Chain gave names to the colonial officials they met that were passed on to subsequent holders of those positions, so that the successor of a colonial governor or Indian agent could be raised up in his place at the council fire. The governor of New York became known as "Corlaer," in honor of Arent van Curler, an early fur trader and broker between the Dutch and Mohawks. The city magistrates of Albany became known collectively as "Quider," an Indian name originally given by the Mohawks to city mayor Peter Schuyler.[45]

In forging these diplomatic relations with outsiders, the Iroquois acted on their own cultural and historical precedents. In particular, the condolence and requickening ceremonies became the paradigms by which they engaged in diplomacy and extended their notions of kinship and reciprocal obligations to outsiders. The Iroquois described such bonds as "linking arms together," a metaphor that expressed perfectly the nonhierarchical, kinship-based manner in which they thought of their relations with colonial and native allies.[46]

The English were slow to accept such notions and took a more top-down approach to the council fire. At an Albany treaty conference in 1688, New York governor Edmund Andros addressed the Iroquois as "children" and pushed them to acknowledge their "submission" to the English Crown. The Iroquois refused to call the New York governor "father," and instead insisted that each side address the other as "brethren." "We are a free people," they reminded Andros, "uniting our selves to what sachem we please."[47] When one of Andros's successors pointed out in a fit of pique that the Iroquois addressed the governor of New France as "father," an Iroquois speaker replied that it was for "no other Reason . . . but because he calls us Children. These names signify nothing."[48] Obviously, the names did signify something, otherwise the Iroquois would have addressed the New York governor as he pleased. Like other Indians of the Northeast, they called the French governor "father" because he played that role properly, as it was defined within their own kinship relations: He provided generous material support for his "children" and helped to mediate their conflicts with others, but never presumed absolute authority over them or expected unquestioning obedience from them.[49]

Over the course of the colonial era, variations and adaptations occurred in Iroquois treaty-making ritual that were clearly the product of their encounter with Europeans. We will explore some of these in much greater detail in later chapters, but it is important to note here the changes that occurred in gift-giving. Gift exchange was an important part of League ritual, but the objects involved were small in quantity and of no economic significance. In their diplomatic encounters with the French, Dutch, and English, on the other hand, the Iroquois came to expect large donations of trade goods in addition to traditional condolence gifts such as wampum and tobacco. They associated the size of these donations with the other party's sincerity and came to rely on them as supplements to the goods they acquired through the fur trade. Chiefs gained prestige and influence at home by redistributing such diplomatic presents among their kin and neighbors.

The Covenant Chain borrowed extensively from the values and customs of the Iroquois League, but it operated independently of it as a framework for Iroquois-European diplomacy. Colonial Europeans such as Weiser, who had extensive experience in Iroquois diplomacy, remained aloof from the League and unfamiliar with its operations. The Covenant Chain, on the other hand, became a bona fide intercultural phenomenon, blending native and colonial customs in an effort to preserve peace and trade between the Iroquois and their Dutch and English neighbors.

THE STRUGGLE WITH NEW FRANCE

While the English would have preferred it otherwise, the Iroquois never conceived of the Covenant Chain as an exclusive relationship. They approached diplomacy with the French in much the same manner as they did diplomacy with the Dutch and English. They addressed the governor-general of New France as "Onontio," meaning Big Mountain, a name derived from the translation of the name of an early holder of that office.[50] They kept a council fire kindled in Montreal, where they negotiated matters of trade and war and expected to receive generous gifts of goods as evidence of the French esteem for their friendship.

Unfortunately, linking arms with the French proved to be difficult in the closing decades of the seventeenth century. Iroquois warfare against the Illinois, Miamis, Ottawas, and other nations from the western Great Lakes frustrated French efforts to extend their fur trade and reignited tensions along the Canadian frontier. As Jesuit missionaries in Iroquoia retreated to Canadian *reserves* with their converts, those Iroquois more inclined to favor alliance with the Dutch and English gained ascendancy within their communities. By 1684, the French missionary endeavor in Iroquoia was over. In that same year, at a treaty conference in Albany, New York governor Thomas Dongan gave the Iroquois banners emblazoned with the arms of the Duke of York, the proprietor of New York and brother of King Charles II, to display in their towns as evidence of their allegiance with England. Meanwhile, the French raised an expeditionary force to invade the western Iroquois nations, but sickness among the troops and timely diplomatic intervention by the Onondaga chief Otreouti stalled them at the eastern end of Lake Ontario. The French returned to Iroquoia with greater purpose in 1687, burning the major Seneca towns and destroying their crops and food stores. This was the expedition in which the Flemish Bastard and other Catholic Iroquois assisted, a portent of more interneccine Iroquois violence to come in the 1690s.[51]

In 1689, events in Europe drew the Iroquois into the emerging transatlantic imperial rivalry between France and England. The ascension of the Dutch Protestant William of Orange to the English throne in 1688 set in motion an Anglo-French conflict known as King William's War in English North America. Colonial governments in Canada, New England, and New York took advantage of the war in Europe to engage in hostilities of their own. Catholic Iroquois in Canada participated in a devastating French attack on the Dutch settlement of Schenectady in the Mohawk Valley in 1690. Those Iroquois who remained in their homelands favored the English, but their colonial allies failed in 1690 and again in 1691 to deliver promised men and arms for a retaliatory invasion of Canada.

The Covenant Chain left pro-English Iroquois exposed and bereft of assistance. In 1693 a combined French and Indian force laid waste to three Mohawk towns in much the same manner as the Seneca invasion six years earlier. The French commander had orders to offer no quarter to Mohawk warriors, but found such carnage unnecessary because "they surrendered at discretion and expressed themselves pleased at having this opportunity to come and live with our Indians, to whom they were closely related."[52] Close to three hundred Mohawk captives, many taken willingly, joined the triumphant invaders on their journey back to Canada. The eastern and western doors of the Longhouse had been breached and its inhabitants humiliated. In 1696, another French and Indian force did the same to the Onondagas and Oneidas in the Longhouse's center.[53]

The French and English ceased their hostilities with the Treaty of Ryswick in 1697, but Iroquoia remained open to the depredations of New France. As a new century dawned, the Iroquois League was battered and beaten. More than a decade of violence had reduced its population to little more than five thousand. About half of the League's warriors had perished during the 1690s.[54] The Longhouse had been invaded and shaken to its very foundations by disease, migration, and war, with no end in sight. If the Five Nations were going to remain united, if they were going to protect their political and territorial autonomy from European intrusion, then they would have to find new sources of strength and cohesion. To make the Longhouse whole again, it would be necessary to cultivate new alliances with outsiders, native and colonial, and to link arms together with them as one people.

2

LINKING ARMS

AT THE START of the eighteenth century, the Iroquois found themselves in a precarious position between two formidable imperial rivals, France and England. A century's worth of war, disease, and depopulation had shifted the military balance of power in favor of the colonizers, but even if the Five Nations had commanded the resources necessary to deal the newcomers a decisive blow, *realpolitik* would have dictated otherwise. The fur trade had wrought material dependence on European goods, while religious conversions and sexual unions had knit other, more intimate bonds across cultural and geographic borders. The question in Iroquoia during the opening decades of the eighteenth century was not "*can* we live with these neighbors?" but "*how* do we live with these neighbors?"

A single violent incident in the opening decade of the new century illustrated this dilemma. Alexander Montour was the son of a French emigrant to Canada and a Mohawk woman. Like the Flemish Bastard a generation before him, Montour put his cross-cultural background to use in diplomacy. He started as a fur trader who traveled the routes between Montreal and the "far Indians,"

Algonquian-speaking peoples—Ottawas, Miamis, Mississaugas, Wyandots, Potawatomis, Illinois, Foxes, and others—who inhabited the Upper Great Lakes region that the French called the *pays d'en haut*.[1] By 1701, the French had anchored their hold on the western fur trade with a string of posts that stretched from Fort Frontenac on the eastern shore of Lake Ontario to Michilimackinac, on the straits between Lakes Huron and Michigan. The fur trade drew the western nations into New France's orbit, but also close enough to Iroquoia to learn that Albany traders offered cheaper and more plentiful goods. Montour was well positioned, geographically and culturally, to negotiate a rapprochement between the Iroquois and the western Algonquians that would allow the latter to trade in Albany.

In April 1709, Montour was escorting ten chiefs from the *pays d'en haut* through Iroquoia. In the parlance of Iroquois diplomacy, he was helping the western nations to "clear a path" so that all three groups—the Iroquois, the western Algonquians, and the Albany traders—might "link arms together" in peace and friendship. Unfortunately, that metaphorical path intersected quite literally with one traveled by Louis-Thomas Chabert de Joncaire, a French soldier and fur trader.

Joncaire had much in common with Montour. He had come to Canada as a soldier in the 1680s, but was taken captive by the Senecas shortly thereafter. Marked for torture and execution, he defied his fate by breaking the nose of one of his tormentors, an act that so impressed his captors that they chose to adopt him instead. Joncaire resided among the Senecas, learned their language, and became an influential agent between them and the government of New France. He spent much of his time shuttling between Montreal and the Senecas, but his meeting with Montour was no accident. The French governor-general of Canada, Philip de Rigaud de Vaudreuil, had learned of Montour's intercessory efforts between the western nations and Albany, and he ordered Joncaire to stop him.[2]

Joncaire and a party of other Frenchmen intercepted Montour's embassy in Cayuga country. Joncaire told Montour to turn back, or he would "oblige the 5 Nations to kill him." Montour, perhaps aware that Joncaire's influence did not extend much beyond Seneca country, through which he had already safely passed, refused to comply. Joncaire changed tactics and offered to smoke with Montour instead. Montour took out his knife to cut some tobacco. Joncaire mocked its small size and told Montour that he would give him a much better knife in its place. When Montour handed his knife over, Joncaire "flung it away" and one of his compatriots took out a hatchet hidden beneath his coat and buried it in Montour's head. So ended the career of one intercultural diplomat. Montour's companions seized Joncaire, intending to kill him, but Montour's brother-in-law, who was among their number, interceded. Perhaps he feared another war with New France or perhaps he had some hidden sympathy with Joncaire's mission, but for whatever reason, he allowed Joncaire to be on his way.[3]

"Opening paths" and "linking arms" were pleasant-sounding metaphors for what could be a high-stakes business on the early American frontier. As Montour's experience illustrated, an open path could easily lead to an early grave. Montour's death was especially brutal because it involved egregious violations of the etiquette that governed intercultural trade and diplomacy. Warning someone out of territory you considered your own was one thing, but inviting that person to smoke and then using a deceptive offer of a gift exchange to kill him was another. Perhaps Joncaire, because of his French background and loyalties, did not feel bound by Iroquoian diplomatic customs, and so was willing to put them to use in committing murder.

His bold move, however, did not succeed in preventing the Iroquois from mediating peace between the western nations and Albany. During the first two decades of the eighteenth century, the Five Nations worked individually and collectively to open

paths in all directions of the compass. Linking arms with some
people invariably involved irritating, offending, or raising the
wrath of others, but as a strategy of self-preservation, it enabled
the Iroquois to play a central role in the intercultural relations
that reshaped eighteenth-century North America.

EDGING TOWARD NEUTRALITY

The seventeenth century produced a division within the Longhouse between those Iroquois allied with the English and those
allied with the French.[4] While members of each faction could be
found in each of the Five Nations, the pro-English Iroquois
tended to be from the eastern half of the Longhouse. They were
motivated by personal and economic ties to Albany and their
suspicion of French missionaries who depleted local populations
by drawing their converts to Canadian *reserves*. The pro-French
Iroquois tended to come from communities in the western half of
the Longhouse, which had absorbed many captives formerly
allied with the French during the seventeenth century.

A host of other factors rooted in Iroquois culture affected
these loyalties. Older men traditionally played the role of peace-
makers in Iroquois diplomacy and thus sought accommodation
with the French and their allies, while young men, anxious to distinguish themselves as warriors, continued to participate in war
parties. Ties of kinship between those Iroquois who emigrated to
Canadian *reserves* and those who stayed behind also dampened
the enthusiasm for war in some quarters, while the potential for
taking of captives among French-allied Indians increased it in
others. Neither the pro-French nor the pro-English faction was
strong enough to overcome the decentralized and autonomous
nature of Iroquois decision-making, so neither side could negotiate for the League as a whole during the tumultuous years of
King William's War.

Signs of a third way emerged during the 1690s. Led by an Onondaga chief named Teganissorens, some Iroquois pushed for neutrality between the French and English. The neutralists gained favor as more Iroquois realized that the English would never deliver more than promises in the war against New France and that the French would welcome peace as a means of extending their western fur trade. After a French army destroyed three Mohawk towns in early 1693, representatives from the Five Nations met in Onondaga and outfitted Teganissorens with wampum belts to carry to the French governor-general, Louis de Buade de Frontenac, to initiate three-way peace negotiations among the Iroquois, French, and English.[5]

The description of three of these belts, as recorded by French missionary Pierre Millet, who had been adopted by the Oneidas, illustrates how the color, design, and size of wampum belts gave meaning to a diplomat's speech-making. The first belt featured five black squares on a white background, representing "the Five Iroquois Nations, who have all unanimously agreed to this embassy." The second, "a large belt and almost entirely black," was for the purpose of upsetting the "war kettle" of the French, or in other words, bringing about a cease-fire while peace negotiations occurred. The Iroquois intended for the third belt, "the longest of all," to be sent to the French king, so that he and his English counterpart might agree to peace "not only between all the Indians but between all their relations." The Iroquois desired an answer to this belt "as soon as possible."[6]

Neither the English at Albany nor the French in Canada were quite ready to upset the war kettle in 1694. In Canada, Frontenac played hardball with the Iroquois messengers sent to clear a path for Teganissorens. Suspecting that their real purpose was to convince those Iroquois living on Canadian *reserves* to return home, Frontenac "kicked away" their wampum belts. Nevertheless, he offered to "tie up his hatchet" for two months on the condition that Teganissorens arrive with "two principal Chiefs of each nation" by the end of that time to make his case for peace. If anyone else came in Teganissorens's place, they would find the path closed, and if captured, they "will not escape roasting."[7]

It was in that air of mutual suspicion that Teganissorens arrived in Quebec in May 1694. Like many other Iroquois diplomats, he impressed his European contemporaries with his combination of a powerful physical presence and an impressive eloquence, even when he spoke in a tongue they did not understand. A French official described him as possessing "as perfect a grace as is vouchsafed to an unpolished and uncivilized people."[8] Years later, a New Yorker who heard Teganissorens speak likened him to the ancient Roman statesman Cicero and noted that his "graceful Elocution" would have pleased listeners "in any Part of the World."[9] In Quebec, Teganissorens made "a good Appearance" dining alongside Frontenac and New France's other leading officials, "cloathed in Scarlet trim'd with Gold and with a laced Bever Hat on his Head." That last item was a gift he had received from New York governor Benjamin Fletcher at an earlier treaty conference in Albany. No doubt, Fletcher would have bristled at the notion of contributing to Teganissorens's sartorial splendor in Quebec.[10]

Teganissorens achieved part of what he had come for. Frontenac accepted his offer to "bury our hatchet" and together they worked out a tentative peace. Frontenac, however, refused Teganissorens's invitation to extend the peace to the English. "My war with them has nothing to do with my war against you," he stated unequivocally. The western Algonquians followed suit, telling Teganissorens, "Know, then, that the peace Onontio accords you for himself and for us, hath no connection with the English, and if our Father turn the hatchet in that direction, ours will turn thither also."[11]

A few months later, Teganissorens treated in Albany with Governor Fletcher and representatives from New Jersey, Massachusetts, and Connecticut. He chided them for failing to prosecute the war against New France effectively: "The Greese is melted from our Flesh, and drops upon our Neighbours [meaning the English colonies], who are grown fat, and live at ease, while we become lean; They flourish, and we decrease." Fletcher refused Teganissorens's offer to help negotiate peace between the two European powers, stating, "Peace could be only made between them by the two Kings." Nor did he warm to the idea of the Iroquois treating with New France independently of the English. However, he was unable to provide "any Assurance of vigorous Assistance" in continuing the war, and so half-heartedly offered his blessing to Teganissorens's efforts.[12]

Teganissorens's shuttle diplomacy between New York and Canada made perfect sense from the perspective of Iroquoia. Linking arms with Frontenac at Quebec offered the added benefits of peace with the Canadian Iroquois and western Algonquians. The Covenant Chain already provided peace with the English, but there was no reason why it could not be used to link arms between the English and French, not only in North America, but in Europe as well. Frontenac and Fletcher disagreed. Neither entertained seriously the notion that an alliance with native peoples in North America might somehow provide a foundation for peace between France and England in America or Europe. The New Yorkers considered the Covenant Chain an exclusive relationship, one that committed the Iroquois to the English at the expense of the French. Teganissorens and like-minded Iroquois saw the Covenant Chain differently, as a relationship that could be extended indefinitely to include any number of other parties, native or European.

The peace that Teganissorens negotiated with Frontenac in 1694 proved to be fleeting. Neither side trusted the other, and further negotiations broke down over the French construction of Fort Frontenac at Cataraqui (modern Kingston, Ontario), a strategic passage between the St. Lawrence Valley and Iroquoia. In a stirring speech intended for Frontenac, one Iroquois orator summed up the neutralists' growing conviction that French arrogance and English indifference came from the same well: "You [the French] thinke your selfes the ancient inhabitants of this countrey, and longest in possession[.] Yea, all the Christian inhabitants of New York and Cayenquiragoé [Governor Fletcher] thinke the same of themselves[.] Wee Warriours are the firste and the ancient people and the greatest of You all, these parts and countrys were inhabited and trodd upon by us, the warriours, before any Christians."[13] In other words, the French and English acted as if they ruled over the Iroquois, but the Iroquois had never surrendered their land or sovereignty to anyone.

The palpable sense of frustration in those words only grew in the years that followed, strengthening the neutralists' position within the League. By 1700, an Iroquois-French rapprochement once again seemed possible. Frontenac had died, passing the governorship of New France to Louis-Hector de Callière. The western Algonquians were expressing interest in making peace with the Iroquois and opening a path to Albany's fur traders. The New Yorkers, aware that the French had made considerable strides into the western Great Lakes region, were stirring out of their lethargy and hoped to build forts and send missionaries among the Iroquois to counter the French influence there.[14] In July 1700, Teganisorrens and a delegation of Onondagas and Senecas conferred in Montreal with Callière, requesting his intercession with the Indians of the *pays d'en haut* "to take the hatchet out of their hands so that they may strike no more." Callière agreed to have a Jesuit and two French soldiers (including the former Seneca captive Joncaire) accompany the delegation back to Iroquoia, as evidence of the sincerity of French intentions.[15] The enthusiastic welcome these French agents received in Onondaga resulted in an invitation for the Iroquois to attend a treaty conference Callière planned to host in Montreal the following summer with the western Algonquians and Indians from the St. Lawrence Valley *reserves*.

While Teganissorens was in Montreal, another delegation of Iroquois conferred with New York governor Richard Coote, the Earl of Bellomont, in Albany. As was the case in Montreal, a conciliatory tone prevailed. The Iroquois asked for Protestant missionaries to counter the influence of the French Jesuits, and hinted not so subtly that "the French give their Converts Victuals and Cloathing." Bellomont agreed to send missionaries in return for permission to build a fort large enough to garrison two hundred men in Onondaga country. He encouraged the Iroquois to make peace with the western Indians so that they might be brought into the Covenant Chain.[16]

Two Cities, Two Treaties

In summer 1701, Iroquois delegations in Montreal and Albany negotiated separate treaties that formalized the Five Nations' neutrality between the French and English. Each treaty was the result of momentum that had been building over the previous year in Iroquois negotiations with the governors of Canada and New York, but taken together, they were also the culmination of an effort within the Iroquois League to quell factionalism and restore a measure of unity in their relations with outsiders.

In June, chiefs gathered in Onondaga received representatives from Montreal and Albany, sent to ensure their attendance at treaty conferences planned at their respective cities for later that summer. According to the report made by the New York agents, Teganissorens revealed in private conversations with them that the assembled chiefs were "extreamly divided" over whether to cultivate ties with the French or English. "Some will have a priest on the one side of the Castle [Longhouse] and a Minister on the other side," he said, presenting a neutralist option that would keep a path open to both sides but not favor one over the other. The New Yorkers' professions of friendship only irritated him. He wanted to know which of the colonial powers would give the Iroquois the best terms in trade and prove the most generous in conducting their diplomacy. "Our Sachims are going some to Albany, [and] some to Canada," he concluded.[17]

From the perspective of visiting Iroquois, Montreal and Albany must have seemed like very similar places in 1701. Both had the appearance of medieval market towns airlifted out of Europe and dropped down on the colonial frontier. Each was located at a junction on a major river route between the North American seacoast and the continent's interior. Albany stood near the confluence of the Hudson and Mohawk, linking New York City to Iroquoia. Montreal was built on an island in the St. Lawrence near the Ottawa River, linking Quebec with the *pays d'en haut*. Within their palisades, the streets of each city were narrow and constantly befouled by livestock. Buildings were tall and narrow, serving simultaneously as homes, workshops, and storefronts, stuffed to the rafters of their steeply pitched roofs with people and goods. Merchants, craftsmen, and tavernkeepers made up the bulk of their populations (each had about one thousand residents in 1701), but all sorts of transients came and went through their gates. Government officers and soldiers came to keep order, conduct treaties, and remind everyone they were subjects of a distant king. Fur traders, adventurers, and Indians passed through to buy, sell, and constantly challenge the authority of that distant king.[18]

Hundreds of Indians, potentially thousands, visited Albany and Montreal each year for days or weeks at a time. Each city had a seasonal fur market that peaked during the late summer, when Indian families arrived in canoes loaded with furs. These Indian visitors took their time, camping outside the city walls at night and spending their days frequenting the homes and workshops of traders and craftsmen. The market was a time of buying and selling, but also of visiting with acquaintances, mourning the deceased, and conducting diplomacy. The Indians' presence brought a touch of the exotic to the rhythms and customs of daily life for the locals, but also added immeasurably to the headaches of city magistrates, who were besieged from all sides by complaints of cheating, brawling, and drunkenness fueled by the brandy and rum that lubricated this business.[19]

Even as the annual fur markets declined in economic significance, diplomacy continued to bring Indians to Albany and Montreal. For Indians, diplomacy and trade went hand-in-hand, so any type of material exchange naturally involved the exchange of customary greetings, ceremonial presents, and related rituals. Europeans were not enamored of the ceremonial apparatus that accompanied trading with Indians—they found it tiresome and expensive—but they could not ignore the expectations that annual convoys of Indians brought with them for a warm reception and generous hospitality. Colonial governors also learned to convene their treaty conferences with Indians during the trading season, because it was the only time of the year when they could rely on Indians to attend. The crowds that trade and diplomacy brought to Albany and Montreal, while not quite captive audiences, were at least susceptible to persuasion by government officials familiar with the rules of Indian diplomacy. If the governor treated his guests right, then he could expect them to carry home reports of his largesse and goodwill that would reap dividends well worth the effort and expense.

French officials in Canada grasped this strategy more readily than their peers in New York. The governors of colonial New York did not acquire their positions by virtue of their expertise in Indian affairs. On the contrary, most were second-rate political appointments, well-connected enough in London to rate a job from the Crown but not talented or reliable enough to be trusted with one at home. When such officials made the trip to Albany to preside at a treaty conference, they often found themselves out of their element. Bellomont, at his first Albany treaty conference in 1698, unwittingly flubbed the opening of the proceedings when instead of greeting his Iroquois counterparts with the customary strings of wampum and words of condolence, he complained that his trip to see them had been "tedious and troublesome, and I am now much indisposed by the Pains of the Gout."[20] Two years later, Bellomont was back in Albany, and his mood had not improved. He complained to a correspondent that treating with the Iroquois was "the greatest fatigue I ever underwent in my whole life . . . shut up in a close chamber with 50 Sachems, who besides the stink of bear's grease with which they plentifully dawb'd themselves, were continually either smoking tobacco or drinking drams of rum."[21] Judging from Bellomont's crankiness, perhaps tobacco and rum were precisely what the Indians needed to endure their councils with him.[22] As for the bear's grease, it made an excellent insect repellent.

Montreal had another advantage over Albany in Indian relations: a strong missionary presence that encouraged close ties with neighboring Indians. Priests and nuns from two missionary orders, the Sulpicians and the Congregation de Notre Dame, lived in Montreal and worked as the spiritual overseers of La Montagne, a *reserve* populated by a mixture of Iroquoian and Algonquian converts that shared Montreal island with the city. Across the water on the south bank of the St. Lawrence, Jesuit missionaries attended the faithful on another *reserve*, Kahnawake. Founded by Iroquoian converts from the Mohawk Valley, Kahnawake was the largest *reserve* in New France and had a population that rivaled Montreal's.[23]

In contrast, seventeenth-century Albany had cultivated much weaker spiritual and social ties with its Indian neighbors. The Dutch colonizers of New Netherland never made converting Indians a priority. Working chiefly on his own initiative, the Reverend Godfridius Dellius converted a number of Mohawks in the 1690s, and they became the core of a Protestant Mohawk population that figured significantly in British-Iroquois relations in the eighteenth century. However, Dellius's converts never rivaled in number those Mohawks who resettled in the *reserves* of Canada, and they often complained of Albany's neglect of their spiritual instruction and material support.[24] Religion worked much more effectively as a bond of intercultural communication and obligation in Montreal, whereas in Albany, it proved to be another bone of contention between colonists and Indians.

About two hundred Iroquois traveled to Montreal in July 1701 to participate in the treaty conference there. They accounted for only a fraction of the thirteen hundred Indians who gathered for this meeting, but figured prominently in its negotiations and outcome. Callière, stepping into the role of Onontio, the French "father" who provided for his Indian children and helped them mediate their differences, used the occasion to make peace between his Indian allies in New France and the Five Nations. A major point of contention concerned the return of prisoners between the western Algonquians and the League Iroquois, but too much was at stake to allow that obstacle to stand. In exchange for agreeing to peace with the western Algonquians, the Iroquois negotiated freedom to trade at French posts in the *pays d'en haut*. The western nations extracted from the Iroquois recognition of their right to hunt and live on disputed territory in the Upper Great Lakes, which the Iroquois claimed they had conquered during the wars of the previous century. The French stood to gain from the revitalization of the fur trade in the *pays d'en haut*, and they also convinced the Iroquois to allow the return of French missionaries to their homelands.[25]

Realizing how much was at stake in these proceedings, Callière made sure to observe all necessary treaty protocol. When Kondiaronk, a Huron who was the western Indians' chief spokesmen, suddenly fell ill and died, Callière oversaw a funeral that combined Native American and European customs. The deceased chief lay in state, dressed in a French officer's uniform and sprinkled with holy water, for colonists and Indians to pay their respects. Callière provided condolence presents to Kondiaronk's kinsfolk and fellow Hurons and then sponsored a funeral parade that was "magnificient and singular." French soldiers and Indian warriors headed the procession, followed by clergy, six war chiefs carrying the deceased's bier, Kondiaronk's family, the chiefs of the assembled nations, and French officials. Observers watched a tableau of New France pass before their eyes: soldiers and warriors, chiefs and clergy and magistrates, symbolically linking arms as they mourned a fallen leader.[26]

A few days later, Callière orchestrated an equally spectacular public assembly for the signing of the three-way peace treaty between the Five Nations, New France, and its allied Indian nations. On a plain outside the city's walls, he had workers build a public enclosure large enough to hold the Indians in attendance plus local citizens. With missionaries acting as his interpreters, the governor took turns addressing each nation and exchanging wampum belts and prisoners with them. One French chronicler confessed that his countrymen found the whole affair "a kind of comedy" because the Indians, especially those from the remote western nations, "were dressed and adorned in a manner quite grotesque, contrasting curiously with the grave and serious demeanor they affected" in their speeches. One Fox gave particular amusement. He painted his face red and wore on his head an old French wig, "profusely powdered and ill combed," creating an appearance "at once frightful and ridiculous." When he took off the wig to "salute the Governor-General in the French style," the crowd burst out in laughter, "which did not disconcert him, for he doubtless took it as applause."[27] One wonders how many jokes the Indians told back in their camps about the foppish costumes and manners exhibited by Montreal's elite.

Despite the death of Kondiaronk and an outbreak of illness in the Indians' camp, the Montreal treaty conference had gone well. Moments of grave solemnity balanced outbursts of hilarity. Condolence rituals and private councils gave way to presents, feasting, and professions of friendship. Onontio had taken "hold anew of all your hatchets and other warlike weapons and put them, together with my own, in so deep a trench that no one can take up again to disturb the peace." For their part, the Iroquois rejoiced in a "Tree of Peace" planted in Montreal, whose roots and leaves would grow "to shelter us."[28]

Meanwhile, another sizable contingent of Iroquois had traveled to Albany to meet with the New York governor. Bellomont had died since the previous year's treaty conference—presumably passing on to an Englishman's heaven without gout, bear's grease, tobacco, or rum—leaving Lieutenant Governor John Nanfan to brighten the Covenant Chain. The New Yorkers were not pleased that the Iroquois had gone against their wishes and sent a delegation to the Montreal conference, but they also knew they were powerless to stop it.

In their speeches to Nanfan, the Iroquois complained of poor prices for their furs at Albany and of French intrusions into their hunting territory, especially at Detroit (to which they were simultaneously acquiescing in Montreal). They offered novel solutions for both problems. To encourage good prices for furs, they gave the governor ten beaver pelts to send to London, so that King William might wear a hat made from them and inspire "all his good subjects" to follow his example. In addition to manipulating London's next fashion season, they proposed giving "all that land where the Beaver hunting is which wee won with the sword eighty years ago" to the king, so that he might "be our protector and defender there."[29]

Nanfan knew a good deal when he heard one: the makings of a fancy hat *and* thousands of acres of prime Great Lakes real estate. What wasn't to like? With the help of the assembled chiefs, he had a deed and map drawn up, placing the "Beaver Hunting Ground" under the Crown's protection. This territory was not Iroquoia proper, but the western Great Lakes region over which the Iroquois had been fighting with the western Algonquians and French for the past twenty years. It stretched from the northwestern shore of Lake Ontario to Lake Huron, westward to encompass the lower Michigan peninsula, and then eastward again to Lake Erie.[30]

The Iroquois had nothing to lose in this deal because they put nothing on the table other than the beaver pelts intended for King William's head. Land they had spent the past twenty years fighting over in a bitter and inconclusive war they now placed under protection of the English, who could start expending their own blood and treasure in defending it. The deed was an insurance policy of sorts, a way of committing the English to fighting for this disputed territory, should the peace being negotiated in Montreal collapse.

Historians have taken to calling the Montreal and Albany treaties of 1701 the "Grand Settlement" because it ended a period of protracted warfare for the Iroquois and ushered in the era of their neutrality between the English and French empires in North America.[31] That is the sort of elevated terminology that can only be used in hindsight, but it does convey a sense of the neutralists' triumph. Teganissorens attended neither the Montreal nor Albany treaties, but his influence was apparent in how each managed to hold its colonial counterparts at arm's length yet embrace them at the same time. In Montreal, the Iroquois finally made peace with Onontio and his Indian allies, but promised only neutrality in future Anglo-French conflicts. In Albany, the Iroquois stood by their peace with the French but drew the English closer by placing their disputed hunting territory under the Crown's protection. The Iroquois remained autonomous, arms linked with the French and English but still standing firmly on their own two feet.

Linking Arms East and West

In diplomatic councils, the Iroquois often referred to the "Tree of Peace," planted over the hole where they buried their hatchets at war's end. As the tree grew, its branches and roots spread outward to encompass more people. Wampum belts occasionally featured representations of the Tree of Peace, and Europeans engraved its image on peace medals and certificates they distributed to allied chiefs. References to the "white roots of peace" (white because that color symbolized well-being) were another variant of this metaphorical expression of alliance.[32]

The "roots of peace," however, could not flourish without time spent on the routes of peace. That is to say, Iroquois diplomacy involved an enormous amount of coming and going by emissaries who traveled by foot and canoe among native and colonial communities in a never-ending cycle of greetings, speeches, and councils. The footpaths of Indian America were not used just by warriors and their captives; they were highways for messengers, fur traders, hunters, families commuting to seasonal camps, and Indians and colonists conducting diplomacy.[33] In the years after the Grand Settlement of 1701, the Iroquois traversed these routes, trying to extend their influence in all directions.

First, the Iroquois turned their attention westward to open a path between the Algonquians of the *pays d'en haut* and Albany. The western nations knew that they could acquire a better variety of goods at better prices in Albany than in New France, and the Albany traders were anxious to tap into the flow of furs out of the Great Lakes. The Iroquois, their own supply of furs having long been depleted by overhunting, stood to gain by acting as diplomatic middlemen in this exchange. To trade in Albany, western Indians would have to pass through Iroquoia and engage in the necessary diplomacy and gift exchanges along the way. At the eastern end of this path, the Albany traders would have to keep hold of their end of the Covenant Chain by supplying the Iroquois with ample presents and low prices.[34] The French tried to prevent the defection of the western Algonquians' trade, but they met with limited success. Even Joncaire's dramatic intervention in 1709 did not keep the delegation of western Algonquians that had been traveling with the ill-fated Montour from making their way to Albany and initiating diplomatic relations there.[35]

The following year, in June 1710, the Iroquois positioned themselves squarely as middlemen in this diplomacy by inviting representatives from Albany to Onondaga to meet with a party of Ottawas. The Ottawas asked to be taken into the Covenant Chain, addressing the New Yorkers as "Father" (as they did the governor of New France). Referring to Montour's mission the previous year, they stated, "I have last summer sucked one of your Breasts but now I am come to suck them both," a reference to sustenance they would draw from the Albany trade. The image of the English father nursing his Indian children might have disquieted some in attendance, but the Iroquois and Albany representatives welcomed the Ottawas, accepting from them two calumets, the traditional peace pipes of the western Algonquian nations, so that "we may smoak on them together in peace as often as we shall meet in this place."[36]

Episodes of Iroquois brokerage like this one enabled Albany's share of the western fur trade to expand. Anglo-French competition grew accordingly, especially after the renewal of warfare between the two powers in Europe in 1702. The Iroquois initially maintained their neutrality during the War of the Spanish Succession, known as Queen Anne's War in the English colonies. Through Joncaire, the French continued to curry the favor of the western inhabitants of the Longhouse, sending Jesuit missionaries among the Onondagas, Cayugas, and Senecas, along with blacksmiths to manufacture and repair their tools and weapons. The English recruited warriors from among those Iroquois disaffected by the French for invasions of Canada in 1709 and 1711, but both expeditions fizzled, contributing in Iroquois eyes to the English reputation for military incompetence. Like the French, the English used missionaries and blacksmiths to cultivate Iroquois support. The successful embassy of the four Indian kings to London in 1710 resulted in the construction of a fort and Anglican chapel near the Mohawk town of Tionon-deroge, known in Albany as the "lower Mohawk castle." A significant percentage of Mohawks were baptized there in the early eighteenth century, strengthening the bond between the keepers of the Longhouse's eastern door and the English.

But missionaries could go only so far in the battle for Iroquois hearts and minds. At an Albany treaty conference in 1713, Iroquois delegates grew impatient with hearing about spiritual rewards in the hereafter when what they needed was material support in the here and now. What they really wanted, they told New York governor Robert Hunter, were lower trade prices and more blacksmiths: "When we consider what fine Cloaths the Christians put on every Sabbath day when they go to church and that goods are still so dear that we cannot purchase good cloaths but would be under necessity to go to Church with an old nasty Bear Skin or Greezy Deer Skin, We defer the receiving of Missionaries till goods become so cheap that we can buy suitable cloaths to go to Church." One colonial commentator found this exchange representative of skewed Iroquois priorities, for "a Smith was in greater Esteem with these politicians than a Parson."[37] Maybe so, but one person's shortsightedness is another's pragmatism. Far more modern Americans are willing to tolerate a marginal clergyman working on their soul than are willing to tolerate a marginal mechanic working on their car.

Ultimately, merchants in New France and New York completed end runs around the Iroquois in the western fur trade. Joncaire convinced the Senecas to allow the French to build a trading post at the Niagara portage between Lakes Erie and Ontario. Impressively rebuilt and expanded in the mid-1720s, Fort Niagara enabled French traders to intercept western Algonquians before they entered Seneca country. From Niagara, the French could send furs by water to Fort Frontenac on the eastern end of Lake Ontario, bypassing Iroquoia entirely. The New Yorkers responded by building their own fort and trading post at

Oswego on the southeastern shore of Lake Ontario in the 1720s. Oswego offered Indians to the north and west an alternative to trading at Niagara or Frontenac, and they would no longer have to go all the way to Albany for the cheaper English goods. In this reconfigured western fur trade, some Iroquois continued to act as middlemen, but now they were reduced to the role of coolies, hauling watercraft and goods around the portages leading to these sites. Senecas near Niagara and Onondagas and Oneidas near Oswego often earned their pay in brandy and rum, which eroded the physical and social health of their local communities.[38]

The Grand Settlement of 1701 also made it possible for the Five Nations to extend their influence eastward among Indians and colonists living along the Canada–New England frontier. The native peoples with whom they were most concerned in this region were their kin on the *reserves* near Montreal and Quebec. When Catholic Iroquois resettled in the St. Lawrence Valley, they mixed with other native peoples—Hurons, Montagnais, Abenakis, Algonquins—converted by French missionaries, but they never lost their cultural kinship with those who remained in Iroquoia. They fought alongside French soldiers and their native allies in Queen Anne's War, but they avoided making war on their cousins, who likewise refused English entreaties to attack them. This neutrality caused no end of frustration for their colonial neighbors, but it also created new diplomatic and economic opportunities.

To avoid warring against their kin among the League Iroquois, the Canadian Iroquois joined French raids along the New England frontier. In February 1704, they were among the warriors and soldiers who attacked Deerfield, Massachusetts, in the most famous raid of Queen Anne's War. The devastation of that raid, which carried many captives back to Canada, infuriated New Englanders. Massachusetts officials had long participated in Covenant Chain diplomacy, which they believed bound the Iroquois to assist them against their enemies. The Five Nations interpreted that relationship differently, offering instead their services as intermediaries in the repatriation of captives.

One instance from 1706 illustrates this process. A boy captured at Deerfield was adopted by a Christian Oneida family at Kahnawake to replace a deceased kinsman. New Englanders enlisted the New York Oneidas to assist them in recovering the boy. The Oneidas' efforts involved several trips to Montreal and Kahnawake, but at last they prevailed, bringing the boy back to Albany and receiving "a reward for their trouble."[39] Such rewards were one of the benefits of the neutrality maintained between the League Iroquois and the Canadian Iroquois. When war broke out between Massachusetts and French-allied Abenakis in the 1720s, the Five Nations refused the New Englanders' pleas to enter the fray as their "fellow Subjects and Allies." In treaty conferences convened in Albany and Boston, they insisted on playing the role of mediators who would "put both Hatchets together" and "endeavour to compromise Matters and conclude a reconciliation and Peace on all sides."[40] Predictably, the New Englanders dismissed such answers as insufficient and pressed for a more bellicose response that never came.

Another material benefit that accrued to the Iroquois from their neutrality with their Canadian kin involved the illicit fur trade between Montreal and Albany. New France and New York forbade trade across their shared border, but merchants on both sides dodged that prohibition by having Iroquois traveling between Mohawk country and Montreal do their smuggling for them. Mohawks from Kahnawake appeared in Albany regularly, ostensibly to "brighten" their peace with the New Yorkers, but also to ferry French furs south and English goods north.[41] The local Albany magistrates charged with managing Indian affairs found this diplomacy a profitable means of keeping the peace along their northern frontier. Those New Yorkers concerned about French competition in the West were less pleased, because the Albany-Montreal trade provided French traders with cheap goods. New Englanders were livid about it, because they claimed it supplied the Canadian Indians with the weapons and supplies they needed to terrorize frontier towns such as Deerfield. Despite their protests, the smuggling continued because it worked so well for its participants, perfectly mixing trade and diplomacy in the traditional Iroquoian manner.[42]

Props to the South

The most important route south from Iroquoia was the Susquehanna River, which flowed from its headwaters in Oneida country through Pennsylvania and Maryland until emptying into the Chesapeake Bay. Borders drawn by royal ministers in London meant little to the native inhabitants of this region. Regardless of colonial jurisdictions, they treated the Susquehanna as a wide north-to-south corridor that connected the eastern Great Lakes to the Chesapeake and regions farther south. The importance of this route and the lack of any clear native or colonial power governing it created a vacuum into which the Iroquois readily extended their diplomacy and power.

During the late seventeenth century, the Iroquois had used the Susquehanna Valley as a warpath for attacking the Susquehannocks, an Iroquoian-speaking people who had migrated out of Iroquoia into the lower Susquehanna Valley about a century earlier. Wars with the Iroquois and English colonists in the Chesapeake region had dispersed the Susquehannocks by 1680. Some assimilated into the Five Nations as captives and adoptees; others joined the Delaware Indians who lived farther east. Still others joined Indian peoples displaced by other seventeenth-century wars—such as the Shawnees from the Ohio Valley, the Conoys from the lower Potomac Valley, and the Nanticokes from Maryland's eastern shore—who began repopulating the lower Susquehanna Valley in the 1690s. By 1710, the town of

Conestoga (in modern Lancaster County, Pennsylvania) had emerged as a new center for Indian trade and diplomacy in that region. Its inhabitants had close cultural ties to the Iroquois and became known collectively to colonial traders and officials as the Conestogas.[43]

The Iroquois abetted the native repopulation of the Susquehanna Valley by allowing refugee peoples who acknowledged their authority to settle there. Colonial observers described this as a tributary relationship forced on weaker nations by their Iroquois conquerors, but that interpretation derived more from English efforts to bolster their own claims to the region than from any definitive Iroquois victories over these groups. The Iroquois themselves, relying on the same metaphor they used to describe their League, referred to these groups as "props" who helped support and extend the Longhouse. As props to the Longhouse, they enjoyed security from Iroquois attack. They were also supposed to assist the Iroquois in fighting their wars, although that ultimately remained a decision made at the local level by warriors, war chiefs, and clan matrons, just as it was in Iroquoia. More important, the Iroquois expected the Susquehanna Valley Indians to defer to them in matters of diplomacy with colonial governments. So long as they acknowledged Iroquois leadership in this regard, they could reap the material benefits of presents and provisions distributed at treaty conferences in New York and Pennsylvania.[44] Precedent for this sort of relationship already existed. The Iroquois treated a group known as the River Indians—remnant Hudson Valley and New England Algonquians—as eastern props for the Longhouse. The River Indians participated in Covenant Chain treaties in Albany, where they received separate, smaller presents granted by the New York governor.[45]

The extension of the Longhouse into the Susquehanna Valley strengthened the hand of the Iroquois in Pennsylvania's Indian relations. William Penn had founded his colony on a combination of Quaker idealism and hardnosed entrepreneurship. During the two trips he made to North America, he gained a reputation for dealing fairly with the Indians, but he also moved quickly against his rivals in New York and Maryland to corner the fur trade and Indian land sales in the Susquehanna Valley. Negotiations between Penn and the Conestogas in 1701 gave the Pennsylvania proprietor a pre-emption right to purchase Susquehanna lands and initiated what became known as Pennsylvania's "Chain of Friendship" with its Indian neighbors, a multiparty diplomatic relationship similar to New York's Covenant Chain but separate from it.[46]

As the Penn family's ambitions grew in the Susquehanna Valley, they found themselves having to deal with the Iroquois. The Onondagas and Senecas took the lead in this relationship, the former because the Susquehanna River cut a natural path from their door to Conestoga and the latter because many of their kin lived among the Indians in that region. The Mohawks, the other nation among the Iroquois League's "older brothers," focused their diplomacy on Montreal and Albany and did not turn their attention to Pennsylvania until the 1750s. The rise of the Iroquois within Pennsylvania's Indian relations, in other words, was not the product of a single League policy or outlook. Rather, it reflected the autonomy enjoyed by individual communities and nations within the League to link arms with whomever they saw fit. At a series of councils in Conestoga in 1710 and 1711, Iroquois delegations met with agents of the Pennsylvania government. Operating independently of the New Yorkers, who liked to think of themselves as the sole custodians of Iroquois relations for the English colonies, Teganissorens and other chiefs took hold of the Chain of Friendship with Pennsylvania and offered security to any Indians wishing to resettle in the Susquehanna Valley.[47]

The Iroquois' assertion of authority over the Susquehanna Valley brought them another significant advantage: the incorporation of the Tuscaroras as the "sixth nation." An Iroquoian-speaking people from the Carolinas, the Tuscaroras had sent emissaries to Conestoga in 1710 to discuss the possibility of removing to the Susquehanna Valley. A year later, war broke out between them and the North Carolina colonists, making that removal a necessity. The Iroquois welcomed their cultural kin, who resettled in the northern reaches of the Susquehanna along the southern edge of Oneida country. By 1723, New Yorkers were describing them as the "sixth Iroquois nation."[48]

The Tuscaroras owed this unique position within the Longhouse to a number of factors. They spoke an Iroquoian language, suggesting greater cultural affinity with the Five Nations than Algonquian speakers like the Conoys and Nanticokes. They were also more populous than other refugee groups settling in the Susquehanna Valley—up to two thousand migrated north from the Carolinas—making it easier for them to retain an identity as a separate, autonomous nation in what had become a polyglot region of native peoples.[49] In welcoming them, the Five Nations appear to have regarded them as long-lost kin, the Iroquoian equivalent of the Prodigal Son. At an Albany treaty in 1714, one Iroquois speaker, most likely Teganissorens, explained it this way: "They [the Tuscaroras] were of us and went from us long ago and are now returned and promise to live peaceably among us."[50]

The Tuscaroras' status as the sixth nation placed them somewhere between the original Five Nations of the Iroquois League and the props who extended the Longhouse to the east and south. The Tuscaroras joined the Cayugas and Oneidas in the "younger brothers" moiety, but when nineteenth-century anthropologists collected the names of the hereditary chiefs of the Grand Council, no Tuscaroras were included among them, and the Oneidas were said to act for them.[51] All indications, in other words, suggest that there was an improvised quality to their incorporation into the Longhouse resulting from the circumstances of their migration into the Susquehanna Valley. Nevertheless, membership had its privileges. As the sixth nation, the Tuscaroras took home a share of

the presents distributed to the Iroquois at colonial treaty conferences. This privilege raised them above other props to the Longhouse, such as the River Indians, who usually showed up at treaty
conferences as hangers-on, content to give obsequious speeches to
colonial officials in return for smaller presents than those doled
out to the Iroquois proper. In the mid-eighteenth century, Iroquois
interaction with some of the props to the Longhouse grew increasingly high-handed, but the Tuscaroras' position as the sixth
nation insulated them from this kind of treatment and prevented
their dispossession by means of Iroquois collaboration with colonial
governments.

The Tuscaroras' incorporation into the Longhouse made
plain a transformation that had been occurring within Iroquoia
for some time. The Iroquois League was gradually being sup-
planted in political importance by something new, often referred
to in treaty records as the Iroquois Confederacy. The Confederacy incorporated not just the Five Nations, but also the props
with whom the Iroquois linked arms during the colonial era.
Metaphorical arms, paths, and chains held it together rather than
lineages and hereditary sachems.[52] It also improvised its rituals
and ceremonies to accommodate the purposes and backgrounds of
its members. At some Confederacy councils, participants smoked
the traditional Algonquian calumet to initiate the proceedings,
while at others, they engaged in the Iroquoian condolence ritual.
On some occasions, they did both. Adaptive flexibility was the
rule of the day.

The distinction between the Iroquois League and the Iroquois Confederacy was never perfect. Documents and records
kept by Europeans made no attempt to distinguish between the
two, in part because Europeans had only the foggiest notion of
what the Grand Council was. Long after the Tuscaroras came
north, colonial agents referred interchangeably to the "Five Nations" and the "Six Nations." What is clear is that as the Iroquois
sphere of influence expanded, Europeans dealt with the Iroquois

through the framework of the improvised and expansive Confederacy, not the traditional League.[53]

ALBANY, 1722

The rising power of the Iroquois Confederacy was apparent at a treaty conference in Albany in late summer 1722. The governors of New York, Pennsylvania, and Virginia traveled to the city on the upper Hudson, each to discuss matters particular to his own colony. In addition, New York governor William Burnet conducted business on behalf of Massachusetts. Teganissorens, now quite old, attended this meeting, and although the proceedings do not indicate whether he served as the Indians' spokesman as he had so often in the past, he must certainly have been pleased with the results of the neutralist diplomacy he had helped set in place almost thirty years earlier.[54] By refusing to align too closely with either the French or the English, the Iroquois had opened new paths and linked arms with new partners, so that now four of the most important English colonies in North America were currying their favor, providing a useful counterbalance not only to New France, but to each other as well.

As governor of New York, Burnet was an imperialist committed to expanding English power in the Great Lakes region. At Albany in 1722, he appealed to the Iroquois to "keep the Path open for the Farr Indians to come to trade with this Province." That request fit squarely with the linking of arms between the Iroquois and the western Algonquians that had cost Montour his life in 1709. The Iroquois told Burnet that they were giving the western Indians "all the encouragement and assistance that lays in our Power" to bring their trade to Albany. They were a bit cagier when Burnet warned them "not to have any correspondence with the French," a perennial complaint by New York governors who expected the Iroquois to act like loyal British subjects.

In response, the Iroquois promised to "adhere and cleave strongly to the English," but noted that some of their chiefs were late in arriving at this Albany conference because they had just returned from one in Montreal. Obviously, Burnet's objections would not prevent them from continuing to negotiate independently with New France.[55]

Speaking on behalf of Massachusetts, Burnet asked the Iroquois to send deputies to Boston to serve as brokers between the warring Abenakis and New Englanders. He promised "a handsome reward to the Messengers" who undertook this mission, as well as "a noble Present to the 5 Nations when the Service is effected."[56] This request was good news to the Iroquois, who had learned their lesson about serving as military auxiliaries for the English during failed expeditions against Canada in King William's War and Queen Anne's War. It was far better to play the role of intermediaries and to acquire the influence and material benefits that came with it.

The governors of Pennsylvania and Virginia had come to Albany to discuss the southward extension of Iroquois power. Governor William Keith of Pennsylvania traveled to Albany to defuse tensions caused by the recent murder of a Seneca Indian by Pennsylvania traders in the lower Susquehanna Valley. Keith had already dispatched agents to Conestoga to investigate the matter with local Indians, but his trip to Albany was indicative of how powerful the Iroquois had become in Pennsylvania's Indian relations. He made condolence presents to the assembled chiefs and presented wampum belts to renew his colony's "strongest Tyes of friendship with the five Nations." The chiefs addressed him as "Brother Onas," the Iroquois name for the Pennsylvania government, meaning "quill" or "pen," a play on words inspired by the memory of William Penn. They thanked him for having "wiped away and covered the blood of our dead friend and brother" and requested that the men jailed for the murder be freed and the affair forgotten.[57]

Virginia governor Alexander Spotswood was concerned about warfare between the Iroquois and their southern enemies. Since the peace negotiated at Montreal in 1701, the Iroquois had redirected their warfare away from French-allied Indians in Canada toward southern Indians, mostly Catawbas in the Carolinas. Under the neutralist policy, the Iroquois extended their diplomacy in all directions, but warfare still served important purposes in Iroquois culture, such as assuaging grief, gaining captives, and providing young men with a means of distinguishing themselves. Linking arms with more immediate neighbors displaced this traditional warfare to distant foes such as the Catawbas. Iroquoian war parties, sometimes now fighting in alliance with Indians from New France, moved south through the Susquehanna corridor, augmenting their numbers with warriors from various allied communities along the way. In southern Pennsylvania, they left the Susquehanna and traveled south along the spine of the Blue Ridge Mountains through Maryland and Virginia and into the Carolinas. Catawba warriors engaged in reprisal raids along the same route. Colonial fur traders and farmers often ended up in the middle of these hostilities, their goods and livestock seized by war parties, their homes and lives sometimes destroyed.[58]

Spotswood came to Albany to create a boundary line intended to keep Iroquois war parties well away from colonists and several small communities of dependent Indians living along Virginia's frontier. He wanted the Iroquois to remain north of the Potomac River and west of the Blue Ridge. The Iroquois addressed him as "Brother Assarigoe," a name meaning "sword" or "long knife" that they had first conferred upon his predecessor Lord Howard of Effingham when he had attended an Albany treaty conference in 1684. They acknowledged that their chain with Virginia had "grown rusty" and brightened it by agreeing to observe the boundary line. In exchange, Spotswood granted presents, including twenty guns and five hundred flints. The irony of providing Iroquois warriors with the very weapons necessary to continue their war-making in his colony apparently escaped him.

Spotswood had hoped to solemnize this agreement with the Iroquois by crowning one of their chiefs with a *"fine Coronet"* he had brought with him from Virginia. He quickly realized, however, that there was no supreme leader of the Iroquois to receive such a handsome gift. In a bit of improvised theater, he held the crown up at the moment the Iroquois collectively shouted their approval of the treaty's terms.[59] The empty crown proved to be a fitting metaphor for the difficulties colonial governors faced when conducting diplomacy with the Iroquois. Like many of his peers, Spotswood resented the time and money expended on such business, and at several points during the treaty, he reminded his Indian audience that he had no intention of repeating the trip any time soon. He brought a crown to Albany because he expected to find an Indian king's head to place it on. But power was broadly dispersed in Iroquois politics, and no single leader—fancy crown or not—had the wherewithal to enforce the treaty terms Spotswood negotiated. The Iroquois and Catawbas continued their warfare for thirty more years.

The 1722 Albany conference anticipated the role the Iroquois would play as intercultural brokers in the years that followed. In matters concerning trade, land, and war, they constantly inserted themselves into colonial relations with other native peoples. Multilateral treaty-making of the kind that went on in Albany became their modus operandi, and their metaphors the shared diplomatic language of these negotiations: Rusty chains needed to be brightened, blocked paths had to be cleared, hatchets buried, and arms linked together. On a more concrete level, the Iroquois would demand greater material benefits for their services as intercultural diplomats, and their colonial partners would seek ways to curb those expenses. Burnet was already thinking that way in Albany in 1722, when he told the Iroquois to limit the size of their delegations at future conferences to only "60–70 persons in all, including Sachims, Warriors, young men, and women," so that he could provision them properly and limit the "desorders" their visits occasioned among the locals.[60] This type of frontier diplomacy, with its metaphorical language masking competing interests and agendas, reached its zenith in the generation that followed.

3

"THE METHOD OF DOING BUSINESS"

THE INDIANS ARRIVED in town on the afternoon of June 22, 1744. They marched past the courthouse, 252 in all, the men carrying "their fire-arms and bows and arrows, as well as tomahawks." The inhabitants of the tiny frontier town of Lancaster, Pennsylvania, founded only a few years earlier along an Indian path between the lower Susquehanna Valley and the Delaware River, must have felt especially vulnerable. Philadelphia was seventy miles away, and there was no local militia because maintaining one would have violated the pacifist principles of the Quaker colony. If they had wanted to, the well-armed Indian warriors could have easily destroyed the town and taken its population captive before anyone in the outside world could have raised a musket in its defense.

Countless Hollywood westerns have trained modern Americans to imagine Indians as warriors on horseback, raising their war whoop and sweeping out of the hills to attack stagecoaches and wagon trains. Long before motion pictures and dime-store novels of the Wild West, captivity narratives presented much the same image of Indians ambushing frontier homesteads. Generations of American writers and filmmakers have generally ascribed only violent motives to Indians who visited white communities and only one result of such encounters: bloody mayhem.

The people of Lancaster in June 1744 did not see it that way. True, there were about 130 well-armed warriors walking down Main Street, the vast majority of them utter strangers to the locals, but they were also accompanied by an equal number of Indian women and children. In fact, in this "great concourse of people," the only ones on horseback were "several of their squaws, or wives, with some small children," hardly the vanguard of a savage horde bent on pillage and bloodletting. On the contrary, the Indians—men, women, and children—marched in "very good order" through town. When they passed the courthouse, their leader, an Onondaga chief named Canasatego, "sung, in the Indian language, a song" inviting the gentlemen who were inside "to a renewal of all treaties heretofore made, and that [are] now to be made." After Canasatego had finished, the Indians continued on their way "to some vacant lots in the back part of the town," where poles and boards had been left for them. Using these materials along with bark and boughs from trees in the surrounding woods, they built their "*wigwams,* or cabins" in an orderly encampment, where they lived for the next two weeks.[1]

The 1744 Treaty of Lancaster does not ring many bells today, but at the time, it attracted considerable notice. Colonial printers published editions of its proceedings in Philadelphia and Williamsburg. Benjamin Franklin, who printed the Philadelphia edition, sent copies to his bookseller in London, suggesting that he might find a market for them there, "as the Method of doing Business with those Barbarians may perhaps afford you some Amusement."[2] The Williamsburg edition included an introduction offering background information on the history and culture of the Iroquois Confederacy.[3] Ultimately, versions of these colonial publications also appeared in London, in the *American*

Magazine and an updated edition of *History of the Five Indian Nations*, written by colonial New Yorker Cadwallader Colden and first published in 1727.[4] As a "Method of doing Business" unique to America, Iroquois treaty-making caught the attention of colonial Americans and their British cousins and aroused their curiosity about Indians in general.

The founding mythology of the United States makes room early on for some Indians, but these are cardboard cut-outs cast in decidedly secondary roles. Squanto and Pocahontas helped save early English colonists from starvation, but after those Thanksgiving-pageant moments, a collective amnesia settles in about the presence of Indians in early American history.[5] This absence of memory may explain why events like the Treaty of Lancaster seem so strange to us today. The inhabitants of Lancaster did not panic when all of those Indians marched into their town because such encounters were commonplace wherever the Iroquois conducted diplomacy with their colonial neighbors. Montreal and Albany had been hosting treaty conferences since the mid-seventeenth century. In the first half of the eighteenth century, as Iroquois influence spread in all directions, such meetings occurred in frontier towns like Lancaster, Carlisle, and Easton (all in Pennsylvania) and in port cities such as Philadelphia, New York, and Boston.

Through years of such intercultural communication, colonial agents had become familiar with the customs that governed Iroquois diplomacy and learned its rituals and metaphorical language. They also left their own mark on these proceedings. The motives and objectives of colonial governments shaped the agenda of treaty conferences, and European goods reshaped the significance of ceremonial gift-giving. While the overall framework of this intercultural diplomacy was unmistakably Iroquoian, its character reflected the "middle ground" that Indians and Europeans created in colonial America to negotiate peacefully with each other.[6] Treaty conferences such as the one at Lancaster in 1744 were a unique hybrid of Native American and European precedents. Franklin was correct in recognizing them as a distinctly American method of doing business, for they illustrated the role the Iroquois played in shaping the colonial world he inhabited.

How They Got Together: Meeting and Greeting

Colonial Americans attended treaty conferences to achieve specific ends—such as a promise of alliance, trade concessions, or a land purchase—which could be documented and archived in a written record of the proceedings. Europeans thought of Indian treaties as texts, contracts that recorded in black and white deals reached with America's indigenous inhabitants. The ceremonies, speech-making, and gift-giving that went on at such meetings were merely steps to achieving this end, a document that could be sent to superiors in London, Paris, or colonial capitals, filed away, and cited as necessary to prove a binding agreement.

The Iroquois did not see it that way at all. The vast majority of those who participated in treaty conferences were not literate, and they talked disparagingly of what Canasatego called the "pen and ink work" that went on at treaty conferences.[7] They knew that the written records of such proceedings could exaggerate, manipulate, and outright fabricate what had transpired there, and years of experience with such chicanery had taught them to place little faith in such documents. Instead, they valued the *process* of treaty-making: the reception hosts provided their guests, the exchange of ritual objects at the council fire, the give and take of speechmaking, and the distribution of presents at the treaty's conclusion. To the Iroquois, linking arms together was not a contractual agreement that once entered into became forever binding. On the contrary, linking arms committed the participants to mutual obligations that could only be met through a perpetual process of negotiation and renewal.

This divergence in perspectives lent a creative tension to Iroquois treaty-making with colonial powers. Europeans convened treaty conferences because they wanted to extract something from the Iroquois, such as assistance in war or a land cession. Iroquois delegations attended such meetings because they wished to make their colonial neighbors honor their responsibilities as friends and allies. Colonial agents sought to minimize the time and money they had to spend on conducting such diplomacy, but in their efforts to secure binding agreements, they did their best to observe the proper customs that would give their negotiations legitimacy before their native audience. The Iroquois, on the other hand, would draw out the proceedings as long as necessary to make sure that their counterparts fulfilled their obligations as hosts, allies, and partners in trade and diplomacy. Each side sought to impress the other with its unity and power, and neither was willing to play the role of a humble client bowing down before a mighty patron. Despite the professions of friendship exchanged throughout a treaty conference, such meetings were at their core a contest of wills.

The methods of Iroquois treaty-making had their roots in the condolence and requickening rituals that were at the heart of the Iroquois League's internal operations. Conducting diplomacy with outsiders involved constantly balancing attention to these time-honored ceremonial forms with improvisation and adaptation to new realities. Treaty conferences mimicked the format of the annual gathering of the hereditary sachems in Onondaga. However, the people who gathered at a colonial treaty conference and the business they transacted there were distinct from the Iroquois Grand Council. The names of hereditary sachems rarely appear in the treaty proceedings, nor do those records contain references to Deganawidah, Hiawatha, or the founding of the Iroquois League. Instead, the Iroquois who took the lead in treating with Europeans, such as Canasatego, were usually men who acquired their influence by virtue of talent and reputation rather than lineage.[8] These were the men (and men they were, because Iroquois gender roles defined diplomacy as a male task) who took the words, forms, and rituals of intra-Iroquois negotiation and turned them into a method for doing business with strangers.[9]

Colonial governors typically initiated treaty conferences because they had a specific issue to address with the Iroquois, and if it was a matter of intercolonial concern, they asked other colonial delegations to participate. From its seventeenth-century origins among the Mohawks and Albany Dutch, the Covenant Chain had become by the 1740s a multiparty alliance that regularly drew Indians and colonists from New England, New York, and Pennsylvania to Albany for treaties, as well as occasional colonial and native delegations from as far south as Virginia and South Carolina. Inviting Indians to such meetings involved a delicate calculus. If too many showed up, they would strain the governor's budget and his ability to manage the agenda, but if too few arrived, all was for naught, because power was broadly dispersed in Iroquois communities and their populations would not feel compelled to observe agreements in which they were not consulted or represented. It was better to err on the side of too many than too few, to endure the time and expense of a well-attended treaty rather than to try limiting negotiations to only a handful of participants. For that reason, treaty conferences in the mid-eighteenth century tended to attract Indians numbering in the hundreds. The 250 or so who arrived in Lancaster in 1744 made it a fairly typical treaty conference in this regard.[10]

Colonial officials publicized upcoming treaty conferences by sending messengers equipped with the necessary wampum and presents into Indian country, where they would meet with village councils and spread the word. Conrad Weiser, the seasoned interpreter who had lived among the Mohawks as a child, undertook many such journeys on behalf of the governments of Pennsylvania and Virginia. He knew the paths and waterways of Iroquoia as well as any colonist, but still relied on Indian guides when he made such trips, which he found hazardous, time-consuming, and exhausting. Such embassies required not only familiarity with Iroquoian languages and the customs, but also a hardy constitution capable of enduring prolonged exposure to the elements.[11] Weiser described the discomforts of the trail best during his 1743 trip to Onondaga. After being welcomed by one of the local chiefs, he replied, "It was enough to kill a Man to come such a Long & bad Road, over Hills, Rocks, Old Trees, and Rivers, and to fight through a Cloud of Vermine, and all kinds of Poisen'd Worms and creeping things."[12]

Treaty conferences usually convened in frontier towns rather than the eastern ports that served as colonial capitals. Iroquois and colonists literally met each other halfway when they traveled to Albany or Lancaster. Colonial delegations left the creature comforts of New York City, Philadelphia, or Boston to endure a few weeks in the hinterlands, while Iroquois parties traveled to colonial frontier settlements that might be hundreds of miles away from their homes. Colonial delegations avoided traveling to Iroquois towns for treaty conferences because that shifted the dynamic of their meeting. Hosting a treaty conference, while expensive, did have its advantages, one of which was setting the agenda.[13]

The Iroquois favored frontier towns for treaty conferences because such locations were less of a health risk than crowded colonial ports. Indians who visited Philadelphia, New York City, or Boston were more likely to expose themselves to smallpox, measles, or other contagious diseases.[14] Referring to the high mortality suffered by Indians at a Philadelphia treaty conference in 1749, one Iroquois chief lamented to Weiser, "When we go down to see our Brother onas [Pennsylvania], we los[e] so many of our people, and particular[ly] last sumer, and all our head men, that we left like a people without a head."[15] Such experiences taught the Iroquois to prefer treaty sites away from colonial capitals. Of course, dangerous microbes could be found anywhere. At an Albany treaty conference in 1746, smallpox broke out among the seven hundred Indians in attendance, the contagion likely spreading from a nearby encampment of colonial soldiers. When word of the outbreak reached a party of Indians approaching from the Susquehanna River, they turned around and went home.[16]

Thus, the middle ground on which treaty conferences convened was more than just metaphorical. Colonial officials, especially those attending such a meeting for the first time, were more likely than their Iroquois counterparts to feel like fish out of water. Visitors to Albany were struck by the foreign quality of this isolated town, whose inhabitants still spoke, dressed, and acted according to their Dutch heritage a century after their supposed conquest by the English.[17] Likewise, Lancaster struck Witham Marshe, the secretary of the Maryland delegation to the Lancaster Treaty in 1744, as a "filthy town," populated by "great sluts and slovens"—Germans, Quakers, Scots-Irish Presbyterians, and Jews—in short, just about as broad a collection of ethnic and religious oddballs as an English gentleman could expect to find in North America. Bedbugs and fleas assaulted him in his sleep, and one night, he returned to his lodgings to find that fur traders more wild than "the most savage Indians" had dispossessed him of his bed. The local elites who tried to show him a good time were comically inept. At a ball they arranged for the visiting treaty commissioners, the ladies "danced wilder time than any Indians." On another occasion, he had to endure the "horrid noise" of a local doctor's organ-playing and singing.[18] Marshe's disdain for the inhabitants of backcountry Pennsylvania was unremitting. In his eyes, at least the visiting Iroquois exhibited manners and decorum of their own style; it was the townsfolk who gave "savages" a bad name.

A hybrid routine of Iroquois diplomatic ritual and British social customs brought the strangers who attended a treaty conference together and placed them in their proper roles. This process started with the woods' edge greeting, the Iroquois practice in which the party arriving to treat paused at the palisades or in a clearing outside a town and announced their arrival. The townspeople welcomed their guests with celebratory songs and music, followed by condolence speeches and ritual smoking at the council fire. After a nourishing meal, the weary travelers retired to their lodgings and rested for a day or two before conducting any business.[19]

Colonial hosts learned to imitate the woods' edge greeting and added their own touches to it, such as cannon salutes and toasts of wine and rum shared with the arriving Indians. At Lancaster in 1744, after the Indians had marched through town and set up their camp, the Pennsylvania governor invited their chiefs to the court-house, where he gave a brief speech of welcome, distributed pipes and tobacco, and drank "a glass or two of wine and punch" with them before they retired.[20] By the 1740s, Iroquois had incorporated such European elements as gun salutes, flying the British colors, and flute and fiddle music when they greeted colonial messengers arriving in their towns.[21] The presiding officers at colonial treaty conferences were always anxious to dispense with what they perceived to be such time-wasting formalities, but they knew that Iroquois diplomatic protocol would not allow hurrying guests, so they provisioned the Indians in their camps and waited on word that they were ready to begin negotiations.

Another ritual designed like the woods' edge greeting to render strangers into friends involved naming newcomers to treaty conferences. This practice had its roots in the Iroquois requickening ceremony. By 1700, the Iroquois had bestowed ceremonial names on the governors of New France (Onontio), New York (Corlaer), Pennsylvania (Onas), and Virginia (Assaraquoa), and the magistrates of Albany (Quider), but the expansion of Iroquois treaty-making in the eighteenth century occasionally brought new participants to the council fire. At Lancaster in 1744, the Cayuga chief Gachradodon bestowed upon the Maryland government the name "Tocaryhogon," which he translated as meaning "living in the middle, or honourable place, betwixt Asserigoa [Virginia], and our brother Onas."[22] At an Albany treaty conference in 1754, delegates from New Hampshire received the name "Sosaquasowane." Witnesses did not record a translation of the name at the time, but a curious eighteenth-century historian inquired about it with a missionary familiar with Iroquois languages, who told him that "*So* signifies AGAIN; *saquax,* A DISH; and *owane,* LARGE."[23] While "A Large Dish Again" is more likely to call to mind disappointed newlyweds opening wedding presents than Indian diplomats gathered at the council fire, the name was most likely a variation of the common Indian metaphor of "eating out of the same bowl," a reference to familial obligations to share resources.[24] In that sense, it reflected perfectly the Iroquoian notion of linking arms by extending kinship roles and responsibilities to strangers.

Colonial participants in treaty conferences accepted Indian names and learned to use them at the council fire. The innovation they brought to this practice was to reward the granting of a name with liberal donations of tobacco, liquor, and provisions. At Lancaster in 1744, the Maryland delegation received its name at a dinner they sponsored for twenty-four Iroquois chiefs. After Gachradodon made a speech in which he presented the name, the Maryland delegates expressed their appreciation with a round of toasting to the king's health. The assembled chiefs finished off their "bumpers of Madeira wine" and raised a shout of "*jo-hah!,*" their customary "cry of approbation." The colonists responded with "three several huzzas, after the English manner," which surprised the Indians, "they having never before heard the like noise."[25] At Albany in 1754, the New Hampshire delegates were not as well-coached in how to reciprocate. The Indians had to hint that "*the[y] Expected Some thing as a Treat*" when they united and gave a Name." The chagrined New Hampshire delegates had a cow delivered to the Indians' camp for a feast.[26]

AT THE COUNCIL FIRE

When the preliminaries of arrivals, greetings, and resting were over, the governor or official presiding over the treaty convened its first public council. Again, Iroquoian custom provided the format, this time in the style of the condolence ritual. Each side took a turn playing the role of the clear-minded moiety, presenting their grieving counterparts across the council fire with three strings of wampum to mourn their kin who had died since they last met, and to open their eyes, ears, and throats so that they might see, hear, and speak clearly once again. If a prominent figure had died in the interim, this process might take considerably longer to accommodate speeches memorializing the deceased and raising up someone new in his place.

Europeans altered this custom by introducing trade goods as condolence gifts. Gift-giving was woven throughout Iroquoian diplomatic ritual, and sacred objects such as wampum had long been used to "cover the graves" of the dead, but that symbolic act blended with more mundane practicality when trade goods became part of this exchange. Colonial officials commonly used strouds, woolen blankets that were a staple of the fur trade, as condolence presents. Blankets were of course perfectly suited for "covering the grave" of the deceased, but they also offered material comfort to the surviving kin. Black strouds, unlike the more common blue and red, made ideal condolence gifts because Iroquois culture associated their color with grief and mourning.[27]

Colonists were inclined to treat the condolence ceremony as yet another time-consuming preliminary before the real business of a treaty conference began, but they could find their purposes easily frustrated if they did not pay it proper attention. The opening of a treaty in Carlisle, Pennsylvania, in 1753 was delayed by an absence of the necessary condolence presents. In traveling to Carlisle, the Pennsylvania delegates had outpaced the goods they had ordered back in Philadelphia. Anxious to get their business underway, they asked the Oneida chief Scarouady "whether the Condolences would be accepted by Belts and Strings [of wampum], and Lists of the particular Goods intended to be given, with Assurances of their Delivery as soon as they should come."

Scarouady replied, "The *Indians* could not proceed to Business while the Blood remained on their Garments, and that the Condolences could not be accepted unless the Goods, intended to cover the Graves, were actually spread on the Ground before them." The frustrated Pennsylvanians had no other option but to send a messenger "to meet and hasten the Waggoners, since every Thing must stop till the Goods came."[28] It is not possible to know whether Scarouady's response was motivated by an insistence on the respectful observation of Iroquoian forms or by a healthy skepticism of European promises. In all likelihood, it was a little of both. After all, treaty conferences were about deal-making, and experienced chiefs were not above manipulating diplomatic customs in order to get what they wanted.

From the colonial perspective, the official business of a treaty conference finally got underway when the governor or presiding officer convened its first public council. A great deal of fanfare was involved on such occasions. Colonial delegates and Indians marched to the meeting place—a courthouse, public square, or other open space—"with Colours flying, Drums beating, and Musick playing" and assumed seats opposite one another.[29] Each side strove to give the impression of unity and order. Ironically, the Indians, whose social and political relations lacked the strict hierarchy of colonial society, did a better job of this. At intercolonial treaty conferences, colonial delegations often worked at odds with each other or chafed under the governor's assertion of authority. At an Albany conference in 1745, New York governor George Clinton found himself at loggerheads with the visiting delegates from Massachusetts and Connecticut, but for the sake of projecting solidarity before the Indians, he asked them to attend his opening speech. The Quakers in the Pennsylvania delegation, who at first demurred because the governor intended to ask the Indians to go to war, finally agreed for the sake of intercolonial amity, but then refused to remove their hats in the governor's presence. Clinton could not condone such a blatant challenge to his authority in front of the Indians, so he ordered all the delegates to don their hats, a show of unity different from what he had originally planned. Later in the same conference, Clinton was humiliated again when the Massachusetts delegation disrupted one of the Indians' speeches because they were displeased with its content.[30]

The Indians, on the other hand, exhibited the highest degree of gravitas and decorum when in public councils. Colonial observers were struck by the attentive silence they granted speakers and the self-possession of orators who combined gesture, pacing, and voice into moving performances. In his journal from Lancaster, Marshe described Canasatego as a striking physical specimen for his sixty years, a "tall, well-made man" with a "very full chest, and brawny limbs . . . a manly countenance, mixed with a good-natured smile . . . very active, strong, and . . . with a surprising liveliness in his speech." Likewise, the Cayuga chief Gachradodon was "straight-limbed" and "graceful," a natural-born orator who presented himself before audiences "without the buffoonery of the French, or the over-solemn deportment of the haughty Spaniards."[31] On the rare occasion when an Indian orator lost his composure, the impact was striking. At the same 1745 treaty conference that caused Clinton so much trouble, the Mohawk chief Hendrick "ran on for above an hour in an harangue" of which no one, the interpreters included, "could make head nor tail." Feeling ashamed of his performance, the other Indians present said " 'twas a matter [that] required sober consideration" and immediately adjourned the session.[32]

The impressive figures cut by the likes of Canasatego and Gachradodon were made possible in part by their adoption of European dress. Colonial observers learned to distinguish chiefs from the "multitude of plebs of their own complexion" by the costume they wore on such occasions—hats laced with gold trim, ruffled shirts, regimental coats, and silver medals, all of which they obtained as private presents from their colonial counterparts.[33] Marshe described the Indian rank and file at Lancaster as "poorly dressed" in old trade blankets and "few, or no shirts," but he found their chiefs to be just the opposite.[34] Like many of his colonial peers, he looked at Indians through the lens of his own society's assumptions about clothing, self-presentation, and status. A well-dressed Indian chief who could hold a crowd's attention with his dignified carriage and eloquence was certainly more deserving of respect and admiration than the backcountry bumpkins who offended Marshe with their rude manners, clumsy dancing, and wretched organ-playing.

The crowd that assembled for a treaty conference's public councils was a feast for the eyes, a multihued tableau of colonial and native society. Colonial officials sporting wigs and dress swords sat across the council fire from chiefs arrayed in scarlet coats and laced hats; a large audience of Indian warriors sat behind them on boards or the floor, constantly toking away on their pipes; on the periphery, a motley audience of onlookers milled about, including Indian women and children, curious townspeople, and hangers-on who accompanied the governor and delegates. All walks of life in colonial America intersected here, from high-born governors appointed to their posts by the king himself to anonymous laborers and tradesmen. The panoply of ethnic, racial, and religious diversity in colonial America was evident as well: Taciturn New Englanders rubbed shoulders with Dutch New Yorkers, abstemious Pennsylvania Quakers came face to face with Chesapeake planters who thought the only bad punch bowl was an empty one. Even the African presence in North America was apparent at treaty conferences. Some black slaves and servants came as attendants to the colonial commissioners, while others were part of the local crowds that gathered to glimpse the visiting Indians. An African presence was occasionally evident among the Indians as well. Marshe noted that one of the most important chiefs to come to Lancaster in 1744 was Tachanuntie, an Onondaga also known as "the Black Prince" because of his African-Indian parentage.[35]

Tracking female participation in treaty conferences is more difficult, but women were there as well. One point of convergence between native and European diplomatic cultures was each one's insistence that diplomacy was a man's job. The colonial officials at treaty conferences were all male, and when they brought along family members, it was sons, not wives or daughters, who joined them. Iroquois women attended treaty conferences, where they wove wampum belts and participated in private councils with Iroquois men, but for the most part, theirs was a silent presence in a treaty's public proceedings.[36]

Notable exceptions to this rule allow us to glimpse the work of native women behind the scenes in Iroquois diplomacy. In 1762, British Indian agent William Johnson tried to curb the costs for a treaty conference by sending advance word that he did not want Iroquois women to accompany their men. The women came anyway, "as it was always the Custom for them to be present on Such Occasions." One Oneida speaker explained it to Johnson this way: The women "[are] of Much Estimation Amongst Us, in that we proceed from them, and they provide our Warriors with Provisions when they go abroad."[37] In Canandaigua, New York, in 1794, "three elderly Squaws made their appearance" at a private council between the U.S. official Timothy Pickering and some Iroquois chiefs. After receiving permission to speak, these clan matrons "expatiated on the importance of their Sex, saying that it was they who made the Men, [and] that altho' they did not sit in council, yet that they were acquainted from time to time with the transactions at the Treaties." Having made their stake in the negotiations clear, they expressed "their principal desire" that Pickering provide redress for land stolen from them after the American Revolution. None of the Indian males present challenged the women's assertion of their political authority at this council.[38]

Some women did work as interpreters, although their numbers paled in comparison to their male counterparts. The most famous of these was Madame Montour, the daughter of a French father and Indian mother who had spent her early life along the Great Lakes frontier (she was the sister of Alexander Montour, the trader who was murdered while escorting Indians from the *pays d'en haut* to Albany in 1709). After marrying an Oneida chief, she worked as an interpreter in Albany, where her knowledge of French, Algonquian, and Iroquian languages facilitated the diplomacy involved with that town's western fur trade. In the late 1720s, she moved with her Oneida family to the western branch of the Susquehanna River and continued to work as an interpreter for Pennsylvania.[39] Although quite old in 1744, she was among the Iroquois who attended the Lancaster Treaty. No longer serving officially as an interpreter at that point (her son Andrew had taken over those duties), she still commanded a high reputation among colonists.[40] Marshe made it a point to seek her out and described her as "a handsome woman, genteel, and of polite address, notwithstanding her residence has been so long among the Indians."[41]

Iroquoian forms and customs provided the framework for the task that took up the bulk of a treaty's public proceedings: speechmaking. One side delivered a speech, its major points visually reinforced with wampum strings and belts, while the other listened in silence. When a speaker finished, his counterpart on the other side responded with a brief recapitulation, to show that all had been understood, then everyone retired while the other side prepared its response. The pacing was slow and deliberate, with answers rarely coming before the next day. Only when issues raised in previous speeches were settled could new ones be raised. As in Iroquois village councils, the objective was to negotiate with an air of amity and gravity, to hear contending voices but also to take the time necessary to forge a consensus.

This type of negotiation was made all the more difficult by the language and cultural barriers between the participants. Over time, the Iroquois and their colonial counterparts had developed their own methods for smoothing and speeding this process. First, they relied on interpreters to render their words comprehensible to the other side. Some interpreters, such as Weiser, enjoyed reputations for linguistic dexterity and cultural expertise. At Lancaster in 1744, Weiser not only translated speeches, but also served as an intercultural coach for the colonial delegations, warning them "not to talk much of the Indians, nor laugh at their dress, or make any remarks on their behaviour" when in their presence, for many of them understood English, even though they would not speak it. He also attended unofficial gatherings such as the Maryland delegation's dinner with the chiefs, to provide on-the-spot assistance with bridging the gap between native and colonial customs.[42]

Weiser was just one of several interpreters who enjoyed long careers as cultural go-betweens between Iroquois and colonial peoples. The French Indian agent Joncaire, who orchestrated the murder of Alexander Montour in 1709, played an indispensable role as New France's emissary to the western Iroquois until his death in 1739. Joncaire's rival was Lawrence Claessen, a Dutch fur trader who had been taken captive by Canadian Iroquois as a youth. During the early decades of the eighteenth century, he undertook numerous embassies from Albany into Iroquoia on behalf of New York's governors, and he served as an interpreter at Albany treaty conferences.[43] Good interpreters spent considerable amounts of time in both Indian and colonial society, cultivating friendships with powerful people on both sides. They familiarized themselves with the necessary ritual forms of communication: gift and wampum exchanges, woods' edge greetings, and condolence rituals. The best ones also cultivated reputations for honesty on both sides of the council fire, so that each could claim him as their own.[44] As Canasatego put it at a 1742 treaty conference, Weiser was one person living in two worlds: "we divided him in two equal Parts: One we kept for ourselves, and one we left for you."[45]

Not every interpreter earned such high praise. Of the one hundred or so that worked in the northern colonies in the mid-eighteenth century, only a handful were acceptable enough to both Indians and colonists to sustain good reputations.[46] Interpreters who gained their expertise in the fur trade were often tarred by that business's association with fraud and avarice. Missionaries and Christian Indians had the language skills necessary for such work, but preferred to devote themselves to preaching rather than diplomacy. The *métis* offspring of European and Indian parents sometimes worked as interpreters, but colonial officials associated biracial or multiracial parentage with moral degeneration and generally distrusted such people. The most successful interpreters were people like Weiser, Joncaire, and Claessen, who had learned Indian languages and customs by living among them as children or young adults, but who anchored themselves firmly in colonial society as adults.[47]

Even the best interpreter faced a Herculean task in making the parties at a treaty conference comprehensible to each other. Depending on the number of parties attending a treaty, speeches might have to pass between two or even three interpreters before reaching their intended audiences. At Albany conferences in the early eighteenth century, it was not uncommon for speeches made by visiting Algonquian Indians to be translated first into an Iroquoian language such as Mohawk, then into Dutch, and then into English. No wonder Cadwallader Colden, who attended such conferences as a member of the New York governor's council, complained that interpreters stripped the eloquence and imagination from Iroquois oratory by rendering their passionately delivered speeches into "one single Sentence."[48]

To compensate for the difficulties of translation, the Indians and colonists learned to rely on such nonverbal forms of communication as wampum belts and gift exchanges. They developed a shared stock of metaphors, practically all of them Iroquoian in origin, that became the *lingua franca* of speechmaking: open or blocked paths, hatchets buried or taken up, war kettles put to the boil or trees of peace planted, arms linked together or chains broken. The colonists also adopted the Iroquoian custom of using kinship terms to address parties around the council fire, yet another means by which Iroquois diplomacy made clear the roles and obligations strangers assumed when they linked arms. Colonial delegates and Iroquois speakers addressed each other as brothers or brethren. Iroquois orators addressed props to the Confederacy as nephews, who in turn called the Six Nations uncles (the uncle-nephew relationship was a significant one in Iroquois kin relations, because in their matrilineal society, a maternal uncle figured more prominently in a child's upbringing than the father). When they could get away with it, colonial officials addressed the weaker props to the Iroquois, such as the River Indians, as children, making clear the expectation that such groups would not act independently of Iroquois or colonial authority.[49]

In the Bushes

Interpreters also helped move the proceedings along by assisting colonial delegates and Indian chiefs in their negotiations away from the public council fire. Such get-togethers were known in Iroquois parlance as meetings "in the bushes." In these private consultations, treaty participants ironed out their differences so that rancor would not disrupt their public speeches. At Lancaster in 1744, Weiser spent much of his time assisting the Maryland delegation in land purchase negotiations conducted in this manner. At Albany in 1754, he did the same for the representatives of the Penn family trying to purchase land in the Susquehanna Valley.[50] On such occasions, colonial agents gave private presents to leading chiefs, who extracted the concessions they wanted before agreeing to terms in public councils.

A few words should be said here about the role of alcohol in treaty conferences. Colonial observers time and again deplored Indian drunkenness on such occasions, attributing it to their savage character. Nevertheless, they supplied the Indians with copious amounts of liquor, believing that there was no other way to lure them into attendance and ensure their cooperation. The issue faced by the colonial officials who managed such conferences was not whether Indians would consume liquor, but how such consumption would be managed and to whose ends. The governor or presiding officers at a treaty conference commonly prohibited local colonists from selling rum to visiting Indians while they were in town, because they knew that the altercations and disaffections that accompanied such transactions soured the proceedings. Experienced Indian diplomats were also well aware that colonists used alcohol to cloud Indian judgment when purchasing furs and land, and asked that the liquor tap be turned off while they were conducting business.

In light of concerns expressed on both sides of the council fire, it became a common practice for colonial delegations to withhold their large donations of rum to the Indians until after a treaty had concluded. Sometimes they arranged for the Indians to receive their present of rum only after they were on the road homeward, a policy intended to minimize the interaction between Indians and local colonists once the taps were opened. Canasatego referred to this practice in 1742, when at the end of a treaty conference he asked Pennsylvania governor George Thomas to "open the Rum-Bottle, and give to us in greater Abundance on the Road." On another occasion, the Indians called this customary grant of liquor their "Walking-stick" for the journey home.[51]

In writing about the Carlisle Treaty of 1753, Benjamin Franklin congratulated himself and his fellow Pennsylvanian delegates for keeping the rum away from the Indians until their business was over. After the closing speeches, they presented the liquor and watched in horror as what today might be called the after-party unfolded:

> We found they [the Indians] had made a great Bonfire in the Middle of the Square. They were all drunk, Men and Women, quarrelling and fighting. Their dark-color'd Bodies, half naked, seen only in the gloomy Light of the Bonfire, running after and beating one another with Fire-brands, accompanied by their horrid Yellings, form'd a Scene the most resembling our Ideas of Hell that could well be imagin'd. . . .
>   And indeed if it be the Design of Providence to ex-tirpate these Savages in order to make room for Cultiva-tors of the Earth, it seems not improbable that Rum may be the appointed Means.[52]

Franklin's lurid description reveals much about the Indians' drinking habits and colonial impressions of them. It is true that the Iroquois, like other Indians of this era, regarded alcohol as one of the spiritually potent goods Europeans brought into their world, and Indian drinkers used it for what they perceived to be its intended purpose: intoxication. Alcoholism ravaged native communities in the colonial era, and they suffered the inevitable consequences of violence, ill-health, impoverishment, and social breakdown.[53]

It should also be remembered that colonists were hardly teetotalers themselves. The punch bowl was an important device by which colonial hosts asserted their authority over their guests, and like many modern business travelers, colonial delegates at treaty conferences considered getting "very merry" or "extremely merry" a prerogative of their work.[54] At a dinner at the Lancaster Treaty in 1744, the Pennsylvania governor set the pace for "jol-lity" with his heavy drinking and the "whole company" of his out-of-town guests followed suit. A raucous night of eating, drinking, and music ended with the younger men "dancing in the Indian dress, and after their manner." Compared to such shenanigans, some Indians were models of self-control. Marshe, who watched the governor set the pace for inebriation at Lancaster, admired how the Iroquois chiefs maintained their sobriety throughout the proceedings: "When ever they renew old treaties of friendship, or make any bargain about lands they sell to the English they take great care to abstain from intoxicating drink, for fear of being over-reached."[55]

Ultimately, no treaty conference could go forward without the rum bottle or punch bowl because both cultures associated alcohol consumption with hospitality and generosity. Indians expected liquor at such meetings, whether it was measured out in drams or gallons, because their diplomatic customs demanded open-handedness from hosts. They felt no compunction when they asked Governor Clinton for a "Barrel of Beer to drink" after a day of public councils in Albany in 1745, but Clinton failed as a host when he "damn'd them and sayd he gave them some the other day." Weiser, who reported this incident, was also flabbergasted when Clinton's secretary refused a gift of venison from some visiting Indians because he thought it a ruse "to get ten times as much Victuals from the Governor."[56] Such mean-spirited attempts at economy offended the Indians' sensibilities and poisoned the air of amity that was supposed to prevail at treaty conferences.

Nothing less was at stake here than the future of the Anglo-Iroquois partnership in North America. The geopolitical implications of drinking at treaty conferences were never more apparent than at the conclusion of the Lancaster Treaty in 1744. After delivering a closing speech to his Iroquois guests, the Pennsylvania governor ordered rum for Canasatego and his fellow chiefs, "to be given to each, in a small Dram-Glass, which the Governor called a *French* Glass." The following day, after the Indians made their final speech, the governor called for liquor again, only this time in "middle-siz'd Wine-Glasses" to prove the "generous Dispositions of your Brethren the *English* towards you."[57] In such a manner, the English impugned their imperial rivals and displayed their superior regard for the Iroquois.

PARTING WAYS

When at last the issues set forth at the beginning of the conference had been settled, it was time for the participants to take leave of each other. Each side delivered a farewell speech, professing friendship and "brightening" the chain between them with more presents. Throughout the colonial era, the Indians' diplomatic gifts remained small and symbolic, usually a bundle of pelts. On the colonial side, these gifts—which were given in addition to condolence presents that opened the treaty and whatever deals may have been struck along the way for land purchases or private presents to chiefs—grew ever larger in response to Indian demand. Occasionally, the treaty proceedings offered detailed inventories of these goods: firearms, ammunition, and gunpowder; hats, linen shirts, strouds, blankets, and other textiles; hatchets, hoes, kettles, knives, awls, scissors, and similar metal wares; hawks' bells, mouth harps, mirrors, tobacco, liquor, and other novelties.[58] As a final order of business at treaty conferences, the presiding official often hired wagons and horses to help the Indians haul all their loot home.

The escalation in gift-giving at treaty conferences reflected both the strength and weakness of the Iroquois in these negotiations. Colonial governments were generally tight-fisted when it came to such expenditures. Indian diplomacy was expensive, and presents could cost in the hundreds of pounds for a single treaty conference. The fact that colonial assemblies continued to shell out for these goods is evidence of the high estimation in which they held the Iroquois. On the other hand, the Iroquois demanded such large donations because a century's worth of contact with colonial neighbors had eroded their traditional economy and left them dependent on European cloth, weapons, and metal wares.

Canasatego described the straitened circumstances of the Iroquois in a speech to Governor Thomas of Pennsylvania in 1742. After examining an inventory of goods the governor had prepared for the meeting, Canasatego told him they were not even sufficient to divide among the Indians in attendance, so "if you have the Keys of the Proprietor's [the Penn family] Chest, you will open it, and take out a little more for us." Anticipating resistance to his request, Canasatego presented his own economic argument for more presents:

> We know our Lands are now become more valuable: The white People think we do not know their Value; but we are sensible that the Land is everlasting, and the few Goods we receive for it are soon worn out and gone. For the Future . . . we will know beforehand the Quantity of Goods we are to receive.

Thomas's reply was unapologetic:

> It is very true, that Lands are of late become more Valuable; but what raises their Value? Is it not entirely owing to the Industry and Labour used by the white People in their Cultivation and Improvement? Had not they come amongst you, these Lands would have been of no Use to you, any further than to maintain you. And is there not, now you have sold so much, enough left for all the Purposes of Living?—What you say of the Goods, that they are soon worn out, is applicable to every Thing; but you know very well, that they cost a great deal of Money; and the Value of Land is no more than it is worth in Money.[59]

Thomas's response dripped with the condescension that typically accompanied European descriptions of the Indians' land use: the men were lazy hunters and the women sloppy farmers; they kept no livestock and thus collected no manure to fertilize their fields; they built no fences or barns and constantly moved about rather than "improving" the land by working it as Europeans did. His statement that "the value of the Land is no more than it is worth in Money" was as foreign a method of valuation as he could offer to Canasatego, who although savvy in the ways of Anglo-Iroquois diplomacy, no doubt failed to attend the same real estate seminar as Thomas.

Here then was the Iroquois dilemma in a nutshell. A century's worth of interaction with Europeans had profoundly upset their lives and made their future even more precarious. Strange diseases decimated their populations, alcohol corroded their well-being, and religious and political factionalism rent their communities. Poverty and hunger threatened everyone. Like it or not, there was no turning back. They needed European trade goods to survive and they used diplomacy to get them, but by the mid-eighteenth century, what the colonial governments wanted most in return was land. Colonial officials perceived treaty-making as a means of permanently transferring land from Indian to European hands; these were deals cut between free and willing participants in public councils, the details dutifully recorded in deeds signed by Indian chiefs. The Iroquois thought differently. They regarded each treaty as part of an ongoing negotiation between peoples who had linked arms and entered into mutual obligations. Yes, they sold land to colonial neighbors, but they expected such deals to increase rather than end the generosity and regard shown to them by those neighbors. Unfortunately, the more land they sold, the more unbalanced this method of business became.

4

PATHS AND CHAINS

IN JUNE 1753, seventeen Mohawks arrived in New York City to treat with Governor George Clinton. Clinton and the Mohawks had encountered each other before, but always at conferences in Albany convened by Clinton. It was extraordinary for an Iroquois delegation to travel to New York City for such a meeting, and even more so for one to come uninvited, as these Indians had.

They were led by a chief named Theyanoguin but known more commonly to the British as Hendrick (scholars have confused him with the earlier Mohawk leader known as Hendrick who visited London in 1710, but the two were in fact distinct figures). Clinton knew Hendrick well enough to be concerned about his sudden appearance in the city. At a series of Albany conferences during the previous decade, Hendrick had been an indispensable broker between Clinton and the Iroquois, but also a constant thorn in the governor's side, pressing him to treat the Mohawks generously and to provide redress for their grievances concerning land frauds and trading abuses. At these meetings,

Hendrick openly received the attention and favors of agents from Massachusetts and Pennsylvania, making plain to Clinton the possibility that the Mohawks might redirect their diplomacy toward another colony and take the rest of the Iroquois nations with them.

Hendrick was well aware that Clinton needed him more than he needed Clinton. In his opening speech, Hendrick told the governor, "I have always been a help and support to you when you have called our Six Nations together at Albany. By my means every thing has gone right, and whilst the five other nations of Indians have promised and not performed, the Mohawks have always proved true." Clinton probably bristled when he heard Hendrick say that "every thing has gone right." Since becoming governor, Clinton's experience with the Iroquois had been one frustration after another, but Hendrick did have a point. What little had gone right for Clinton in his Indian relations could not have occurred without the Mohawks' cooperation.

Hendrick cut to the chase quickly: "The indifference and neglect shewn towards us makes our hearts ake, and if you don't alter your Behaviour to us we fear the Covenant Chain will be broken." He enumerated the Mohawks' complaints. The British had failed to protect the Six Nations from the French, to perform the necessary condolence rituals for Mohawk warriors killed in battle, or to secure Mohawk lands from grasping speculators and squatters. He reminded Clinton of the New Yorkers' obligations to the Covenant Chain. If they did not make good on them, "the rest of our Brethren the 5 Nations shall know of it and all Paths will be stopped."[1]

Hendrick's speech was a bold gambit to break a stalemate between Clinton and the Mohawks over who would control the Covenant Chain. The Mohawks' uninvited appearance in New York City upset the traditional method of treaty-making and allowed the Indians to seize the initiative against the governor. Hendrick couched his speech in the traditional metaphors of the

Covenant Chain, but that language barely contained the threat he was making to his colonial counterparts: Settle the Mohawks' grievances now or face the defection of the Iroquois. He backed up this threat by asserting the Mohawks' priority within the Longhouse ("we Mohawks are called the Head of the Five Nations") and their role as keepers of the eastern door. He did not threaten war or invoke the legendary ferocity of Mohawk warriors to make his point. Instead, Hendrick raised the specter of a broken Covenant Chain and blocked paths to Iroquoia. The New Yorkers would lose communication with the Iroquois and have to defend their long, exposed frontier with Canada alone.

Hendrick's performance in New York City was one example of how the Iroquois manipulated diplomatic language and ritual to achieve their ends. Open paths and linked arms promised trade and peace, but threats of blocked paths and broken chains were also powerful symbols in Iroquois diplomacy. Blocked paths prevented the exchange of information and goods; broken chains disrupted the mutual obligations that bound friends together against common enemies. As the Anglo-French rivalry in North America intensified, neither side could afford to alienate the Iroquois. Chiefs such as Hendrick and Canasatego used that dependence during the mid-eighteenth century to extend Iroquois influence into new regions and populations well beyond Iroquoia.

Their diplomacy also made plain some of the problems facing the Iroquois Confederacy. The farther Iroquois diplomats carried their business, the more obvious it became that their pretensions to power over distant lands and peoples were just that, pretensions. Colonial agents were happy to describe the Six Nations as the rulers of a vast inland empire when it suited their purposes, and Iroquois diplomats endorsed this idea because it added to their prestige and influence. Other native peoples, however, were skeptical of Iroquois authority, and as time passed, they became more willing to assert their own interests. Hendrick, Canasatego, and other Iroquois leaders of their generation walked a fine line as they conducted their diplomacy. Their success rested in bluffing without overreaching, in maintaining the appearance of power without having to use it. If, as the creation myth described, the world grew from a bit of earth placed on the back of a turtle, then the trick was to stand astride that turtle without losing your footing.

THE CHAIN OF FRIENDSHIP BINDS IN PENNSYLVANIA

Like many other native peoples in North America, the Iroquois faced increasing pressure on their land base from a growing colonial population in the eighteenth century. A solution they found to this problem was to sell other people's land rather than their own, and nowhere did the Iroquois practice this tactic more successfully (at least in the short run) than in Pennsylvania. At a series of treaty conferences in the 1730s and 1740s, the Six Nations asserted their authority over native peoples and lands south of the Longhouse and became the most important participants in Pennsylvania's "Chain of Friendship" with its Indian neighbors.

Geography accounts in part for the rapid ascent of Iroquois power in Pennsylvania. The Susquehanna River flowed out of the heart of Iroquoia into Pennsylvania, and the Quaker colony had no choice but to cultivate the goodwill of its neighbors to the north if it wanted a secure frontier. Bald-faced opportunism also figured on both sides of this relationship, and no Indian nation felt the brunt of it more than the Delawares. Although never conquered in war by the Iroquois, the Delawares found themselves dispossessed by a combination of Iroquois bravado and colonial legal chicanery. By choosing to cast their lot with the Penn family rather than the Delawares, the Six Nations strengthened their own hand in the mid-Atlantic region, but at the cost of sowing dissension among native peoples who were supposed to be props to the Longhouse.

"Delaware" was a collective term used by the English to describe a number of Algonquian-speaking Indian groups living in or near the river valley of that name. These Indians had been in contact with Europeans since Dutch and Swedish fur traders arrived in the region in the 1620s. As the colonial populations of New York, New Jersey, and southeastern Pennsylvania grew, the Delawares found their economic and political independence squeezed by the fur trade and colonial land-grabbing. During the 1720s, some Delawares moved west into the Susquehanna, Allegheny, and Ohio valleys, entering into the web of Iroquois diplomacy that extended southward from the Great Lakes along the Appalachian frontier. Another group of Delawares remained rooted in northeastern Pennsylvania. The Forks Delawares, so-called because they lived near the confluence of the Lehigh and Delaware rivers, earned a meager subsistence by selling brooms, baskets, and other native crafts to their colonial neighbors. Some welcomed Protestant missionaries to the Forks region and converted to Christianity.[2] Before the 1730s, the Forks Delawares had little to do with the Six Nations, but the precariousness of their material lives left them vulnerable to outsiders.

Two other native communities bolstered Iroquois power in Pennsylvania. The residents of Conestoga, the polyglot Indian town in the lower Susquehanna Valley, had close ties with the Senecas. To the north, the Indian town of Shamokin sprang up at the juncture of the Susquehanna River's north and west branches (near modern Sunbury, Pennsylvania). Its inhabitants included Delawares, Shawnees, and Iroquois, as well as other props to the Longhouse from farther south in the Chesapeake Bay region, including Tutelos, Conoys, and Nanticokes. The Oneida chief Shickellamy, who guided Weiser's party to Onondaga in 1743, worked in conjunction with Iroquois leaders to represent the Confederacy's interests in Shamokin. Colonial contemporaries often referred to him as an Iroquois viceroy sent to rule over this populous but fractious town, but his role was closer to that of a diplomatic observer and mediator. Like most other Indian communities of this era, Shamokin was autonomous, and the composite nature of its population made its inhabitants even more independent-minded. Shickellamy served as the eyes and ears of the Longhouse there, but he could not compel the locals to heed his words or those he relayed from Onondaga.[3]

James Logan, the provincial secretary of Pennsylvania and private land agent to the Penn family, found in Shickellamy a congenial partner for conducting land purchases. At a series of diplomatic councils in Philadelphia in 1728, Logan and Pennsylvania governor Patrick Gordon shifted their attention away from Sassoonan, an eastern Delaware chief who had grown disgruntled with the Penn family for its land-grabbing, and toward Shickellamy. Logan and Gordon acknowledged Iroquois authority over Pennsylvania's Indian neighbors, and in return asked Shickellamy and the Iroquois Confederacy to use a more forceful hand in managing them.[4] Four years later, a party of Iroquois chiefs led by Shickellamy arrived in Philadelphia to light a council fire with Gordon, Logan, and Thomas Penn, who had just arrived in the colony he had inherited from his father. The 1732 treaty in Philadelphia cemented the new Iroquois partnership with Pennsylvania. The tempo of diplomacy between these parties quickened, as the Iroquois exploited the Pennsylvanians for diplomatic presents and the Penn family used the Iroquois to dispossess less powerful natives. The Six Nations proved to be very amenable to selling territory to colonial officials so long as they did not occupy it themselves. By engaging in such purchases, they enriched themselves without endangering their own homelands north of the Pennsylvania border.[5]

Emboldened by their support from Shickellamy and other Six Nations chiefs, the Penns moved against the Forks Delawares. In 1735, agents for Thomas Penn produced a copy of a deed that had supposedly been signed by Delaware chiefs in 1686, conveying lands in the vicinity of Tohickon Creek on the Delaware River to

William Penn. According to the deed, the size of the purchase was to be determined by a day and a half's walk from an agreed-upon starting point. Nutimus, the leader of the Forks Delawares, reacted with skepticism. No one among his people had been party to the agreement or had any memory of it. Logan and Penn worked around Nutimus by finding more pliable Delawares to recognize the deed as legitimate. In the meantime, the Pennsylvanians hosted the Iroquois at another treaty conference in Philadelphia.[6] No Delawares attended this meeting, and the Iroquois had never claimed the Forks region as their own, but the Penn family wanted them on board. Working through Weiser and Shickellamy, Logan convinced the Iroquois to release the lands in question to Pennsylvania. As always, presents eased the way. When the day appointed for the "walk" finally arrived in 1737, Penn's agents hired trained runners who followed a path specially prepared for them. Such chicanery allowed them to engross far more territory than the disputed deed had originally entailed. The Delaware observers who were supposed to accompany the walkers quit en route out of disgust.[7]

Nutimus and the Forks Delawares had been flagrantly cheated. They appealed to the Iroquois for redress but found no sympathy. The matter came to a head at a Philadelphia treaty conference in 1742 attended by a large number of Iroquois, Delawares, and Indians from Conestoga and Shamokin. Nutimus and Sassoonan represented Delawares disaffected by the Penn family's land purchases, and Shickellamy and Canasatego led the Iroquois delegation. Canasatego did all the talking while the Delawares and other "props" remained silent. In a speech he delivered before Nutimus and Sassoonan, Canasatego chastised the Delawares for their failure to remove from the lands involved in the Walking Purchase:

> You ought to be taken by the Hair of the Head and
> shak'd severely till you recover your Senses and become

Sober; you don't know what Ground you stand on, nor what you are doing . . . you are maliciously bent to break the Chain of friendship with our Brother Onas.

As Canasatego continued, his language grew more blistering, and he claimed an unqualified authority for the Iroquois over the Delawares:

We conquer'd You, we made Women of you, you know you are Women, and can no more sell Land than Women. Nor is it fit you should have the Power of Selling Lands since you would abuse it. This Land that you Claim is gone through Your Guts. You have been furnished with Cloaths and Meat and Drink by the Goods paid you for it, and now You want it again like Children as you are.

Canasatego offered the Forks Delaware two options: return eastward to their homelands in New Jersey ("but we don't know whether, Considering how you have demean'd your selves, you will be permitted to live there"), or remove to new homes at Shamokin or along the northern branch of the Susquehanna, where "we shall have you more under our Eye, and shall see how You behave."[8]

Canasatego's novel reinterpretation of Iroquois history and diplomacy worked to the considerable advantage of the Pennsylvanians. While it is true that sometime during the late seventeenth century, the Delawares had accepted the status of "women" in their diplomatic relations with the Iroquois, this role did not involve the sort of debasement and powerlessness implied by Canasatego. The Iroquois had warred with plenty of native peoples in the Susquehanna Valley during the early colonial period, but they had never conquered the Delawares nor laid claim to the Delaware Valley. The Delawares' status as "women" in intertribal relations appears to have emerged not out of their military conquest but from the role they played as mediators between the Iroquois and other native peoples. Contrary to Canasatego's assertions, it did not imply a loss of political autonomy or control over their lands.[9]

Why then did Canasatego use this occasion to humiliate the Delawares and claim such an absolute authority over them? The simple answer is because he could. Sassoonan and Nutimus, whose reactions to this speech are not recorded in the proceedings, lacked the resources and numbers to challenge him. They had staked their hopes for countering the Penn family on Iroquois support, but instead found themselves facing an Iroquois-Penn juggernaut. Canasatego and his fellow Iroquois chiefs made a calculated decision when they abandoned Sassoonan and Nutimus to the Pennsylvanians: Neither of these two Delaware chiefs had political or material capital the Iroquois needed, but the Penns had plenty to offer of both. Together, the Iroquois and the Pennsylvanians used the Chain of Friendship to reduce the eastern Delawares to tributaries.

Canasatego's drubbing of the Delawares in 1742 made him a prominent figure in Pennsylvania's Indian affairs. Working on behalf of the Penn family and occasionally other colonial governments, Weiser undertook multiple embassies to Iroquoia during the following decade, where he made private presents to Canasatego and other chiefs.[10] In this manner, Iroquois power continued to grow in Pennsylvania and colonies to its south, but it was never exercised in the sort of brute manner implied by Canasatego's threat to take the Delawares by the hair and shake them. On the contrary, it rested on the foundation of the personal diplomacy that Weiser conducted with Shickellamy in Shamokin and Canasatego in Onondaga.[11]

This relationship was in full bloom at Lancaster in 1744, where the Pennsylvanians served as mediators between the Six Nations and the governments of Maryland and Virginia. As had been the case with the Delawares and the Walking Purchase two years earlier, negotiations focused on contending colonial and native land claims, and once again, Canasatego proved willing to cut deals for territory far removed from Iroquoia. The Marylanders had come to Lancaster because they wished to secure the release of all Iroquois claims to land within their colony. An irritated tone seeped through their opening speech, in which they expressed doubt about such claims to begin with ("nor can we yet find out to what Land or under what Title you make your Claim"), but they were prepared to make suitable compensation for the sake of amity with the Six Nations.[12] As was his wont, Canasatego responded to questions about the extent of Iroquois authority with an oratorical barrage designed to dismiss all such doubts:

> Brother, the *Governor* of Maryland,
>   When you mentioned the Affair of the Land Yesterday, you went back to old Times, and told us, you had been in Possession of the Province of Maryland above One Hundred Years; but what is a Hundred Years, in Comparison of the Length of Time since our Claim began? Since we came out of the Ground? For we must tell you, that long before a Hundred Years, our Ancestors came out of this very Ground, and their Children have remained here ever since.
>   You came out of the Ground in a Country that lies beyond the Seas; there you may have a just Claim, but here you must allow us to be your elder Brethren, and the Lands to belong to us long before you knew any Thing of them.[13]

Put less diplomatically, Canasatego and his fellow chiefs cared not one whit about previous treaties or deeds the Marylanders may have signed with other Indians. Right now, the Six

Nations were the native power with whom they would have to deal, and no prior claim to the lands in question made by Europeans could supersede that of "our Ancestors [who] came out of this very Ground."

Once more, Canasatego reinterpreted Iroquois history to his own advantage. Where exactly was "this very Ground" out of which his ancestors had come? It certainly was not in Maryland or Lancaster, Pennsylvania. His ancestors had waged long, inconclusive warfare in the lower Susquehanna Valley in the seventeenth century, but that was even more recent than the founding of the Maryland colony in the 1630s. In that same speech to the Marylanders, Canasatego recounted in detail the founding of the Covenant Chain, the story of how the Dutch had arrived in a ship full of useful goods, which the Iroquois had anchored first with a rope and then with an iron chain and finally a silver one, so that the bond between them and the English "wou'd last for ever."[14] He failed to explain how this economic partnership forged in the upper Hudson Valley gave the Iroquois claim to Maryland, but the implication was clear. If Maryland wanted to hold fast to the Covenant Chain, it had better cough up for Iroquois claims within its borders, no matter how improvised or specious they were.

When it came the Virginians' turn to raise the issue of disputed lands and borders with the Iroquois, the Cayuga chief Gachradodon gave a similar speech:

Brother *Assaraquoa,*
The World at the first, was made on the other Side the great Water, different from what it is on this Side, as may be known from the different Colours of our Skin, and of our Flesh; and that which you call Justice, may not be so amongst us: You have your Laws and your Customs, and so have we: The great King might send you over to conquer the *Indians,* but it looks to us, that

God did not approve of it; if he had, he would not have placed the Sea where it is, as the Limits between us and you. . . . Tho' great Things are well remembered among us, yet we don't remember that we were ever conquered by the great King.[15]

In other words, the Virginians might not understand the Iroquois claims to land within their borders, but in Lancaster, they were playing by Indian rules, not English. Like the Marylanders, they had no choice but to negotiate a new deed with Gachradodon, Canasatego, and their fellow chiefs for land hundreds of miles distant from Iroquoia.

There is something seamy about the real estate transactions conducted at the Treaty of Lancaster. Colonial delegates from Maryland and Virginia paid much to purchase title to lands from the Iroquois, all the while knowing that these Indians did not occupy the territory being sold and had a questionable right over it. Who is the guilty party in such transactions, the con artist who sells the Brooklyn Bridge or the dupe who enters into the bargain with eyes and wallet wide open? We can easily condemn the Iroquois for engaging in a real estate racket, selling land they did not legitimately own and dispossessing weaker native peoples in the process. But blame must also be assigned to colonial agents who approached such purchases with a cynical "that's the cost of doing business" attitude that allowed them to shrug off the suspicions that arose whenever these deals failed to pass their own sniff test.

If we look beyond each side's opportunism, we can gain some insight into the Iroquois perspective on this diplomacy. The speeches of Canasatego and Gachradodon share an admirable assertion of Iroquois independence from colonial governments and laws. In their eyes, the land in question was theirs to sell simply because it did not belong to Europeans: What possible right could the king or his colonial subjects claim to it before the Iroquois? Had not nature itself placed an ocean between the Old

World and the New to make plain the Indians' primacy in the matter? Were not Indian and European notions of ownership and justice as different as "the different Colours of our Skin, and of our Flesh"? Canasatego and Gachradodon felt no compulsion to explain themselves to their colonial counterparts beyond this assertion of their cultural differences. The same held true for an offer the Virginians made at the end of the Lancaster Treaty to take three or four Iroquois boys back with them, where they would be educated in the "Religion, Language, and Customs of the white People." Canasatego replied, "We must let you know, we love our Children too well, to send them so great a Way.... We allow it to be good, and we thank you for your Invitation; but our Customs differing from yours, you will be so good as to excuse us."[16] Thanks, but no thanks. That polite but firm rejection, a proud expression of Iroquois cultural difference from their colonial counterparts, could only have come from someone confident of his people's place at the center of the world on the turtle's back.

THE COVENANT CHAIN BREAKS IN NEW YORK

While Canasatego was so confidently extending the Longhouse's authority in Pennsylvania, Iroquois power waned on another frontier. At the eastern door, the Mohawks' relations with New York had deteriorated considerably since the intercolonial treaty conference held in Albany in 1722. The opening of Oswego, the British post on the southeastern shore of Lake Ontario, had eliminated the economic and diplomatic advantage the Mohawks held as the gatekeeper between Albany and the Indians of the *pays d'en haut*. The long peace between Britain and France that followed the Treaty of Utrecht in 1713 had reduced the significance of the Mohawks to New York's security and also emboldened speculators and settlers to purchase and occupy land in the Mohawk Valley. Furthermore, the Mohawks' population had never recovered from the migration of so many of their kin to Canadian *reserves* in the late seventeenth century. By 1740, about five hundred souls lived in Canajoharie and Tiononderoge, the two remaining Mohawk towns in the Mohawk Valley, where they were crowded by a growing population of German and Scots-Irish neighbors.

Canajoharie and Tiononderoge were closely linked to each other, but they were also a study in contrasts. Canajoharie, known as the "upper Mohawk castle" to colonists, was about sixty miles west of Albany. Despite that distance, its inhabitants had plenty of colonial neighbors, mostly Germans from the Rhine River Valley who had established several communities in the upper Mohawk Valley during the 1720s. Canajoharie was also on the route between Albany and Oswego, a mixed blessing for its people. Traders wishing safe passage to and from Oswego needed to keep the upper Mohawks happy, but this traffic also brought a great deal of rum into Mohawk country. In the mid-eighteenth century, the inhabitants of Canajoharie had a reputation for drunkenness and poverty, and their relations with colonial neighbors grew belligerent whenever they felt they had been cheated in their wages, trade, or land sales.[17]

Tiononderoge, known as the "lower Mohawk castle," stood on the west bank of the Schoharie Creek, near its confluence with the Mohawk River, about thirty miles west of Albany. During the 1710s, the British built Fort Hunter on the opposite bank of the Schoharie. The soldiers and traders who frequented this post brought the usual problems associated with an increased availability of rum, but Fort Hunter was also home to a minister sponsored by the Society for the Propagation of the Gospel, the missionary arm of the Church of England. The SPG mission was the most enduring result of the four Indian kings' trip to London in 1710. Long after the "four kings" had slipped back into their normal lives, the missionaries who worked at Fort Hunter continued to provide the lower Mohawks with spiritual instruction and material assistance. They described the lower Mohawks as poor but acculturated Indians who lived in huts rather than traditional longhouses, dressed in English-style clothes, kept livestock, and practiced the Anglican faith, although never to the behavioral standards of their teachers.[18] While most of the lower Mohawks led hardscrabble lives, the standard of living for some had clearly improved with these changes. When Conrad Weiser and fellow German émigré Daniel Claus passed through Tiononderoge in 1750, they stayed with a local chief who lived in a two-story house furnished like that of a middle-class colonial family: "There was nothing wanting in our food or drink or in our beds."[19] Looking downriver at their cousins in Tiononderoge, the Canajoharie Mohawks could glimpse their future. Survival would depend on finding colonial patrons with deep pockets while they adapted to the encroaching colonial population around them.

The inhabitants of Tiononderoge and Canajoharie had one complaint in common against the government of New York: fraudulent land patents. The city corporation of Albany claimed that a late-seventeenth-century patent gave it title to "Tiononderoge flats," the fertile bottomlands on which the lower Mohawk town stood. The Canajoharie Mohawks protested the Livingston patent, a dubious deed to their river lands claimed by one of New York's most powerful families. Both Mohawk towns also complained about a third deed known as the Kayaderosseras patent, which encompassed an enormous swath of Mohawk hunting territory in the Adirondacks region.[20] In all three of these cases, the suspect deeds dated back at least one generation, if not two. In a manner similar to the Penn family's handling of the Walking Purchase, it was the heirs of the original holders of these supposed deeds who stirred trouble by acting on what they said were deals made a long time ago. Not surprisingly, the Mohawks found their claims highly suspect.

Unlike the Delawares dispossessed by the Walking Purchase, the Mohawks at least had a diplomatic leg to stand on. No other

Indian nation had ever claimed to speak for them in such matters, and they still held their position as the preeminent Iroquois nation in the Covenant Chain alliance with New York, although even that status was weakening by the 1730s. While a flurry of Iroquois diplomacy was underway in Pennsylvania during those years, the pace and nature of treaty-making in Albany changed. So long as peace between the French and English allowed, the royal governor of New York avoided the tiresome and expensive trips up the Hudson to brighten the Covenant Chain, delegating that job instead to the Albany Commissioners of Indian Affairs, a board of local magistrates and merchants who conducted such business with far greater expertise and economy. The Albany Commissioners operated according to their own priorities, the chief of which was preserving the city's profitable but illicit trade with French Canada.[21]

Despite official prohibitions against it, the Albany-Montreal trade flourished, in part because of the role played by the Catholic Mohawk community of Kahnawake, located on the south bank of the St. Lawrence across from Montreal. Kahnawake Mohawks arrived each trading season in Albany with beaver pelts and returned home laden with goods destined for the Montreal merchants. With their own fur trade sidelined by the construction of Oswego, the Canajoharie and Tiononderoge Mohawks resented the diplomatic attention the Albany Commissioners devoted to the Canadian Indians, and for good reason. In a typical year, the Albany Commissioners spent £170 on Indian presents.[22] As the Kahnawake Mohawks grew more important in Albany's Indian relations, the Canajoharie and Tiononderoge Mohawks received smaller slices of that pie.

That indignity was compounded when the Albany Commissioners negotiated openly with the Kahnawakes. On one such occasion in August 1735, several Kahnawake chiefs appeared before the Albany Commissioners with a "Pipe of Peace," or calumet, "to renew and strengthen the Antient Peace, Friendship, and

Intercourse between their Constituents, this Government, and the 6 Nations." The Commissioners circulated the pipe, taking "each a Whif," and promised to send it to Onondaga "to be there laid up as a Memorial to Posterity of this Solemn Treaty."[23] To the Mohawks who had remained in their homelands and never abandoned their alliance with the Dutch and British, this was really just too much. Their role as the Iroquois Confederacy's eastern door was being usurped by their Catholic kin in Canada, and with the full cooperation of the Albany Commissioners. If the Mohawks were going to retain their diplomatic power, they would have to find new channels through which to exert it.

That opportunity came with the renewal of Anglo-French warfare along the Canadian frontier. Like previous imperial wars in North America, King George's War (1744–48) was a spillover from a much larger European conflict, the War of the Austrian Succession. British and French ministers paid little attention and devoted even less resources to North America during such conflicts, but the state of war between the two powers gave royal officials in the colonies a chance to seek plunder, fame, and preferment in campaigns they organized and financed themselves. Although Albany shared an exposed frontier with French Canada, its inhabitants preferred to remain neutral in such conflicts. War threatened their trade with Montreal and their peaceful relations with the Kahnawakes. Locally, neutrality made sense. It insulated Albany from the devastating raids that plagued other remote New York and New England communities (Saratoga, a small settlement north of Albany, was sacked by French-allied Indians in 1745). But Albany's neutrality infuriated colonial officials who believed that the Covenant Chain alliance should be put to more aggressive use against New France.[24]

That anger with Albany's management of the Covenant Chain led to a revival in intercolonial treaty-making under the aegis of Governor Clinton of New York. Clinton convened four treaty conferences in Albany between 1744 and 1748, where at various times he was joined by delegations from Massachusetts, Connecticut, and Pennsylvania. These treaty conferences were a material and diplomatic boon to the Canajoharie and Tionon- deroge Mohawks, who used them to air their complaints of land fraud, trading abuses, and diplomatic neglect and to link arms with new colonial partners.

Clinton convened these treaty conferences because he was concerned about the security of New York's western frontier. New York's fur trade and western settlements had extended con- siderably westward into Iroquoia since the last Anglo-French war in North America had ended in 1713. If the Mohawks and other Iroquois abandoned the Covenant Chain, all of that wealth and territory could be lost to the French. The New Englanders, who suffered the brunt of French and Indian raids into the British colonies, wanted the Six Nations to declare war against New France. The Iroquois were inclined to stick to their policy of neutrality. When pressed in 1745 to accept a wampum belt "with the figure of a Hatchet hung to it," they insisted on playing the role of intermediaries instead, stating that they would keep the hatchet "in our bosom" until they had first sent peace delegations into Canada.[25] They played hard to get with the British, giving indefinite responses that left their commitment to the Covenant Chain unclear and made more treaty conferences and presents necessary. While representatives from all six Iroquois nations usually attended these meetings, the Mohawks benefited the most from them. As keepers of the eastern door, they sent larger dele- gations to Albany, exerted more influence there, and engrossed a larger share of the presents.[26]

Hendrick emerged as the spokesman for the Mohawks at these treaty conferences. Like Canasatego, he cut an impressive figure: He was older, in his fifties, and dressed himself in the laced hats, ruffled shirts, scarlet coats, and other finery he received from colonial agents. His reputation as a "bold, intrepid fellow" derived in part from his oratory in public councils, which featured the usual inventory of Iroquoian diplomatic metaphors, but also carried a fiery edge that denounced the Albany Commissioners and predicted dire consequences for the British if they did not appease the Mohawks.[27] Hendrick used King George's War as an opportunity to break the Mohawks' diplomatic dependency on the Albany Commissioners. Everywhere he went—including Boston, Montreal, and Philadelphia—he denounced them. He told Weiser the "Albany people . . . have Cheated us out of our Land, Bribed our Chiefs to sign Deeds for them. They treat us as Slaves. . . . We could see Albany burnt to the Ground, or every Soul taken away by the Great [French] King and other people planted there."[28] He repeated these sentiments to Governor Clinton and New England treaty delegates in October 1745, describing how, if current conditions continued, the Mohawks would "become the property of the Albany people . . . their dogs."[29]

Hendrick's rise to prominence in New York's Indian relations was abetted by his partnership with William Johnson, an Anglo-Irishman who had settled in the Mohawk Valley in 1738 and become a prosperous merchant and landlord.[30] Johnson established himself on the north side of the Mohawk River, between Tiononderoge and Canajoharie. He enjoyed a good reputation in both communities for his generosity and hospitality, but he worked especially closely with the inhabitants of Canajoharie, perhaps because the Mohawks at Tiononderoge already had a colonial patron in their SPG missionary, the Reverend Henry Barclay. Regardless of the reason, Johnson had by 1746 emerged as the new diplomatic partner the Canajoharie Mohawks so desperately needed. In that year, Johnson rode into an Albany treaty conference at the head of a party of Mohawk warriors, "dressed and painted after the Manner of an *Indian* War Captain."[31] His influence among the Mohawks so impressed Governor Clinton that he immediately made Johnson his sole agent for Indian affairs and appointed him colonel and commissary for all Iroquois warriors who joined the British cause.[32]

As his grand entrance to Albany suggests, Johnson had a flair for the dramatic that complemented Hendrick's fiery oratory, and the two forged an enduring partnership. Hendrick, the Mohawk elder statesman dressed in the style of a colonial gentleman, found in Johnson a local agent who could supply the Mohawks' material needs and serve as their advocate to colonial officials beyond Albany. Johnson, a gentleman merchant who delighted in dressing like an Iroquois warrior, used the Canajoharie Mohawks in the manner that a landlord in his native Ireland might have used his tenants, as a retinue of loyal dependents who provided living testimony to his wealth and influence. While he doled out enormous quantities of goods—clothing, arms, gunpowder, kettles, knives, hatchets, tobacco, food, and drink—to his Mohawk neighbors, he also lined his own pockets, because the mercantile business he was patronizing was his own. In one year during King George's War, Johnson spent almost £3,500 on goods and services for his Indian agency, a remarkable sum when compared to the £170 the Albany Commissioners typically spent per year on Indian presents or the £400 the New York Assembly allotted to the governor for treaty conferences. Clinton had appointed Johnson his agent to all six of the Iroquois nations, but during King George's War, the Mohawks (and especially the residents of Canajoharie) received the bulk of his largesse.[33] In a statement reminiscent of Canasatego's description of Conrad Weiser, one Iroquois orator, probably Hendrick, told Governor Clinton in 1751 that "one half of Colonel Johnson belonged to His Excellency [Clinton], and the other to them [the Mohawks]."[34]

Hendrick's alliance with Johnson reinvigorated the Mohawks' significance in New York's Indian affairs, but not without cost. While the other Iroquois nations remained neutral during King George's War, Johnson used his influence and material resources to recruit and outfit Mohawk war parties against the French. The Mohawks complied, their young men anxious for the chance to distinguish themselves in war, but they also expected the British to attack the French with vigor. As had happened during Queen Anne's War thirty-five years earlier, colonial troops raised for an invasion of Canada never moved past Albany. Meanwhile, the Mohawks suffered heavy casualties in their raids, and were enraged when Clinton told them in 1748 that they were to put down their hatchets because Britain and France had negotiated a peace.[35]

In the aftermath of King George's War, the Mohawks again felt the sting of diplomatic neglect. They complained bitterly that Governor Clinton had declared the war over before they had opportunity to avenge their losses and then compounded the insult by failing to make the necessary condolence presents to them. Johnson, who had difficulty getting his expenses reimbursed by the New York Assembly, threatened to resign his office unless it was put on a more secure financial footing. Matters came to a head at an intercolonial Albany conference in 1751. Johnson resigned as Indian agent in advance of the meeting, hoping to force the Assembly's hand. In a maneuver probably planned by him and some Mohawk associates, the Indians at the conference insisted on sending their own messengers to plead for Johnson's attendance. Clinton relented and Johnson came, his reputation as the indispensable man in the Covenant Chain greatly enhanced.[36]

Clinton left this treaty conference abruptly, without bidding a proper farewell to his Indian guests. According to Weiser, the governor's actions left the Iroquois "very Much exasperated."[37] A few months later, Clinton reinstated the Albany Commissioners of Indian Affairs because of Johnson's steadfast refusal to continue serving as an Indian agent without a royal appointment and salary. For the Mohawks, this was the last straw. Hendrick undertook his embassy to New York City, where he confronted Clinton. Displeased with the governor's evasive answers, he declared the Covenant Chain broken.

Hendrick made this statement unilaterally, with no apparent consultation among any Iroquois other than those Mohawks who accompanied him. His single-handed shutting down of the

Covenant Chain was consistent with the Iroquois penchant for playing a diplomatic bluff when the occasion called for it. He had not gone so far as to declare war between the Iroquois and New York. Rather, he had merely observed that the Covenant Chain was broken and that the path between Albany and Iroquoia blocked. "You are not to expect to hear from me any more, and Brother we desire to hear no more from you," he told Clinton.[38]

ALTERNATIVE PATHS IN CANADA AND THE OHIO COUNTRY

In Pennsylvania and New York, Canasatego and Hendrick proudly asserted Iroquois autonomy in the face of colonial authority, but within the Iroquois Confederacy, both of these men aligned themselves with the British and reaped considerable benefits from their partnerships with British colonial agents. Not all Iroquois shared their sympathies. Iroquois who distrusted the British and favored closer ties with the French could be found throughout the Confederacy. They engaged in treaty conferences in Montreal and Quebec, where they received presents and favors from the governor-general of New France and welcomed French traders and blacksmiths into their towns (although not missionaries, whose presence they found too disruptive). New France provided the Longhouse with an important counterbalance to the British, one that could be used time and again to preserve the independence exhibited by the likes of Canasatego and Hendrick.

The Six Nations' relations with New France were also affected by the movement of Iroquois peoples beyond their traditional homelands. The Iroquois never observed the imperial boundary France and Britain drew between their colonies in northeastern America. They traveled between Canada and New York frequently to conduct diplomacy, trade furs, visit kin, and recruit participants for war parties against common enemies.

Migration to mission communities along the St. Lawrence also strengthened Franco-Iroquois ties and communication. Catholic Mohawks dominated the populations of the three *reserves* near Montreal—Kahnawake, Kanehsatageh, and Akwesasne—but Iroquois from all of the Six Nations, as well as other northeastern tribes, could be found in those communities. During the 1740s, the French also established a new mission town at Oswegatchie (modern Ogdensburg, New York) in the upper St. Lawrence Valley, not far from Onondaga. It attracted many Iroquois from the center of the Longhouse.[39]

After 1720, another path of migration affected Iroquois relations with New France. The Allegheny–Ohio River watershed, known as the "Ohio Country" during the colonial era, had been emptied of many of its native inhabitants during the seventeenth century by the combined ravages of warfare and disease. The Iroquois claimed the region by right of conquest, but in the early eighteenth century, it was a virtual no-man's-land, albeit an attractive one of fertile bottomlands, wide rivers, and plentiful game. Such resources attracted native emigrants from the east. Senecas and other western Iroquois followed the natural corridor that the Allegheny River provided from the Longhouse into the Ohio Country. Delawares dispossessed in eastern Pennsylvania arrived there via the Juniata River and the west branch of the Susquehanna. The Shawnees followed a similar route, moving out of the lower Susquehanna Valley to return to what were probably their homelands before seventeenth-century wars with the Iroquois had displaced them.[40]

The French exhibited an early interest in the native repopulation of the Ohio Country. Animal pelts could leave this region for European markets either by moving north through French posts at Detroit and Niagara or by moving east on overland routes to Philadelphia. The geographic advantage was to the French, but Pennsylvania fur traders, who had access to cheaper and more plentiful goods, moved aggressively into the region.[41] The governor-general of New France sent Joncaire, the long-standing French agent among the Senecas, into the Ohio Country in 1731 to cultivate relations with the Shawnees. By the time of his death eight years later, Joncaire had opened a path between Montreal and the Ohio Indians.[42] After his death, an Iroquois delegation traveled to Montreal to mourn Joncaire's loss and request that his son Philippe-Thomas be raised up in his place.[43]

The diplomacy the Iroquois conducted with New France had always made New Yorkers nervous, but the budding relationship between the Shawnees and the French spread the alarm to Pennsylvania's colonial officials as well. At a treaty conference in 1732, the Pennsylvanians asked the Iroquois to intercede by ordering the Shawnees in the Ohio Country to return to the Susquehanna Valley. The Iroquois responded equivocally, telling the Pennsylvanians that they could do the job by reining in their traders; the chiefs' reluctance to confront the Shawnees may have indicated that they exerted far less authority over the Ohio Indians than they liked to claim. The issue returned during subsequent treaty conferences, but as time passed it became increasingly clear that Iroquois dominion in the Ohio Country was a convenient diplomatic fiction.[44]

In November 1747, ten Ohio Indians appeared unexpectedly in Philadelphia. With the help of Weiser, government officials hastily arranged a treaty council to hear what these strangers had to say. They introduced themselves as "Warriors living at Ohio" who spoke "on behalf of ourselves and the rest of the Warriors of the Six Nations." It is noteworthy that they did not claim to be chiefs and that the colonial secretary recording the proceedings did not identify them as such. In Iroquois culture, it was usually the old men—the likes of Canasatego and Hendrick—who conducted diplomacy. Young men were supposed to fight, not talk. But fighting was clearly on the mind of this small delegation. They wanted to take up the British hatchet against the French, but the "old men" at Onondaga insisted on adhering to the neutrality they had declared at the start of King George's War. At last, "the Young Indians, the Warriors, and Captains" from the Ohio region had decided to take up the hatchet "against the will of their old People, and to lay their old People aside as of no use but in time of Peace." The bellicose tone of this speech continued as the visiting Indians chastised the British for not fighting the French with greater vigor. When they went to war, the warriors explained, they "put a great deal of Fire" under the war kettle, so that the "French Men's Heads might soon be boil'd," but the "English Kettle . . . hardly boil'd at all."[45]

This speech, intriguing for its taunting rhetoric directed at both Onondaga and the British, can be interpreted two ways. On the one hand, its metaphors reflected a generational divide common in colonial Indian communities between young warriors spoiling for a fight and old men counseling peace. On the other, it also contained an implicit declaration of independence by the Ohio Indians from the Iroquois in New York. When Canasatego and other Confederacy chiefs conducted diplomacy in Pennsylvania, they liked to assume a generational authority over the Ohio Indians, calling them their "nephews." These warriors from the Ohio did not seem interested in deferring to their Iroquois uncles any longer. The Ohio Indians had grown considerably in numbers since the 1720s, and they had developed their own economic and diplomatic interests. Now they were in Philadelphia to open their own path to the Pennsylvanians and to ask for arms and ammunition to use against the French.

The colonial officials who heard this speech were intrigued. They adjourned to confer privately with Weiser and learn what he could tell them about "the particular History of these Indians, their real disposition toward Us, and their future designs." Weiser counseled that the Ohio Indians were too numerous to be ignored. It behooved Pennsylvania to seek their alliance, and he volunteered to journey to the Ohio the following spring to deliver a sizable present to them.[46] From this point forward, Pennsylvania's

Indian diplomacy shifted away from Onondaga and took a western tack toward the Ohio Country.

The Ohio Indians had good reason to light a council fire with Pennsylvania in 1747. King George's War had disrupted the flow of French goods into the Great Lakes region, leaving traders at Niagara and Detroit unable to supply their Indian clients. Meanwhile, Pennsylvania traders made inroads into the Ohio Country by offering cheap woolens, metal wares, and rum. New partnerships emerged out of these shifting alliances. On the Indians' side, two transplanted Iroquois assumed the role of spokesmen in diplomatic councils with the British. Tanaghrisson, a Catawba taken captive and adopted by the Senecas as a youth, lived at Logstown, a polyglot Indian community near modern Pittsburgh. British Indian agents called him the "Half-King," a reference to his supposed authority as the voice of the Six Nations in the Ohio Country. Much like Shickellamy at Shamokin, Tanaghrisson had no coercive powers over his neighbors at Logstown, only useful connections and access to material goods that gave him influence. Scarouady, who was also known as an Iroquois "half-king" on the Ohio, was an Oneida who maintained ties to Confederacy leaders in Onondaga. Yet he acted independently of the Longhouse when conducting diplomacy for the Ohio Indians (in fact, he led the warriors who visited Philadelphia in 1747). On the British side, the most significant agent in the Ohio Country was the Irish fur trader George Croghan. Like Weiser, Croghan spent a tremendous amount of time plying the Indian paths of Pennsylvania, getting to know influential Indians and colonists and sitting in the councils of both. Like William Johnson in the Mohawk Valley, he exhibited a gregariousness and hospitality that won the Indians' trust, which he was not above using to enrich himself by purchasing their lands.[47]

The pace of the Ohio Indians' diplomacy quickened as King George's War ended. The Pennsylvanians convened a treaty conference in Lancaster in July 1748 attended by fifty-five Indians from the Ohio Country, representing the Iroquois, Delawares, Shawnees, Nanticokes, and Miamis. This last group, an Algonquian-speaking nation from the Wabash River region in western Ohio, presented a calumet pipe wrapped in wampum to link arms in Pennsylvania's Chain of Friendship. This interesting combination of Algonquian and Iroquoian diplomatic artifacts, a material blending of the calumet and condolence ceremonies, symbolized the improvised nature of the Ohio Indians' diplomacy. They were piecing together their own confederacy in the Ohio Country, acting independently but not disavowing their connection to the Iroquois entirely. Scarouady, speaking through a proxy because an injury had rendered him unable to join the proceedings, presented the Miamis on behalf of "the Indians of the Six Nations living at Ohio," a clear distinction from those Iroquois associated with the traditional Confederacy to the north. The Pennsylvanians, mindful of the western fur trade and the security of their own frontier, accepted the Miamis' calumet and thanked Scarouady for the role the Ohio Iroquois had played as intermediaries in the Chain of Friendship.[48]

Not long after this treaty, Weiser made his journey to Logstown, where he was greeted warmly by Iroquois, Delawares, Shawnees, Miamis, and Wyandots (an Iroquoian-speaking nation inhabiting the region around Detroit). The scene was one of raucous celebration. Weiser flew the British colors from an improvised flagpole while Indians and British traders exchanged gun salutes and toasts to the king's health. Rum and whiskey flowed so much that "a great many Indians got drunk" and Weiser, with help from George Croghan, had to destroy some of the traders' stock to restore order. Scarouady and Tanaghrisson presented the Wyandots to Weiser for admission into the Chain of Friendship. Weiser asked the Indians he met to tally their fighting men, and they gave him a total of 789, indicating a total population between three and four thousand. He was impressed. "You are now become a People of Note," he told them, "and are grown very numerous of late Years." Returning to the generational metaphor the Ohio Indians had used in Philadelphia a year earlier, Weiser advised them, "There is no doubt some wise Men among you, it therefore becomes you to Act the part of wise men, and for the future be more regular than You have been for some Years past, when only a few Young Hunters lived here." Weiser and Croghan expected Scarouady and Tanaghrisson to assume the roles of level-headed "wise men" who could keep the peace in this volatile region. But even those two "half-kings" were self-described "new beginners" in such arts. Everywhere in the Ohio Country, Indians and colonists alike seemed to be making it up as they went along.[49]

With the arrival of peace in 1748, the French were anxious to counter the British advances made in the Ohio Country during the war. In 1749, a French expedition under the command of Pierre-Joseph Céloron de Blainville moved south of Lake Erie along the headwaters of the Ohio, harrying British fur traders as trespassers, burying lead plates claiming the region for France, and generally aggravating the Indians they encountered. This obtrusive action was out of character for the French, who were usually much more subtle in their efforts to win and preserve Indian customers and allies.[50] Two years later, Philippe-Thomas Joncaire appeared in Logstown to make the French case again. He pressed the Ohio Indians to expel the British traders from their country, but expressed privately his expectation that this would never be accomplished but by the use of French force. The Indians responded coldly, lambasting the French for presuming to make prisoners of British traders and claim dominion over the Ohio. "Is it not our Land?" one Iroquois orator asked, stamping the ground with his foot and "putting his Finger to his [Joncaire's] Nose."[51] George Croghan delighted in witnessing this confrontation, which he took as evidence of the Ohio Indians' attachment to the British.

The rise of the Ohio Indians in Pennsylvania's Indian diplomacy did not sit well with the New York Iroquois. Considerably more than prestige was at stake here; during the 1730s and 1740s, the path between Onondaga and Philadelphia had provided a great deal of material wealth to the Six Nations. In August 1749, Canasatego led his last embassy, uninvited, into Pennsylvania. His arrival with almost three hundred Indians was deeply resented by Weiser and Governor James Hamilton, both of whom tried to get the Indians to turn around and go home, but Canasatego would have none of it. In a rambling speech, he reminded the Pennsylvanians how important the northern Iroquois were as a buffer between them and the French, but also admitted that "we [have] . . . no other Business with you than to pay you a Brotherly Visit."[52] Hamilton and his councilors were not in the mood for chitchat. They took advantage of the occasion to purchase additional lands east of the Susquehanna River, moving the Penn family's claims ever closer to Iroquoia proper.

The sting of Canasatego's reception in 1749 must have been compounded by the attention Pennsylvania was then devoting to the Ohio Indians. Confederacy chiefs who had assembled in Onondaga in 1750 to treat with Weiser told him plainly, "The Ohio Indians were but Hunters and no Counsellors or Chief Men, and they had no Right to receive Presents that was due to the Six Nations, although they might expect to have a Share, but that Share they must receive from the Six Nations' Chief under whom they belong." Weiser had thought otherwise, as "the Ohio Indians were one and the same with the Six United Nations and of their Blood." Consanguinity went only so far when it came to receiving the largesse of colonial governments.[53] Unfortunately, the chiefs in Onondaga were fighting a losing battle. By Weiser's estimate, one-half of the Onondagas' population had moved to Oswegatchie by 1750, leaving behind communities torn apart by alcoholism and poverty.[54] In the Anglo-French rivalry for dominion in North America, the Ohio Indians now sat on the pivot. As with the Mohawks to the east, a palpable air of desperation had seeped into the self-aggrandizing rhetoric coming out of Onondaga.

ENDINGS AND BEGINNINGS

By 1750, there was much uncertainty in Iroquoia, and colonial and native observers alike questioned whether the Six Nations had lost their foothold on the turtle's back. The Ohio Indians were acting independently of Confederacy leaders in Onondaga and exhibiting considerable belligerence toward the French. Relations with New York had deteriorated rapidly in the wake of King George's War, and the Mohawks appeared permanently alienated from their longtime diplomatic partners in Albany. Some Iroquois were expressing their sympathies with their feet by removing to French mission communities, while those who remained home were wracked by poverty and alcoholism. The deaths of Shickellamy and Canasatego within a short time of each other had left the Confederacy's relations with Pennsylvania adrift. Shickellamy died from an illness he contracted in December 1748. He had lived just long enough to see his partnership with Conrad Weiser fade in significance as the Pennsylvanians turned their attention toward the Ohio Country. Canasatego died in summer 1750, days before Conrad Weiser and Daniel Claus arrived in Onondaga to deliver a message on behalf of the governor of Virginia. The circumstances of his death were mysterious; Claus thought he had been poisoned by French agents masquerading as traders in Onondaga. Whether a result of political assassination or not, Canasatego's death delivered a blow to British sympathies within the Confederacy. His successor, Tohaswuchdioony, also known as The Belt, was a Roman Catholic convert and friend of the French.[55]

Old partnerships gave way to new ones. At the Confederacy's eastern door, Hendrick and William Johnson emerged as the paramount brokers in the Covenant Chain. In the Ohio Country, George Croghan was taking over from the aging Conrad Weiser as Pennsylvania's leading Indian agent, working closely with Tanaghrisson and Scarouady. In such relationships, "linking arms" remained a viable metaphor for Iroquois relations with outsiders. Iroquois influence may have expanded beyond the homelands of the Six Nations in the first half of the eighteenth century, but Iroquois power remained just as dispersed as it ever was, allowing enormous latitude to brokers like Hendrick, Tanaghrisson, and Scarouady and their colonial partners. The world in which they operated was changing, but their "method of doing business" remained similar to that of their predecessors: long days spent traveling the paths of diplomacy, giving speeches at council fires, and cutting deals in the bushes, balancing eloquence and gravitas with bluster and bluffs. The greatest challenge these leaders faced was about to unfold in a climactic battle between the French and British for dominion in North America that would change forever the rules of frontier diplomacy.

5

PARTNERS IN EMPIRE

FOR A FELLOW who had been dead five years, Canasatego looked pretty good when he showed up in London in 1755. He appeared "in all the Bloom of Manhood," standing six feet tall, "the most perfect Height in Human Nature," with ramrod posture and eyes that "flashed forth the Beams of Courage and Compassion." Just as impressive was his noble heart, which beat "with honest Throbbing for his Country's Service." He had come to England on a mission of peace. Back home in Onondaga, the chiefs of the Iroquois had grown tired of land frauds and cheating traders, and they wanted to declare war against their English brethren. But Canasatego thought differently. As a boy, he had learned from missionaries about the splendor of England, the liberty of its people, and the wisdom of its king. Those stories had convinced him that the Britons who came to America must have been exiles from their homeland, banished because they were unfit to live in so great a country. Surely, if he could share his wampum belts and calumet pipe with the king and explain how his subjects were abusing the Iroquois, war could be averted.

The scales fell from Canasatego's eyes when he arrived in England. Everywhere he looked, he saw not peace and prosperity, but poverty and inequality, all of it contrary to his notions of liberty and justice. He wandered London, penniless and friendless, but remained committed to his mission. Finally, a kind-hearted gentleman befriended Canasatego and went to see the king on his behalf. "Do the Indians have votes in Parliament?" the king wanted to know. When informed that they did not, he lost interest and sent Canasatego's benefactor away empty-handed. The noble Indian chief sailed for America shortly thereafter, bidding "adieu, perfidious Land; farewell, degenerate Race, farewell." When seated back at the council fire in Onondaga, he told the chiefs about the "faithless Men" and "pamper'd sons of Ease" he had encountered in England. The time had now come for war: "The Chain is broken; let the War-kettle be boiled, and arm yourselves to your Defence and Honour."[1]

This Canasatego was a fictional one, invented by the English author John Shebbeare for his 1755 novel *Lydia, or Filial Piety*, a picaresque comedy of marriage and manners. In creating his fictional Canasatego, Shebbeare anticipated the Indian characters who would populate James Fenimore Cooper's famous *Leatherstocking Tales* more than seventy years later: eloquent Indian chiefs and warriors, the unlettered nobility of the American forest, whose courage and honesty contrasted sharply with the knavery and hypocrisy of the supposedly more civilized whites. Shebbeare was not the first writer to use Indians to satirize European society, but the fact that he drew his Indian characters and settings from the Iroquois is indicative of how eighteenth-century Britons had come to see the Iroquois as the prototypical natives of North America. In all likelihood, Shebbeare drew Canasatego's name from a published edition of the 1744 Treaty of Lancaster. He borrowed other Indian names for the novel from other works on the Iroquois available at that time in Britain. Shebbeare knew as much about the Iroquois as any well-read Englishman of his time could have known, but that was in fact very little, just enough to give a gloss of authenticity to his stereotypical noble savages.

Not long after the publication of *Lydia* in 1755, the Iroquois and the British got to know each other much better. The Seven Years' War (or French and Indian War, as it came to be known in America) fundamentally altered Britain's relations with its American colonies and their Indian neighbors. The scale of military mobilization in North America was unprecedented. For the first time in their long imperial rivalry, Britain and France committed thousands of regular troops to America and spent fortunes recruiting and arming Indian allies. Back in Britain, readers of newspapers and magazines avidly followed reports on the war, including the role played in it by Native Americans.[2] Year after year, military campaigns focused on the contested borderland that stretched from the St. Lawrence River to the Ohio Valley, territory that the Six Nations claimed as their own. The Iroquois encountered by British and French armies during this war were not the cardboard cut-outs from Shebbeare's novel. They were flesh-and-blood men and women stuck between two clashing imperial powers, each trying to win their alliance.

By the time Quebec fell to the British in 1759, the choice made by the Iroquois was obvious. Either by active participation, or in some cases by purposeful inactivity, the Iroquois had become partners in Britain's American empire. Their commitment to the British cause, however, had at no time been unanimous. Reflecting the dispersed and localized nature of power within their communities, different Iroquois peoples supported the British and French with differing degrees of enthusiasm over the course of the war.[3] Nevertheless, by war's end the British had come to regard the Iroquois as indispensable allies against not only the French but other native peoples in North America. In this reconfigured relationship, British agents cast the Iroquois as rulers of a vast Native American empire, with the power to speak for other Indians and to sell their land out from under their feet.

From the Iroquois perspective, the Seven Years' War and its aftermath carried a new set of challenges and opportunities. Britain's conquest of New France eliminated the ability the Iroquois had enjoyed for so long to play one imperial power against the other. Since 1701, Confederacy chiefs had stood between the British and French like a clever maiden enjoying the attention of two suitors, never giving one a firm answer so that both would continue to seek her favor. After 1760, the British were the only game in town. Furthermore, the British Crown decided to centralize its diplomacy with the Iroquois under a single Indian superintendent, a measure that closed the relationships the Iroquois had enjoyed with multiple colonial governments. In the parlance of Iroquois diplomacy, the war blocked paths the Six Nations had worked hard to open and keep clear with their colonial neighbors. Fewer paths meant fewer options, fewer channels of communication, and fewer ways to bring pressure to bear on their European counterparts across the council fire.

Diplomacy continued to provide an important means for bringing material wealth into Iroquois communities, and so long as the Iroquois could position themselves as intermediaries between the British empire and other native peoples, they could continue to extract goods from British agents in exchange for selling land distant from their own. The trick was to convince the British that Iroquois intercession was necessary if the colonies were to remain at peace with other Indians and continue their westward expansion.

As time passed, that notion of Iroquois power became a fiction worthy of the efforts of John Shebbeare. Victory in the Seven Years' War pushed the focus of Britain's Indian relations out of Iroquoia and into the Ohio Country and western Great Lakes region. The Indians who inhabited those regions chafed at the notion of Iroquois supremacy and established themselves as forces to be reckoned with in their own right. The challenge the Iroquois faced in the 1760s was to remain relevant in Britain's

Indian relations, even as the locus of those relations moved past them. They did so by making wampum, not war. Real Iroquois took up the mission of the fictional Canasatego, using their skills in diplomacy to convince the British that their empire could not flourish without them.

THE CHAIN RESTORED

When news of Hendrick's declaration that the Covenant Chain had been broken reached London, it set in motion a series of events that culminated in the most famous Iroquois treaty of the colonial era, the Albany Congress of 1754. British ministers may not have been well versed in the metaphors of Iroquois diplomacy, but they knew bad news when they heard it. Hendrick's angry denunciation of the New Yorkers threatened to disrupt Britain's claim to dominion over the Iroquois just as Anglo-French tensions were heating up in the Ohio Country. A breach with the Six Nations at this time, especially one as significant as Hendrick's speech suggested, would have fatal consequences for Britain's imperial pretensions in North America. The Crown traced its claim to the Great Lakes and Ohio regions to the 1701 Albany treaty at which the Iroquois had placed their hunting territory under British protection (a deal subsequently reaffirmed at another Albany treaty in 1726).[4] A broken Covenant Chain raised the possibility of the Six Nations' abandoning the British and allying with the French, at precisely the time when Britain needed to assert its control over those contested territories.

The Board of Trade, the Crown's advisory council on colonial affairs, responded by ordering the governor of New York to oversee "one general Treaty" between the colonies and the Iroquois to mend the broken chain. This treaty conference, which convened in Albany in June 1754, attracted unprecedented intercolonial representation. Seven colonies sent delegations: the stalwarts of Albany Indian diplomacy, New York, Massachusetts, and Connecticut; occasional previous participants Pennsylvania and Maryland; and newcomers New Hampshire and Rhode Island. Its most famous colonial participant, Benjamin Franklin, attended as a delegate from Pennsylvania and brought with him the blueprint for a plan of union intended to help the colonies prepare for the coming war.

The Albany Congress gave the Mohawks a forum for venting their grievances about the diplomatic neglect they had suffered at the hands of the New Yorkers. The other colonial delegates delighted in hearing this, for they wanted desperately to see the Covenant Chain put to uses other than protecting New York's fur trade. The New Englanders wanted to pressure the Iroquois into declaring war against the French and their Indian allies in Canada. The Pennsylvanians, at least those attached to the Penn family, wanted to complete land purchases in the Susquehanna Valley before other colonies got to the Iroquois first. With such clashing interests at the table, it is no wonder that Franklin thought greater intercolonial cooperation was necessary to meet the French threat to the British colonies.[5]

New York lieutenant governor James DeLancey opened the treaty by inviting the 150 Iroquois in attendance to take hold of the Covenant Chain again. In an angry reply, Hendrick threw a stick behind his back and condemned the New Yorkers for having "thus thrown us behind your back, and disregarded us" while the French were at work using "their utmost endeavours to seduce and bring our people over to them." He turned his attention to the Albany magistrates in the audience and upbraided them for their partnership with the Canadian Iroquois: "Look about you and see all these houses full of Beaver, and the money is all gone to Canada, likewise powder, lead and guns, which the French now make use of at Ohio." After Hendrick's tirade, his brother Abraham (also a chief from Canajoharie) presented a wampum belt and requested that William Johnson be reinstated as the Mohawks' agent. Then, turning to face the Albany magistrates directly, he stated plainly, "The fire here is burnt out."[6]

In that speech, the Mohawks accomplished what they had come to Albany to do. They publicly humiliated the New Yorkers before the other colonial delegations, assuring that their grievances would receive a hearing well beyond the Hudson Valley. They made clear that their alliance, and thus the Covenant Chain as a whole, rested on Johnson's restoration as their agent. They continued to parry with DeLancey through several more public councils, but regardless of the words spoken, the condition the Mohawks had set for restoring the Covenant Chain was clear to anyone within earshot: The Albany Commissioners must go, and Johnson must replace them.

While embarrassing the New Yorkers in public councils, Hendrick and his fellow Mohawks pursued other interests in the bushes. Working on behalf of the Penn family, Conrad Weiser had come to the Albany Congress to negotiate a purchase encompassing the northern and western branches of the Susquehanna Valley, land that was occupied by Delawares, Shawnees, and other Indian peoples who were props to the Longhouse. The Pennsylvanians had not negotiated land purchases in Albany before, nor had the Mohawks figured in any of their previous transactions with the Iroquois, but desperate times called for desperate measures. The Penn family knew that agents from the Susquehannah Company, a group of Connecticut land speculators, were going to be in Albany, trying to complete their own purchase in the same region. Each of these parties raced to pre-empt the other.

The Pennsylvanians' efforts are better documented, because they sought a sheen of legitimacy for their purchase by making the negotiations as public as possible. Weiser initially tried to keep Hendrick and the Mohawks out of the transaction on the grounds that they had no previous stake in the territory in question, but in coming to Albany, Weiser and his colleagues had walked onto the Mohawks' home court. As soon as he arrived at the treaty, Hendrick asserted the Mohawks' primacy in all Iroquois affairs conducted through the Longhouse's eastern door, and he inserted himself into negotiations Weiser already had underway with the Oneidas and Tuscaroras. At first, Hendrick counseled his fellow Indians not to sell as much land as the Pennsylvanians requested. Weiser replied that the Penn family would cancel the purchase altogether rather than reduce its size.[7]

His bluff called, Hendrick relented. Perhaps he was anxious to cement the Mohawks' place in Pennsylvania's Chain of Friendship, or perhaps he wanted to capitalize on the Pennsylvanians' reputation for generosity while he had them in town. Either way, the deal was completed, and the Pennsylvanians arranged a public signing of the deed. Afterward, they sponsored an "entertainment" for the cooperative Indians, the bill from which included charges for fifteen gallons of wine, seven gallons of beer, and five quarts of cider, as well as one "China Bowl Broke" and "8 Drinking Glasses Carried away" by the partygoers.[8] The celebration may have gotten a bit rowdy, but it must have appeared downright somber compared to what the Susquehannah Company was up to. Its agents hired a local fur trader named John Henry Lydius to do their dirty work. Lydius conducted his negotiations by closeting Indians in his home, plying them with liquor and cash, and convincing them to sign a deed that overlapped considerably with the Pennsylvania purchase.[9]

The land purchases conducted at the Albany Congress reflected the harsh reality of Iroquois diplomacy at midcentury. Once again, the Iroquois enriched themselves, at least temporarily, by selling distant lands inhabited by other Indians. Hendrick and the Mohawks took the lead this time, but they followed a precedent that had been set by Canasatego a decade earlier, when he sided with the Penn family in their dispossession of the Forks Delawares and sold vast swaths of western territory to the Virginians and Marylanders at the Treaty of Lancaster. The Pennsylvania and Susquehannah Company deeds became controversial during the Seven Years' War, as Shawnees and Delawares in the Susquehanna Valley fought to defend homelands sold out from under them at the Albany Congress, but at the time, only Lydius's irregular methods raised eyebrows among colonial observers. For everyone else, including Weiser and Hendrick, the treaty conference had been business as usual, and good business at that. When the treaty ended, the Indians went home with thirty wagons loaded with presents, including four hundred quality guns, a ratio of about two and half guns for every Iroquois man, woman, and child present.[10] They had come to town to mend the broken Covenant Chain; they left looking like an NRA road show.

In the year that followed, the impact that the Albany Congress had on the Covenant Chain became clearer. The colonial delegates debated and adopted a version of Franklin's plan of union, but despite their efforts, the plan sank with barely a trace when it was submitted to the colonial legislatures and British Crown.[11] Franklin was disappointed by its ignominious defeat. The Albany Plan, as it became known, was his brainchild and as far he was concerned, the most important work transacted in Albany. In contrast, the negotiations with the Indians barely deserved a mention in a summary of the proceedings he wrote on his way home. "Nothing of much Importance was transacted with them," he reported to his friend Cadwallader Colden.[12]

The Crown, however, took seriously the Mohawks' discontents. The Board of Trade received the proceedings of the Albany Congress as the Crown was debating how to respond to the crisis in North America. While the Iroquois and colonists had been mending the Covenant Chain in Albany, a small force of Virginia militiamen led by George Washington had been handed a humiliating defeat by French troops at Fort Duquesne on the Forks of the Ohio (modern Pittsburgh). The Crown decided to send two regiments of regular troops commanded by General Edward Braddock to North America to accomplish what the Virginians had been unable to do: force the French out of the Ohio Country and claim the region as their own. The Board of Trade also recommended that the management of the Covenant Chain be removed from the hands of the Albany Indian Commissioners. When Braddock arrived in Virginia in spring 1755, he appointed William Johnson his sole agent to the Six Nations. The Crown formalized this office a year later by creating two royal Indian superintendents for North America, one for the northern colonies and one for the southern. Johnson assumed the northern superintendency.[13] Johnson and his Mohawk neighbors were at last victorious in the battle for control of the Covenant Chain.

Unlike the Albany Commissioners, Johnson had wedded his political and economic interests to the British imperial project in North America. His wealth derived from Mohawk Valley lands he rented to tenants who needed security from French and Indian enemies in Canada and from his mercantile business supplying his Indian diplomacy. An expansive British empire in North America promised to enrich Johnson for years to come. In June 1755, almost a year to the date after the Albany Congress convened, Johnson held a treaty conference at his home, known as Mount Johnson, where he relit the council fire that the Mohawks had declared "burnt out" in Albany. Johnson's secretary counted 1,106 Iroquois in attendance, "a greater number . . . than were ever before known at any public Meeting."[14] At the time Johnson opened the meeting, Braddock's army was cutting its way through the Pennsylvania wilderness on its way to lay siege to Fort Duquesne. Braddock had placed Johnson in charge of raising a colonial force to march against another French post, Fort St. Frédéric in the northern Champlain Valley.

Johnson immediately set to work recruiting Iroquois warriors to assist his and Braddock's armies. The Mohawks were ready, but the other Iroquois nations balked. They were not anxious to break their neutrality with the French, and hard experience had taught them not to place much faith in British military prowess. Ever since Hendrick's unilateral declaration of the broken Covenant Chain in 1753, some Iroquois had suspected that his partnership with Johnson may have grown too cozy for the good of the rest of the Longhouse.[15] At Johnson's conference, they also expressed concern for their cousins the Kahnawakes, who would most certainly be fighting alongside the French. As a party of Cayuga chiefs explained to Johnson, the Canadian Iroquois were "our own flesh and blood and many of us have Brothers, sons, etc who live amongst them." Johnson did his best to overcome such doubts, promising to avoid spilling Kahnawake blood and even taking the lead in a war dance, but his audience was not persuaded. They asked leave to go home and set their affairs in order first, "as we left our families unprepared for this event." Johnson told them their objections were more "evasive than just." The chiefs shot back that they hoped the British would not conduct this war as they had in the past, by raising armies to attack the French but then never marching them past Albany.[16] Such sharp exchanges were not typical for Covenant Chain diplomacy, but Johnson managed to hold things together. He knew he could not compel Iroquois participation in his or Braddock's expedition, so he consented to the Indians' vague promises to join him after they had consulted at home first. On the other side of the council fire, the Iroquois were too enamored of Johnson's hospitality and presents to deny him outright.

By early September, Johnson had assembled an army of about three thousand colonial soldiers on the southern end of Lake George, just north of Albany. His recruiting among the Iroquois had yielded only about two hundred warriors, almost entirely Mohawks. News of the crushing defeat that the French and Indians handed Braddock's army on the banks of the Monongahela River in early July fueled Iroquois skepticism. Meanwhile, the governor-general of New France sent a force of soldiers, militiamen, and warriors—about half of whom were Kahnawakes—under the command of Jean-Armand, the Baron de Dieskau to counter Johnson's advance. On the morning of September 8, Mohawks and colonial militiamen from Johnson's army walked into an ambush set by Dieskau's force. On seeing Hendrick "dressed after the *English* manner" at the head of the Indians, some of the Kahnawakes tried to tip off their Mohawk brethren by firing their guns early, but the warning came too late. Hendrick, described by one observer as a "heavy old Man as grey headed as silver," was among the first killed. He rode into the ambush on horseback, but dismounted in an attempt to find safety.[17] Instead, he stumbled into the French force's baggage guard, composed of "young Lads and women" who stabbed him to death and took his scalp.[18] The survivors rushed back to Johnson's camp, which on hearing the gunfire had wisely started erecting barricades and positioning cannon for their defense. Dieskau pressed his advantage by sending his troops against this fortified position. His Indian allies thought better of attacking a well-entrenched enemy and took the afternoon off. In the ensuing battle, casualties on both sides were about equal, but the French withdrew first, enabling Johnson to claim victory.[19]

The Crown rewarded Johnson handsomely for his leadership at the Battle of Lake George. Although the engagement resulted in heavy casualties and ended Johnson's plans to attack Fort St. Frédéric, it was the only battle that could be interpreted as a victory in what was otherwise a disastrous year for British arms. Johnson received a baronetcy and a grant of £5,000 sterling, as well as his official appointment as the Crown's Indian superintendent for the northern colonies, at a salary of £600 sterling per year.[20] His star was now permanently fixed in the firmament of the British empire. Hendrick's was, too, albeit posthumously. Stories and engravings of the Battle of Lake George circulated in British newspapers and magazines, lionizing Hendrick for his loyalty to the British. Ironically, the Indian who had declared the Covenant Chain broken in 1753 became in death the personification of the Anglo-Iroquois partnership.

The reality of Anglo-Iroquois relations in the aftermath of the Battle of Lake George was more sobering than the elevation of Hendrick to imperial sainthood might suggest. The Mohawks had suffered about thirty casualties in the battle, and the survivors lost interest in the war. Johnson may have been fighting for the glory of the British empire, but these warriors had more traditional motives: They wanted captives, scalps, and personal reputation. Heavy casualties like those suffered at Lake George defeated such purposes. They went home to mourn their dead, and Johnson was powerless to stop them.[21] He learned later that Mohawk clan matrons discouraged them from returning by telling them to stay home and "take Care of their Wives and children."[22] It would be several years before another sizable contingent of Iroquois joined a British campaign.

Johnson and Hendrick had succeeded in breaking the Covenant Chain and then putting it back together on their own terms. For the Mohawks, this meant seeing Johnson restored as their agent and reclaiming their preeminent position within the Confederacy as the keepers of the eastern door. Johnson had different priorities. Now that he was vested with a royal office and salary, he had to put his diplomacy to work for the Crown, and his influence among the rest of the Six Nations would be limited if they perceived him to be the tool of the Mohawks. To make the Iroquois effective partners in the British empire, Johnson needed to turn their multiple paths of diplomacy into one, leading only to him.

PATHS OF WAR

One of the paths Johnson worked assiduously to close led from Iroquoia to New France. Since 1701, the Six Nations had engaged in periodic treaties in Montreal and Quebec and allowed French traders, blacksmiths, and agents to travel and live among them. With the return of Anglo-French warfare to the Canadian frontier in 1755, the Iroquois were anxious to keep this path open, even as Johnson pressed them to close it. In addition to maintaining peace with their kin living on Canadian *reserves*, the path to New France provided the Iroquois with another source of diplomatic presents and a means of protecting their lands should a rupture occur with the British.

As he lighted the council fire at Mount Johnson in 1755, Johnson told the Iroquois, in a thinly veiled reference to the French, that it was "absolutely necessary for you, totally to extinguish all other deceitful and unnatural fires which are made to mislead and in the end destroy both you and yours."[23] Johnson had cause to fear that these words would go unheeded. He had learned that the previous fall, not long after the Albany Congress, a party of Oneidas, Cayugas, and Tuscaroras had traveled to Montreal and treated with that city's governor, Charles Le Moyne de Longueuil. While in Montreal, the visiting Iroquois also met secretly with the Indians in the neighboring *reserves* of Kahnawake and La Montagne. "Your blood is the same as ours," they stated. To avoid internecine hostilities, they would reject the hatchet offered by Johnson and "forbid our young men not only to touch it, but even to look at it." The Canadian Iroquois accepted the wampum belts that accompanied this speech, but not without chastising the Six Nations for selling land to the British in the Ohio Country. Their speech contained a prescient comparison of French and British methods of colonization:

> Brethren, Are you ignorant of the difference between our Father [the French] and the English? Go see the forts our Father has erected, and you will see that the land beneath his walls is still hunting ground, having fixed himself in those places we frequent only to supply our wants; whilst the English, on the contrary, no sooner get possession of a country than the game is forced to leave it; the trees fall down before them, and the earth

becomes bare, and we find among them hardly wherewithal to shelter us when the night falls.[24]

Apparently, the shady real estate deals the Iroquois had been
making in Pennsylvania and New York were compromising
their reputation among other Indians.

As British and French armies campaigned against each other
along the Canada–New York border, the Iroquois held on to
their neutrality with New France. Two French agents with personal influence and expertise to rival Johnson's helped them in
this regard. Philippe-Thomas Chabert de Joncaire, who had
taken over for his father as the French agent among the western
Iroquois in the 1740s, worked out of Niagara to promote the
Senecas' and Cayugas' attachment to the French, and he escorted
a party of Senecas to Montreal in fall 1755 to mend the rift opened
between the French and Iroquois in the Ohio Country.[25] Nearer
the center of the Longhouse, Abbé François Picquet was the
French priest at Oswegatchie, the mission community on the
St. Lawrence to which a considerable number of Onondagas had
relocated in the early 1750s. In a stunt reminiscent of the four
Indian kings' embassy to London, he traveled to Paris in the winter of 1753 with four Iroquois to drum up royal support for his
mission. The Indians returned "dressed like Frenchmen from
head to foot," arrayed in wigs and "lace-covered garb." When
war broke out between the French and British in the Ohio Country, Picquet's diplomacy among the Iroquois took on a more militant air. According to one French officer, the missionary taught
and drilled his converts "in the French military exercises."[26]
Working with Joncaire, he extracted from the Iroquois a promise
not to interfere with the French campaign against Oswego in
1756, which ended in the successful siege and demolition of the
fort, a crushing blow to the British war effort.

Despite close relations with Joncaire and Picquet, the Iroquois remained fiercely protective of their political independence.

In 1757, chiefs and clan matrons at Oswegatchie became indignant when the French governor-general Pierre Rigaud de Vaudreuil de Cavagnial, Marquis de Vaudreuil sent them a chief to install on their council. "Although we have been reborn through this same baptismal water which has washed the great Onontio," they explained to Vaudreuil, "we have not renounced our liberty or the rights we hold from the Master of Life. . . . It is only we who can give ourselves chiefs."[27] The French suspected the Iroquois were standing aloof from the conflict so that they could extract maximum material benefit from it, or as Vaudreuil put it to the Onondagas and Oneidas in 1756, "You pretend to be friends of the French and of the English, in order to obtain what you want from both sides, which makes you invent lies that an upright man would never think of."[28]

Some Iroquois warriors did participate in French campaigns against the British, but the Confederacy chiefs held firm to the neutrality they had staked out in Montreal at the war's outset. When pressed by either side to explain why their warriors were fighting for the other, the chiefs repeated their ages-old explanation that the young men were impossible to control. About 350 Canadian Iroquois accompanied the French army that besieged Fort William Henry on the southern end of Lake George in 1757, but their force was dwarfed by the more than 1,200 warriors from the *pays d'en haut* recruited by the expedition's commander, General Louis-Joseph, Marquis de Montcalm. This campaign, which gave the French their greatest victory in the northern theater of the war, was also the high-water mark for participation from their Indian allies. The Six Nations had managed to weather the French offensive campaigns of the war without abandoning their path to Montreal or their neutrality.[29]

The outbreak of the Seven Years' War also jeopardized the path between Iroquoia and Pennsylvania. While Johnson was collecting the reins of the Covenant Chain in New York, the Quaker colony continued to conduct its own diplomacy independently with the

Iroquois. Tanaghrisson and Scarouady, the Iroquois "half-kings" in the Ohio Country, grew increasingly concerned about the security of their homelands as they watched the French construct a series of posts from Lake Erie to the Forks of the Ohio in 1753 and 1754. Scarouady convened treaty conferences in Winchester, Virginia, and Carlisle, Pennsylvania, to solicit military aid from those two colonies, while Tanaghrisson delivered to the French the customary three warnings the Iroquois made to an enemy before going to war.[30]

Virginia and Pennsylvania failed to match the enthusiasm Tanaghrisson and Scarouady expressed for driving the French out of the Ohio Country. Washington's 1754 expedition against Fort Duquesne ended with his capitulation at Fort Necessity. Shortly thereafter, Tanaghrisson, Scarouady, and about three hundred other pro-British Ohio Indians left the Forks region and relocated eastward to Aughwick Creek on the Juniata River, where Pennsylvania Indian agent George Croghan kept a trading post. In councils with Croghan, Weiser, and the interpreter Andrew Montour, these disaffected Indians invoked the Chain of Friendship's origins story ("when William Penn first appeared in his Ship on our Lands") and asked for assistance against the French. They reported receiving wampum belts from the Senecas, ordering them "not to meddle with the French . . . but stand Neuter and keep their Ears and Eyes towards the Six United Nations." Such advice did not sit well with them; they were anxious to strike back at the French, regardless of the neutrality preached by their northern kin.[31]

Tanaghrisson died in the fall of 1754, but Scarouady spent much of 1755 trying to drum up native and colonial support for taking up the hatchet against the French. He visited Iroquoia in the winter of 1754–55 to see if he could swing the Confederacy into a more militant anti-French posture, but his efforts were for naught. He was among a party of Ohio Indians who treated with Edward Braddock that May, as the general gathered his forces at

Fort Cumberland on the Potomac River for his ill-fated expedition against Fort Duquesne. The Ohio Indians were ready to assist Braddock so long as he guaranteed the security of their lands after the French were removed. Braddock, who doubted that he needed the Indians' help, told them plainly that "No Savage Should Inherit the Land."[32] Frustrated, Scarouady moved on to Philadelphia, where he tried to convince the Pennsylvanians to supply the Ohio Indians. In November, with the spectacular French and Indian victory over Braddock's army well-known, Scarouady's tone turned ominous. Addressing the Pennsylvania governor, he stated, "I must now know if you will stand by us; to be plain, if you will fight or not. . . . I must deal plainly with You, and tell you if you will not fight with us, we will go somewhere else." At that time, the governor was caught in a stalemate between the Pennsylvania Assembly and the Penn family over who would pay for the colony's defenses. With this impasse unbroken, he had nothing to offer Scarouady: "I therefore cannot give you a positive answer . . . to know whether we Will fight or not."[33]

The Pennsylvanians paid dearly for turning their backs on Scarouady. Most of the Ohio Indians saw no option other than to join with the French after Braddock's defeat and Scarouady's dismissal by the governor. Supplied out of Fort Duquesne, warriors from the Ohio, Allegheny, and Susquehanna valleys attacked Pennsylvania's frontier communities, burning homesteads, destroying livestock, and taking more than one thousand captives.[34] Pennsylvania's Governor Morris declared war on the Indians and offered bounties for their scalps. Rather than be complicit in this abnegation of the Chain of Friendship, Quaker politicians established the Friendly Association for Regaining and Preserving Peace with the Indians by Pacific Means. The Friendly Association, as it became known, challenged the governor's authority in Pennsylvania's Indian relations (and in time that of William Johnson), by conducting its own shadow diplomacy in an effort to restore peace.

From the war in Pennsylvania's backcountry emerged one of the most enigmatic characters in eighteenth-century Iroquois diplomacy, a Susquehanna Delaware chief known as Teedyuscung. His life is well-documented, but the historical record goes only so far in explaining the motives and personality behind the man who placed himself at the center of the Chain of Friendship during this critical time. Teedyuscung had lived among those Delawares dispossessed by the Walking Purchase and told by Canasatego to resettle in the Wyoming region of the northern Susquehanna Valley. During those difficult years, he had joined some of his Indian neighbors in converting to Christianity under the tutelage of the Moravians, a German Protestant sect that came to the Forks of Delaware region in the 1740s. For a time, he lived among other converts in the mission town of Gnadenhütten, but by the outbreak of the Seven Years' War he had grown discontented with this life and moved west into the Wyoming Valley.[35]

With the coming of war, Teedyuscung seized the opportunity to act as a broker between Indians living in the northern Susquehanna Valley, the Iroquois Confederacy, and the Pennsylvania government. The Iroquois expected the Susquehanna Indians to act appropriately as props to the Longhouse and follow whatever lead or instructions they received from their "uncles" in Onondaga. The Susquehanna Indians—a conglomeration of Delawares, Mahicans, Nanticokes, and others—thought otherwise. Angered by the land purchases conducted by their supposed protectors at the Albany Congress, they wanted more control over their territory. Many vented their rage by participating in the French-sponsored war parties that ravaged the Pennsylvania frontier after Braddock's defeat. In early 1756, at the behest of William Johnson, a delegation of Six Nations chiefs traveled to Otsiningo (near modern Binghamton, New York) to tell these disaffected Indians to put down the hatchet. Meanwhile, Quakers in Philadelphia enlisted Scarouady to carry a message of peace to the same Indians on their behalf.[36] The Quakers attributed the

Indians' hostilities to the Penn family's long train of fraudulent land purchases, and they believed the Chain of Friendship could be restored if those abuses were exposed and corrected by the Crown.

The meeting at Otsiningo resulted in a series of treaty conferences in the northeastern Pennsylvania town of Easton that would eventually involve a large cast of colonial officials and Delaware, Iroquois, and related Indians. Teedyuscung asserted his leadership at the first of these meetings in July 1756, claiming he represented "ten Nations, among which are my Uncles the *Six Nations*, authorizing me to treat with you" (the other four were the Mahicans and three branches of the eastern Delawares). In claiming his authority devolved from the Six Nations, Teedyuscung appears to have stretched the truth for the sake of gaining an entrée into Pennsylvania's Chain of Friendship. At Easton in 1756, he told his colonial audience that Iroquois chiefs had given the Delawares a wampum belt at Otsiningo signifying the end of their status as "women" and making "Men of us," so that they could conduct diplomacy on behalf of the Iroquois Confederacy, because "we are in the Middle, between the *French* and the *English*."[37]

Much of the subsequent diplomatic intrigue involving Teedyuscung hinged on whether his description of the Otsiningo conference was correct. The Friendly Association, led by Philadelphia merchant Israel Pemberton, supported Teedyuscung's claim to speak for the "ten nations." They knew he was anxious to prevent the Wyoming Valley from being peddled away by the Iroquois, and they expected him to serve as an effective native voice for publicizing the Penn family's sordid record in Indian relations. Unfortunately for the Quakers, Teedyuscung was prone to verbal outbursts and bouts of drunkenness that upset the decorum of treaty councils; the confident authority he exhibited in one moment easily gave way to overwrought self-pity in the next.[38] Governor Morris was as suspicious of Teedyuscung as he was of the

Quakers. His preference was to seek peace with the Indians through the intervention of William Johnson and the Six Nations, both of which had proven themselves more amenable to the Penn family's interests in the past.

Trying to fathom the extent of Teedyuscung's authority, Morris asked the Seneca chief Newcastle to explain what had happened at Otsiningo. Newcastle had a different story. The Six Nations had chastised the Delawares for acting as "a common Bawd" by "laying with the French," that is to say, taking up their hatchet against the English. "We now give you a little Prick," the Iroquois chiefs told the Delawares, "and put it in your private Parts and so let it grow there, till you shall be a compleat man. We advise you not to act as a Man yet but be first instructed by us and do as we bid you."[39] In other words, the Six Nations may have made "men" of the Delawares at Otsiningo, but they still expected them to act as nephews to the Six Nations.

Several months later, Teedyuscung was back in Easton to treat with the new governor of Pennsylvania, William Denny. His speeches at this meeting suggest that he had been emboldened by his alliance with the Quakers to speak more directly about the Delawares' discontents. When asked by Denny why the Delawares had gone to war against the colony, Teedyuscung responded by referring to the Walking Purchase: "This very Ground that is under me (striking it with his Foot) was my Land and Inheritance, and is taken from me by Fraud." These accusations ignited a controversy between the Penn family's agents, who accused the Friendly Association of planting Teedyuscung's speech, and the Quakers, who accused their critics of trying to cover up the Indians' legitimate complaints.[40]

Ordered by his London superiors to investigate why the Pennsylvania Indians had gone to war, William Johnson entered the fracas through his deputy, the fur trader George Croghan. The favor Johnson had shown toward the Penn family in previous Indian negotiations had by now evaporated, but he was even less inclined to tolerate the Quakers, whom he considered unwarranted interlopers in Indian diplomacy.[41] Likewise, Teedyuscung's maverick negotiations were challenging the authority Johnson expected the Iroquois to exert over their props in the Susquehanna Valley. Acting on Johnson's behalf in 1757, Croghan attempted to convene a "more general treaty including the Six Nations" in Pennsylvania, but upon gathering a sizable number of Indians, Croghan discovered that Teedyuscung was nowhere to be found. The self-proclaimed "king of the Delawares" had stayed away, apparently to avoid meeting his critics. Two Six Nations chiefs, the Oneida Thomas King and the Mohawk Little Abraham, told Croghan yet another version of what had happened at Otsiningo the previous year. According to them, when the Six Nations told the Delawares to cease their warfare in Pennsylvania, the Delawares had proclaimed, "We are Men, and are determined not to be ruled any longer by you as Women . . . so say no more to us on that Head, lest we cut off your private Parts, and make Women of you." This version put a much more defiant face on Teedyuscung's diplomacy in Pennsylvania, and may explain why he wished to avoid a showdown with the Iroquois chiefs assembled by Croghan.[42]

Two months after those chiefs had returned home, Teedyuscung appeared in Easton with three hundred other Indians from the upper Susquehanna, once again presenting himself as the spokesman for the "ten nations." Encouraged by sympathetic Quakers, Teedyuscung presented his terms for peace. He wanted all the deeds from the Penn family's land purchases examined for instances in which they bought land from Indians who had no right to sell it or engrossed more land than the Indians intended to sell. Delegates from the Pennsylvania Assembly produced the deeds in question, but Denny insisted that the investigation of the Delawares' complaints could go no further because the Crown had charged William Johnson with that task. Teedyuscung flatly refused to take his case to Johnson because of his partnership with the Iroquois who had sold away Susquehanna Valley lands at Albany in 1754.[43] Here was the crux of the matter: Teedyuscung and his fellow Susquehanna Indians knew that they would find no redress in the Covenant Chain because it represented the interests of those who had sold them out in the first place. Instead, Teedyuscung wanted to take hold of the Chain of Friendship and pursue his own diplomacy independently with the Pennsylvanians.

After the inconclusive negotiations of 1757, Denny and Croghan decided to call Teedyuscung's bluff. Was he in fact the powerful broker between the Six Nations and Pennsylvania that he claimed to be? Croghan convened another conference to find out. The Easton Treaty of 1758 brought together representatives from Pennsylvania and New Jersey, the Friendly Association, and Johnson's Indian Superintendency, and more than five hundred Indians from the Six Nations and the Susquehanna and Delaware valleys.[44] Teedyuscung's day of reckoning was at hand. According to Benjamin Chew, a member of the governor's council who witnessed the proceedings, Teedyuscung attended Denny's opening speech to the Iroquois, but "seemed low spirited and eclipsed." A few days later, a "very drunk" Teedyuscung disrupted a public council, "swearing that he was King of all the nations and of all the world, and the Six Nations were fools" who did not realize that the best way to deal with the English was "to make war on them and cut their throats."[45] In a private conference with Denny, chiefs from the "elder brothers" of the Iroquois Confederacy—the Mohawks, Onondagas, and Senecas—disowned Teedyuscung, stating one by one that they did not know who had made him a great man or appointed him to speak for ten nations. Later, when Teedyuscung rose in public council to address the chiefs of the Six Nations, they walked out on him, "seeming much displeased."[46]

The public and private denials of Teedyuscung at Easton allowed Denny to refocus his diplomatic attention on the Six

Nations. He agreed on behalf of the Penns to return the lands west of the Allegheny Mountains that had been purchased at the Albany Congress, but he conveyed them to the Iroquois, not the Delawares. On behalf of the Crown, he agreed that no further settlements would occur in these disputed lands until the Indians approved their sale, and that a well-regulated trade would be restored in the Ohio Country as soon as peace returned. These promises were aimed at winning over the Ohio Indians, who at that time were wavering in their attachment to the French.

When Teedyuscung spoke again at this conference, his tone changed from defiant to humble. He returned to his original concern: the security of the Wyoming Valley. "I sit there as a Bird on a Bough; I look about and do not know where to go," he told the audience of colonial officials and Indians, "let me therefore come down upon the Ground; and make that my own, by a good Deed; and I shall then have a Home for ever."[47] His eloquent plea fell on deaf ears. The Oneida Thomas King responded with a condescending refusal to grant the Delawares a deed to their land, but an allowance for them to continue living there so long as the Six Nations saw fit.

Teedyuscung remained active in Pennsylvania's Indian affairs for a few more years (he died in 1763 in a house fire probably set by colonial squatters in the Wyoming Valley), but he never reclaimed the stature he lost at Easton in 1758. Likewise, the Friendly Association continued to advocate on behalf of the Delawares, but at Easton in 1758, they lost the same gamble as Teedyuscung to keep Pennsylvania's Chain of Friendship from being swallowed up by William Johnson and the Six Nations.[48]

The 1758 Easton Treaty coincided with a seismic shift in the fortunes of war for Britain. In July of that year, Generals Jeffrey Amherst and James Wolfe engineered a successful siege of Louisbourg, the French fortress on Cape Breton Island that guarded the approach to the St. Lawrence River. This was the culminating victory of the British naval blockade that had been strangling

New France's access to fresh troops, munitions, and supplies. Also that summer, another important link in New France's supply chain gave way when Colonel John Bradstreet's army of colonial soldiers took Fort Frontenac on the northeastern shore of Lake Ontario. Johnson's work among the Iroquois in the eastern end of the Longhouse showed some evidence of paying off in this victory. Although Iroquois participation in Bradstreet's force had been small, no word of his mission had leaked from Iroquois sources to French military officers in time for them to defend the post. The Six Nations had not violated their neutrality, but their handicapping of the war now clearly favored the British.[49]

In 1758, the British also exorcised Braddock's ghost by taking Fort Duquesne. General John Forbes spent the summer cutting a road from Carlisle, Pennsylvania, to the Forks of the Ohio, taking care to build fortifications along the way so he could not be forced into the sort of rapid retreat that had ruined Braddock's army. While his slow advance irritated the Cherokee warriors recruited for his expedition and eventually led to their desertion, it worked to his advantage in another way. His caution gave time to the Moravian missionary Christian Frederick Post, who traveled between Philadelphia and the Ohio Country with a message of peace. Post's mission benefited considerably from two chiefs of the western Delawares, Pisquetomen and Tamaqua, who led a peace faction that had grown discontented with the wartime dearth of trade goods at Fort Duquesne. They were now willing to talk peace with the British, provided they would restore a good trade to the Ohio Country and leave the land in the hands of its Indian inhabitants. Pisquetomen traveled east with Post to attend the Easton Treaty in October, where Governor Denny promised to honor the western Delawares' conditions. With those assurances, Post and Pisquetomen returned west in time to sway opinion among the Ohio Indians in favor of the British. Abandoned by their native allies, the French retreated northward toward Lake Erie and blew up Fort Duquesne as Forbes's army approached.[50]

With the fall of Louisbourg, Frontenac, and Duquesne, the pendulum had swung decisively in Britain's favor, and for the Iroquois, that meant it was time for neutrality to give way to alliance. In April 1759, Johnson convened a treaty conference with the Six Nations and several affiliated tribes at Canajoharie. Invoking the Treaty of Easton completed a few months earlier, he hand-delivered to an Onondaga chief the "Instrument of Release and Surrender" for the "Lands on the Ohio" that the Penn family had purchased at the Albany Congress. He then threw down a war belt and asked for warriors to join the British in the coming campaign season. A delegation of Senecas accepted the war belt, signaling that the western Iroquois were ready to support the British, and they pressed Johnson to attack the French at Niagara. Johnson hosted a grand feast and distributed presents the following day. The Indians reciprocated with a wampum belt "with the Figure of Niagara at the end of it, and Sir William's name worked thereon."[51]

The Senecas had long been partners with the French at Niagara, but they had two good reasons for severing the relationship in 1759. First, the French could no longer supply their western fur trade. Second, the war had endangered the Six Nations' claim to the Ohio Country. The Delawares, Shawnees, and transplanted Iroquois living there had acted independently by going to war against the British, and they had paid little heed to calls from the Six Nations to put down the hatchet until it suited them to do so. A timely alliance with the British would give the Six Nations the leverage they needed to reassert their claim to authority over the Ohio Indians and the disposition of their lands.

Approximately one thousand Iroquois warriors, mostly Senecas, joined the British expedition against Niagara in July 1759. A diplomatic interlude that occurred early on in the three-week siege showed the fragility of Johnson's influence. About one hundred local Senecas led by a chief named Kaendaé were among the defenders of the fort when the British arrived. William

Johnson and his French counterpart, Captain Pierre Pouchot, allowed these Senecas to have a three-day parley with their cousins in the British force. Each commander expected his Indian allies to convince the others to switch sides. Instead, Kaendaé's Senecas withdrew from the fort and decamped upriver to La Belle Famille, where a portion of Johnson's warriors joined them, persuaded by Kaendaé that it was best to let the French and British fight it out by themselves. Johnson prevented the loss of the rest of his warriors by promising them the chance to pillage the fort once it fell, but even these stalwarts stood back as the siege proceeded, leaving the hazardous, back-breaking duty of digging trenches and placing artillery to the British and colonial soldiers. The fate of Niagara was sealed a week later, when the British destroyed a French and Indian force arriving to lift the siege. The Iroquois warriors who had moved to La Belle Famille contributed to this victory by organizing their own ambush of the reinforcements, but not before engaging in some more diplomacy across enemy lines to avoid fighting their kin.[52]

The independence the Senecas exhibited in the Niagara campaign did not bode well for Johnson's efforts to turn the Iroquois into reliable auxiliaries of the British empire in North America. Generals Amherst and Wolfe and other senior British officers regarded Indians as expensive and fickle allies, who demanded vast material rewards up front and then abandoned expeditions whenever they grew weary of the delay, hardship, and military discipline that inevitably accompanied them. Despite the long history of Anglo-Iroquois relations in the Covenant Chain and Johnson's significant personal influence, the Iroquois seemed to be no different from other Indians in this respect. For Amherst's 1760 campaign against Montreal, Johnson gathered about seven hundred Iroquois warriors. In their honor, Amherst named two of the gunships he had built to accompany the expedition down the St. Lawrence the *Onondaga* and the *Mohawk*. The enthusiasm with which the Indians greeted the christening of these vessels soon dissipated. The warriors were "universally dissatisfied" when Amherst denied them entry into a French fort that had surrendered, and they took out their frustration by engaging in unauthorized pillage and plunder. When they had had enough, they went home. Only about one-quarter of those who left with Amherst and Johnson in early August were still with them when Montreal fell six weeks later.[53]

In terms of Anglo-Iroquois relations, the war ended much as it had begun. Britain's military fortunes had turned around considerably between Braddock's defeat and the capitulation of Montreal, but the enormous expense of Johnson's Indian diplomacy had paid small dividends on the field of battle. British military officers had been constantly frustrated by their inability to capitalize on what they thought was the loyalty and dependence of the Six Nations. The Iroquois saw it differently. Alliance was a matter of reciprocity, and they expected the British to show them generosity when they linked arms. Furthermore, they refused to fight on anyone's terms except their own. They had no interest in enduring the brutal discipline, endless marches and sieges, and high casualties that were integral parts of eighteenth-century European warfare. Nor were they willing to spill the blood of their cultural kin, even if they fought on opposing sides. The lines that the British and French drew on maps of North America meant little to them. In Iroquois eyes, it was still all Iroquois country.

The war had nonetheless reshaped the world of the Iroquois by closing important paths for their diplomacy. The British decision to retain Canada rather than restore it to the French at the Treaty of Paris in 1763 meant that Onontio was no more; the French father who had always provided a counterweight to the British could no longer receive his children in Montreal, grant them presents, or mediate between them and the Algonquians of the *pays d'en haut*. For that matter, neither could Massachusetts nor Pennsylvania, the longtime thorns in the side of the New Yorkers. All roads now led to William Johnson, or as his Mohawk neighbors had named him, Warraghiyagey, "A man who undertakes great Things." Johnson started construction on a new home in 1763 to serve as the centerpiece of his Mohawk Valley fiefdom. Known as Johnson Hall, this Georgian mansion became the seat of Covenant Chain diplomacy until the eve of the American Revolution.[54]

The war also witnessed the passing of a generation of leaders on both sides of the cultural divide who might have checked Johnson's ambitions. Tanaghrisson had died among the Ohio Indians who took refuge with George Croghan in 1754. Hendrick was killed a year later at Lake George. Scarouady succumbed to an illness he contracted while conducting his diplomatic missions in Pennsylvania in 1757. Conrad Weiser, for so long Johnson's more experienced and knowledgeable rival, died after a short illness in 1760, worn out from years spent traversing Indian paths, real and metaphorical. By 1763, the future of the Covenant Chain rested squarely in Johnson's hands.

The Path to Fort Stanwix

In retrospect, the Iroquois weathered the Seven Years' War fairly well. They had managed to preserve their neutrality while the British and French spilled unprecedented blood and treasure around them, and they kept marauding armies and militias away from their towns. They entered the conflict only when it became clear who the winner would be. Most important, the war had not severed the ties of kinship that connected Iroquois peoples across political boundaries imposed by others. Throughout the war, the path between the Canadian Iroquois and the Six Nations remained open, and both of those groups maintained their diplomatic ties with Iroquois in the Ohio Country.

Yet, the Iroquois Confederacy was a sickly giant at war's end, the balance of its diplomacy with outsiders upended by Johnson's rise to power. During the war, the largesse Johnson showed the

Iroquois outpaced any precedents established by the colonial governments. Johnson made presents valued in the thousands of pounds at treaty conferences as well as countless individual disbursements to Indians who visited his home. He outfitted chiefs for councils and warriors for war parties and supplied their women and children with clothing, tools, and food.[55] Diplomacy, the means by which the Iroquois had always preserved their political and territorial independence, had become a corrosive force on their economic independence, leaving them dangerously exposed to the vagaries of British imperial policy.

Iroquois power in the postwar era was further weakened by Johnson's shifting priorities. While the base of his operations remained in the Mohawk Valley, Johnson spent a great deal of time, energy, and material resources after the war on Indians north and west of Iroquoia. This redirection began immediately after the fall of Montreal with a conference Johnson held with the "Seven Nations" of Canada, a loose confederacy of Indians living on *reserves* in the St. Lawrence Valley. A year later, Johnson traveled to Detroit to admit Indians from the *pays d'en haut* into the Covenant Chain. On the way, he stopped at Onondaga, where the chiefs were surprised to find him traveling so far to treat with nations so recently allied with the French. "You know that the chief and only council fire burns at your house and Onondaga," they told him, "besides, these Indians you are going to, ought rather, as being aggressors, to come to you." Johnson's reply did nothing to smooth their ruffled feathers. The fall of New France, he explained, changed everything: "As our conquests in this country are now great . . . it will be necessary to have other meetings and places of trade, than Oswego and Onondaga." It was his job to "keep up a good understanding" with the western Indians, and he warned the assembled chiefs that "it will be for your good to keep up a good understanding with them also."[56]

Indian diplomacy during the 1760s pulled Johnson in many directions, some of which challenged the Six Nations' preeminent

claim to his attention and generosity. At the 1761 treaty conference in Detroit, Johnson treated with five hundred Indians from
the *pays d'en haut*.[57] The language he used in doing so made clear
that the Chain now centered on him, not the Iroquois:

> The great King George my Master . . . directed me to
> light up a large Council fire at my House in the Mohocks
> Country for all Nations of Indians in amity with his Sub-
> jects. . . . This fire yields such a friendly warmth that
> many Nations have since assembled thereto, and daily
> partake of its influence. I have therefore now brought a
> brand thereof with me to [this] place with which I here
> kindle up a large Council fire made of such Wood as
> shall burn bright and be unextinguishable, whose kindly
> Warmth shall be felt in, and shall extend to the most
> remote Nations, and shall induce all Indians, even from
> the setting of the Sun to come hither and partake
> thereof.[58]

At treaty conferences such as this one, the Iroquois who attended with Johnson took on the characteristics of an entourage.
Johnson understood better than most of his colonial contemporaries that power in Indian communities was broadly dispersed
and maintaining it depended more on persuasion than coercion.
He constantly hosted Indians at his home because he knew that
cultivating such personal bonds was the best means of attaching
them to his interest, and when he traveled to sites such as Montreal, Detroit, Niagara, and Oswego to treat with distant Indians,
he recruited large retinues of Iroquois chiefs and warriors to
accompany him and serve as visual evidence of his power. These
Indians tapped Johnson's generosity, but they lost something in
the bargain, appearing more like clients than partners in the
reconfigured Covenant Chain that now supposedly stretched as
far as "the Setting of the Sun."

After the Seven Years' War, Johnson had to contend with an increasingly volatile situation in the trans-Allegheny West. The Indians of the Ohio Country and *pays d'en haut* were not pleased with the new order of things imposed by the British after 1760. Contrary to promises made in 1758, the British army did not withdraw from the Forks of the Ohio after dislodging the French. Rather, they built Fort Pitt at the site of the ruined Fort Duquesne, which in turn attracted traders, military contractors, and squatters who arrived via Forbes Road and built homes and cleared fields in the fort's shadow. Their presence stoked the militancy of the Ohio Indians, who were also inspired by the visions of Neolin, a Delaware prophet who preached pan-Indian unity against the triple threat of colonial society: liquor, Christianity, and land-grabbing.[59]

Amherst added to the western Indians' discontent by cutting back on the expenses associated with their diplomacy. He told army officers at frontier posts to stop giving presents to Indians and to limit the amount of gunpowder sold to them, now that it was no longer necessary to secure their alliance against the French. Amherst expected these changes to wean Indians from their dependence on Britain's diplomatic largesse while also pacifying them. Instead, the policy enraged Indians who believed that the British were trying to enslave them. In spring 1763, nations along the Great Lakes and Ohio frontiers took up the hatchet again, laying siege to Detroit and Fort Pitt, overwhelming a number of smaller posts, and raiding the Pennsylvania and Virginia backcountry. Pontiac's War, so named for the Ottawa war chief who led the attack on Detroit, threatened to undo the foothold in the continent's interior that the British had so recently wrestled from the French.[60]

Much as they had during the Seven Years' War, the Six Nations officially remained neutral during Pontiac's War, but warriors joined the conflict as they pleased. In particular, many Senecas took up the hatchet and dealt the British army its worst defeat in the conflict when they ambushed a supply train on the portage road around Niagara Falls. Johnson tried to get the rest of the Six Nations to rein in their militant Seneca brothers. At a conference at Johnson Hall in September, his rhetoric grew high-handed as he told the three hundred Iroquois present to bring the Senecas to heel before General Amherst marched against them. To the Kahnawakes, Johnson gave "a good English Axe, made of the best stuff," for them to use in "cutting off the bad links" in the Covenant Chain. Less attached to the Senecas by ties of kinship and sympathy than the other Iroquois, the Kahnawakes accepted the hatchet with enthusiasm. The rest of the Indians in attendance promised to sit still if Amherst brought the fight into their country to subdue the renegade Senecas, but added, "Knowing your foot is large and broad, we earnestly desire you will take care and not touch us your Friends therewith in passing."[61] Once the driving force behind the Covenant Chain, the Six Nations now feared being stepped on as bystanders while Johnson and Amherst prosecuted their Indian war.

The continuing Indian hostilities along the Appalachian frontier convinced British imperial officials that it was necessary to fix a firm boundary between colonial and Indian territory. Johnson argued that drawing such a line was imperative if the Crown wished to establish a lasting peace in its new American dominions. The Ohio Indians believed that the 1758 Treaty of Easton had guaranteed them security in their homelands, and they, too, endorsed the idea. In October 1763, the Crown committed itself to such a boundary when it issued a proclamation placing the trans-Appalachian West off-limits to any further settlement or land purchases by private individuals or companies. From now on, only royal officials acting on orders from the Crown would conduct land purchases in this Indian territory.[62]

The Proclamation of 1763 did not sit well with the colonists, who believed the Crown was denying them the fruits of their victory over the French, but Johnson was firmly behind it, and he brought the Six Nations onboard as well. For Johnson, securing the boundary line was part of a wider effort to centralize Indian affairs, including the regulation of the fur trade and land purchases, under his management.[63] For the Iroquois, collaboration with Johnson would help them bolster their claims to the Ohio Country. At a treaty conference at Johnson Hall in May 1765, Johnson and the Six Nations hashed out a boundary line from the upper Susquehanna River through western Pennsylvania to the Ohio River. Everything east of the line was in possession of the colonies; everything west was Indian territory that the Iroquois would dispose of as they saw fit.[64]

In early 1768, Johnson received orders from his London superiors to complete the boundary line to the Great Kanawha River, a tributary of the Ohio in western Virginia, so that it might be joined with a similar line being negotiated with the Cherokees by John Stuart, the Indian superintendent for the southern colonies. Johnson convened this treaty at Fort Stanwix, a British post in Oneida country. Over three thousand Indians attended, mostly from the Six Nations and their props in the Susquehanna Valley, making it the largest treaty conference of Johnson's career. Delegations from New York, New Jersey, Pennsylvania, and Virginia also attended, some openly mixing private and public business because of their involvement in speculative land ventures. Johnson's chief deputy, George Croghan, who was also present, led a syndicate of investors known as the Suffering Traders, who were seeking a land grant in the Ohio Country as compensation for losses they had suffered at the hands of the Indians during Pontiac's War. The Suffering Traders lined up several important colonial officials, including Johnson, to advance their scheme by granting them shares in the venture.[65]

The public proceedings at Fort Stanwix followed the standard format of Covenant Chain diplomacy, but the final agreement on the boundary line involved two glaring peculiarities. First, before entering into an agreement with the Crown for land cessions that completed the boundary line, the Iroquois entered into a private transaction with the Suffering Traders, giving them a substantial grant of land in the contested region around the Forks of the Ohio. Second, in negotiating the boundary line, Johnson extended it westward along the Ohio from the Kanawha River to the Tennessee River, a move that transferred considerably more territory south of the Ohio into colonial hands. In these two instances, Johnson violated instructions from the Crown, first by allowing a private party to negotiate a land purchase from the Indians, and second, by ignoring his orders to terminate the boundary line at the Kanawha. The handprints of private land speculators, including Johnson's, were all over these cessions. The boundary line drawn between colonial and Iroquois territory in New York favored Johnson's speculations in the Mohawk and Susquehanna valleys. In Pennsylvania, the boundary line ceded valuable territory in the Susquehanna Valley and the Forks of the Ohio to colonial interests, and the westward extension of the boundary line along the Ohio River favored Virginia speculators anxious to secure claim to the Kentucky region. In exchange for their open-handedness, the Indians gathered at Fort Stanwix received more than £10,000 sterling in trade goods and cash, the latter of which was "piled on a Table" as the chiefs signed the deeds.[66]

If as the old saying goes, history repeats itself, first as tragedy and then as farce, it is hard to say whether the Fort Stanwix Treaty qualifies as a first or second act. The farce was evident from the outset. The entire episode might have been lifted out of *The Wizard of Oz,* with Johnson playing the man behind the curtain whose fraud was evident to everyone except himself (admittedly, no one involved in the proceedings exhibited a Dorothy-like innocence). The Iroquois sold thousands of acres of land hundreds of miles away from them to agents whose official credentials barely disguised their private interests. The treaty even offended Johnson's London superiors, whose sensibilities regarding conflicts of interest between private gain and public office could hardly be described as refined. Upon learning of the new boundary line, they censured Johnson and told him to give the land acquired in excess of his original instructions back to the Iroquois.

It took a bit longer for the tragedy of what occurred at Fort Stanwix to unfold, but Indians and colonists in the Ohio Country felt its repercussions broadly and deeply. The native peoples most gravely affected by the complaisance of the Iroquois at Fort Stanwix were the Shawnees who lived in the southern Ohio Valley. A smattering of Ohio Indians attended the Fort Stanwix Treaty, but Johnson considered them subordinate to the Six Nations and did not invite their input or signatures on the deeds. Back in the Ohio Country, the Shawnees felt no need to honor the treaty. In 1774, they went to war with the Virginians invading their homelands, initiating a Shawnee-led struggle for Native American control of the Ohio Country that did not end until forty years later.[67] Whether tragedy or farce, the Treaty of Fort Stanwix most certainly resembled a recurring bad dream to other Indians who had taken hold of the Covenant Chain in the mid-eighteenth century. Once again, Iroquois and colonial interests had conspired to dispossess them.

The Treaty at Fort Stanwix closed the book on one era of treaty-making in early America and opened it on another. Before Johnson cut his boundary line, Anglo-Iroquois diplomacy had involved a variety of issues and relationships that brought natives and newcomers together: managing the fur trade, renewing alliances, making war and peace, and sometimes transferring land from Indian to colonial hands. After 1768, it came to focus on keeping Indians and Europeans apart, preferably by confining the former to reservations while the latter engrossed their lands. In the tumultuous years ahead, the Iroquois would face the reckoning for this method of doing business.

6

NEW NATIONS

In January 1776, at the same time that colonial Americans were reading Thomas Paine's *Common Sense* and nodding along vigorously to its indictment of the British monarchy, a Mohawk war chief named Thayendanegea, more famously known as Joseph Brant, arrived in London to meet King George III. Brant had come to England with Guy Johnson, the nephew of Sir William Johnson who had taken over as the Crown's agent to the Six Nations after his uncle's death in 1774. When hostilities broke out between Britain and its rebellious colonies in spring 1775, Johnson relocated to Canada with a large contingent of loyalist and Mohawk supporters. There he tangled with other royal officials over control of Indian affairs, and decided to take his case directly to England, where he could personally press for the Crown's support. Johnson could not have found a better partner to help him in this enterprise than Joseph Brant.

Brant cut a fine figure in London. Along with a Mohawk warrior named Ohrante, he attended the royal court at St. James's Palace and met the king. He also met with Lord George Germaine, the secretary of state for the colonies, to whom Brant presented the Mohawks' grievances about land frauds in New York. When not engaged in such business, Brant toured the city's sights and socialized with London's elite. He had his portrait painted by the artist George Romney, posing in the costume and accoutrements of an Iroquois diplomat, including linen shirt, silver gorget, and pipe tomahawk. The *London Chronicle* published flattering updates on the comings and goings of Brant and Ohrante, and James Boswell, one of the city's literati, met personally with Brant and wrote a laudatory description of him for the *London Magazine*.[1]

Boswell saw in Brant the results of the civilizing mission that Queen Anne had initiated among the Mohawks sixty-six years earlier, after the visit of the four Indian kings. In 1710, he wrote, "The Mohocks were a very rude and uncivilized nation," their name capable of striking terror in the hearts of Londoners. Now these same Indians were "so well trained to civility" that they lived in "good commodious houses," tilled the earth with "assiduity and skill," and took the Anglican Church's sacraments. To Boswell, Brant offered living proof of the "tameness which education can produce upon the wildest race."

Truth be told, Brant was a bit *too* civilized for Boswell. Only when arrayed in "the dress of his nation" rather than the "ordinary European habit" did this chief become an imposing figure, so when Boswell hired an artist to draw Brant, he made sure that the subject posed in a feathered headdress and with a scalping knife clasped to his chest.[2] The four Indian kings had been a hit in London because they provided an exotic spectacle. Brant, on the other hand, attracted attention because he exhibited the habits of a refined Englishman. An ocean away, American colonists disguised themselves as Mohawks and threw shiploads of tea into Boston harbor, but here in London, a bona fide Mohawk was taking tea and joining the Freemasons. Brant, it seemed, exhibited more British character than all the patriot rabble put together.

Just as they had done with the four Indian kings, Canasatego, and Hendrick, eighteenth-century Britons treated Brant as an empty canvas onto which they projected their image of the perfect Indian: an eloquent, dignified, and loyal subject-in-the-making, a reliably pliant partner in empire. But like his Iroquois predecessors, Brant was also a flesh-and-blood human being with his own agenda. He was a prominent chief, but he did not lead or speak for all Iroquois. He allied himself with the British, but for reasons that had more to do with extending his own power than that of the British empire. He fought hard to preserve the political and territorial sovereignty of his people from Europeans, regardless of their political affiliations.

During the Revolutionary era, the outside pressure on the Six Nations reached its zenith and splintered their confederacy. The American Revolution was a period of prolonged trial for Native Americans in general, but for the Iroquois it was especially damaging, causing dispossession, dispersal, and a permanent fracture in their political union. With the undeniable force of a chemical chain reaction, the creation of the new United States unleashed an equally destructive force on the Iroquois, but from this impact, other new nations arose. Under the aegis of Brant and a rising generation of chiefs, the Iroquois established new homelands and forged new partnerships to preserve their native identity in the postwar era.

DEATH OF A SACHEM

In the years following the Fort Stanwix Treaty of 1768, William Johnson's work as the Crown's Indian superintendent had become only more nettlesome. He spent much of his time trying to keep the peace with the Indians of the Ohio Country, whose resistance to British expansionism had failed to recede after Pontiac's War. During the early 1770s, Johnson moved constantly to quell the violence that erupted between colonists and Indians over trading abuses, alcohol consumption, and shady land deals. When not putting out those fires, he tried to keep the Six Nations from linking arms with the increasingly restive Ohio Indians. The Senecas, some of whom had taken up arms against the British in Pontiac's War, remained particularly difficult in this regard. They were the most populous of the Iroquois nations—by Johnson's own estimate, they outnumbered the other nations combined—and many of them had kin in the Ohio region.[3] Without their alliance, Johnson's hold over the Covenant Chain mattered little.

The growing crisis in the Ohio Country figured on the agenda when Johnson, visibly weakened by poor health, convened a treaty conference with about six hundred Iroquois at Johnson Hall in July 1774. In the Indians' opening speech, a Seneca chief told Johnson, "Your People are as ungovernable, or rather more so, than ours." The fur trade had been thrown into "utter confusion" by traders who ignored regulations imposed at frontier forts and invaded the Indians' hunting grounds peddling rum. The boundary line established at Fort Stanwix that was supposed to "forever after be looked upon as a barrier between us" was being ignored by squatters who "come in vast numbers to the Ohio, and gave our people to understand that they wou'd settle wherever they pleas'd." An exasperated Johnson could offer only familiar excuses in response to these familiar grievances: The Crown had taken the regulation of the fur trade out of his hands and restored it to the individual colonial governments; the squatters invading the Ohio Country did so without his consent; and the Six Nations' security rested in recalling their kin from that troubled region to their homelands. He ordered his Indian audience pipes, tobacco, and liquor and then retired to his chambers, where he "was seized with a suffocation" and died two hours later.[4]

Johnson's death was exquisitely timed. The world he had made for himself was unraveling, and the repercussions were coming hard and fast for all those who had been a part of it. Johnson Hall was a fantastic anomaly, the country seat of an Irish baronet transported to the Mohawk frontier. In the style of a feudal lord, Johnson used the patronage of his king to enrich himself, but he had also exhibited great generosity to his own dependents. He recruited Irish and Scottish immigrants to work his land and established for them the community of Johnstown. For the Canajoharie Mohawks, he built a church and sent their children to mission schools. He took one of their leading women, Mary Brant (more commonly known as Molly, and older sister to Joseph) as his common-law wife and provided liberally for their eight children. He turned his Indian agency into a source of employment for his intermarried native and colonial family. In these and innumerable other day-to-day encounters, Johnson made real the spoken metaphors that were the tools of his trade: opened paths and linked arms, the Tree of Peace growing to embrace all peoples under its branches. For those Indians in his orbit, he embodied the king's pretensions to being the father, benefactor, and protector of the Iroquois.

At the time of Johnson's death, a rebellious spirit among Indians and colonists alike threatened to upset the world he had made. The challenges to his authority came on two fronts. In the Ohio Country, the Shawnees ignored the Covenant Chain and organized a new confederacy of western nations to resist the colonial invasion of their homelands. The Iroquois living in the Ohio region were party to these intrigues and acted as a conduit of disaffection back to their kinsfolk at the western door of the Longhouse. Writing to his London superiors in spring 1773, Johnson described the Ohio Indians as "disaffected and troublesome people, who dislike a Confederacy [the Iroquois] on whom they have been so long dependent." Johnson worried that their discontent would seep backward into the heart of the Longhouse and deal a fatal blow to British influence along the Great Lakes frontier.[5] When war broke out between the Shawnees and

Virginia in fall 1774, Iroquois chiefs in Onondaga symbolically shut the western door of the Longhouse and agreed that "it was bad policy to meddle in this affair," but some Cayuga warriors anxious to aid the Shawnees had already slipped out.[6] Such dissension made clear the growing fissures within the Iroquois Confederacy.

Closer to Johnson's base of operations, a mixture of religion and politics was driving a wedge between the Mohawks and Oneidas. The two Mohawk towns, Canajoharie and Tiononderoge, remained staunchly allied with William Johnson. The inhabitants of both, about five hundred people in total, had acculturated considerably to colonial society by 1770. Both towns were east of the Fort Stanwix boundary line, and the Mohawks found themselves surrounded by European neighbors pecking away at their land. Many had adopted European-style methods, tools, and livestock in their agriculture and attended churches and schools sponsored by the Anglican missionary John Stuart.

Joseph Brant and his sister Molly personified these changes. As children, the Brants had lived in the Ohio Country for a number of years until their father died and their mother returned to her native Canajoharie. There she married a prominent chief, securing a place for herself and her children in the community. Molly probably received some education from an Anglican schoolmaster before having her first child with Johnson in 1759 and moving into his home as wife, housekeeper, and hostess to his innumerable guests.[7] Joseph, her junior by about seven years, distinguished himself while still a teenager in Johnson's service during the Seven Years' War. In 1761, Johnson sent him to an Indian school in Connecticut run by the Congregational missionary Eleazar Wheelock. For two years, Brant was Wheelock's star pupil, but his talents and connections led him away from a missionary career and back into Johnson's orbit. He married one of the Indian daughters of George Croghan, Johnson's deputy in the Ohio Country, and because of Joseph's facility with English and several Iroquois languages, he became an important interpreter and agent for Johnson. Despite his obvious attachment to Johnson, Joseph's identity remained rooted in Canajoharie, and he became that community's leading voice in its land disputes with local colonists.[8]

During his two years in Connecticut, Brant crossed paths with Samuel Kirkland, one of Wheelock's colonial protégés. Swept up in the colonial religious revival known as the Great Awakening, Kirkland decided at an early age to devote his life to missionary work among Indians. At Wheelock's school, Brant taught him the Mohawk language. Kirkland's first missionary foray, a sojourn among the Senecas in 1765–66, was a physical and spiritual trial that nearly cost him his life. A Christian Oneida known as Good Peter warned him that it was "too soon" to seek converts among the Senecas, for "their minds were not yet calmed, after the tumults and troubles of the late war."[9] Kirkland found himself spurned by the Senecas, including one chief who made the following inflammatory speech in his presence:

> This white man we call our Brother has come upon a *dark design* . . . or he would not have travelled so many hundred miles. He brings with him the white peoples *Book,* which they call . . . the *holy Book.* Brothers, you know this book was never made for *Indians. . . .*
>
> Brethren, attend! You may be assured, that if we Senecas . . . receive this *white man* and attend to the Book which was made solely for White people, we shall become *miserable abject people.* It has already ruined many Indian tribes by embracing what is contained in this book. . . . The warriors, which they boasted of, before these foreigners, the white people, crossed the great Lake, where are they now? Why their grandsons are all become *mere women*![10]

Such hostility toward Kirkland made plain how much some Senecas were identifying with the militancy of the Ohio Indians rather than the more conciliatory diplomacy practiced at the eastern end of the Longhouse.

Kirkland's luck changed when he arrived in the Oneida town of Kanowalohale in 1766. The Oneidas were not as acculturated to colonial society as the Mohawks, but they had many years of experience in dealing with fur traders who passed between Albany and Oswego. To strengthen their hold on their land in the years preceding the American Revolution, they used the familiar Iroquois tactic of inviting other native peoples to relocate among them. Mahicans from the missionary town of Stockbridge in western Massachusetts answered their call, as did other Christian Indians from New England and Long Island, eventually forming the communities of New Stockbridge and Brothertown, respectively. These newcomers, already accustomed to using missionaries as intermediaries with colonial officials and neighbors, widened the door to Oneida country for Kirkland and other New England missionaries. Kirkland also found fertile ground for his evangelical message in Oquaga, a community near modern Binghamton, New York, made up of Oneidas, Tuscaroras, Mohawks, and refugee peoples from the northern Susquehanna Valley.[11]

Johnson had initially supported Wheelock's and Kirkland's missionary efforts among the Iroquois, but by 1768, he was having second thoughts. At the Fort Stanwix Treaty, the New Englanders backed the Oneidas' resistance to Johnson's efforts to set the boundary line well into Oneida territory, and they worked independently of him in trying to get the Oneidas to cede land for a new mission community and school.[12] In 1770, Kirkland and Wheelock parted ways when the latter decided to abandon his Indian school in Connecticut and establish Dartmouth College in New Hampshire. Kirkland then turned to Boston supporters to fund his mission, a move that displeased Johnson. The New

Englanders' fiery evangelism ran counter to his own more pragmatic view of Christian missionary work, and he tried unsuccessfully to prevent Kirkland from building a new church at Kanowalohale.[13] The last thing Johnson wanted to see was the Oneidas' and Tuscaroras' flowering Christianity tied to the politics of rebellious New Englanders. After all, the religious conversion of Indians was supposed to make friends for the Crown, not enemies.

Several factors explain the Oneidas' receptivity to Kirkland's message. They had reason to feel slighted by the attention and presents Johnson lavished on the Mohawks, as well as by his efforts to push the Stanwix boundary line into their homelands. True to his spiritual roots in the Great Awakening, Kirkland was also an effective preacher dedicated to reaching his Indian audiences in their native languages. He brought a message of spiritual and social renewal to communities wracked by alcoholism and its attendant ills. He also delivered significant material benefits to his converts: assistance in feeding and clothing their families in times of want and tools and livestock for those wishing to take up European-style farming. The Oneidas and Tuscaroras who heeded his message were following in the footsteps of the Tiononderoge and Canajoharie Mohawks, only using New Englanders rather than SPG missionaries to meet their needs.

By the time the first shots of the American Revolution were fired at Lexington and Concord in April 1775, no consensus existed within the Six Nations over which way to turn. At the western end of the Longhouse, the Senecas and Cayugas looked toward the Ohio Country and sympathized with the Shawnees trying to defend their homelands. At the eastern end, the Mohawks mourned the loss of William Johnson and wondered about the loyalties of the colonists who surrounded them. Oneidas and Tuscaroras who had cultivated strong spiritual and political alliances with New Englanders were moving away from the heirs of Johnson's politics and diplomacy. The Onondagas remained in the middle, tending the Longhouse's ceremonial council fire, but as the tide of rebellion swelled no one could be certain that the center would hold.

A FAMILY QUARREL

After the battles of Lexington and Concord on April 19, 1775, tensions within Iroquoia escalated. At public councils, agents for the Crown and the colonial rebels spoke the language of neutrality, urging the Six Nations to stand aside during this "family quarrel," but in the bushes, each side pressed a more aggressive agenda, promising substantial material rewards to those chiefs and warriors who would ally with them.[14] As they had done during the Anglo-French colonial wars, parties of Iroquois men and women attended these treaty conferences, exchanged speeches and wampum at the council fire, and gathered up presents to take home, but they avoided outright declarations that would have committed them to making war on someone else's terms. This strategy had worked effectively in the past, but circumstances had changed since the fall of New France. Iroquois material dependence on European goods had increased, and their borders in the Mohawk Valley and Susquehanna region had become more vulnerable to colonial speculators and settlers. The presence of New England missionaries and Christian Indians had increased the degree of acculturation in the eastern half of the Longhouse, while Senecas and Cayugas in the west had become more resistant to such influences. The Six Nations had never been especially centralized or uniform in pursuing their politics and diplomacy, but the divisions among them were more pronounced in 1775 than perhaps at any previous time in the colonial era.

Guy Johnson, who took over as the Crown's agent to the Iroquois shortly after his uncle's death, acted first. Not long after Lexington and Concord, he detained Kirkland, effectively preventing his direct communication with the Oneidas and Tuscaroras. Fearing arrest by the local patriot militia, Johnson traveled in May 1775 to Oswego with about two hundred Mohawks and loyal tenants from his uncle's estate. There he convened a treaty conference with about fifteen hundred Iroquois, distributed presents, and received vague assurances of support from those in attendance. Johnson then left for Montreal, where he convened a similar conference with the Iroquois and Algonquian communities in the St. Lawrence River Valley. While some of these Canadian Indians expressed an interest in war parties Johnson intended to raise against patriots in the Mohawk Valley, the governor of Canada, General Guy Carleton, insisted that they remain nearby for Canada's defense.[15]

The patriots had a harder time initiating their diplomacy with the Iroquois, in part because it had been so long since anyone other than William Johnson or his deputies had conducted such business. With Guy Johnson in flight to Canada, Kirkland escaped his house arrest in the Mohawk Valley and headed for Philadelphia, where he helped the Second Continental Congress formulate its Indian policy. Following the regional model inherited from the British, the Continental Congress established northern and southern Indian departments and created a third for the middle colonies. Philip Schuyler, a wealthy patriot from one of Albany's most distinguished Dutch families, emerged as the leader of the five commissioners appointed for the northern department. Armed with practical advice from Kirkland and a speech drafted by Congress, he arranged to treat with the Iroquois in Albany.

Although this was the first Albany conference to convene in more than twenty years, the participants fell into their old roles quickly, the inexperienced colonists following the lead of their Indian counterparts. The proceedings began in German Flats, a small farming community in the western Mohawk Valley. Two of the congressional commissioners traveled there to issue the invitation to Albany. They were greeted mostly by Oneidas; many of the Mohawks from nearby Canajoharie had already departed with Guy Johnson for Canada. Aided by an interpreter, the commissioners spoke in the customary metaphors of clearing a path to Albany and rekindling the council fire there. The Indians accepted the invitation, but with two caveats indicative of the political uncertainty then pervasive in the region. First, they could not extend the invitation to their brethren in Canada, because Guy Johnson was already among them, pressing "hard upon their minds another way." Second, the Indians wanted a guarantee of safe passage to Albany, as they would have to pass through country now divided between loyalists and patriots. "All people do not meet so much like brothers as formerly," they lamented, "on account of the present state of affairs."[16]

The conference in Albany got underway in late August. The commissioners did not count the Indians in attendance, but the crowd heavily favored Oneidas, Tuscaroras, and transplanted Stockbridge Indians drawn by their attachment to Kirkland.[17] Tench Tilghman, a young Philadelphia gentleman acting as the secretary of the Indian commissioners, kept a journal that offers an engaging glimpse of the proceedings.[18] Like many European novices to Iroquois treaty-making, Tilghman was at once attracted to and repulsed by what he witnessed. He thought the Indians came primarily to eat and drink on Congress's tab. Under the guise of diplomatic ceremony, they used every occasion to cadge liquor, such as when they hinted that the drink provided for a toast should be "in proportion" to the greatness of the united colonies or when they granted Tilghman an Indian name, for which they expected "a bowl of punch or two" in return.[19] On the other hand, Tilghman found much to admire about the Indians. He was impressed by the Indians' inherent sense of good manners:

> The Behaviour of the poor Savages at a public Meeting ought to put us civilized people to the Blush. The most

profound silence is observed, no interruption of a speaker.
When any one speaks all the rest are attentive. We gave
them a large Roll of tobacco. Two of their people cut it
into pieces of two or three inches, and then distributed
them all around. No man rose from his seat to snatch.
When drink was served round it was in the same manner,
no Man seemed anxious for the Cup.[20]

Like many of his colonial peers, Tilghman enjoyed the spectacle of treaty-making but grew weary of what seemed like the
endless preliminary and ancillary engagements necessary to
please the Indians. In addition to various rounds of meeting and
treating the visiting chiefs, he attended a nighttime dance by the
Indians through the streets of Albany, a bull-baiting and foot race
sponsored by the commissioners for Indian warriors, and two
singing performances by Oneida and Stockbridge Indian women.
When the treaty's official business finally got underway, the
public councils provided "but dull entertainment" because of the
"delay and difficulty of getting what you say, delivered properly
to the Indians."[21] His impatience with the cultural apparatus
attached to Anglo-Iroquois treaty-making, if shared by the other
colonial officials present, must have made the Indians long for the
days when the council fire burned at Johnson Hall.

The commissioners' primary objective was to have the Six
Nations affirm their neutrality in the war now underway between
the colonies and Britain. The patriots were planning a preemptive
invasion of Canada for the fall, and a promise from the Iroquois
not to interfere would help considerably. For this purpose, the
Continental Congress composed a speech for the commissioners to
deliver at the treaty, but conveying the rebellious colonists' message proved harder than anyone thought. According to Tilghman,
the speech gave the commissioners "a great deal of trouble" as they
tried to translate the patriots' grievances against the Crown into
the idiom of the Covenant Chain. Congress wanted to "read a

Chapter out of Locke" to Indians who had little use for lawyerly arguments about natural rights and liberties.[22] Tilghman's observation laid bare the problem with selling the patriots' cause on the frontier: How were they to gain the sympathy of Indians for whom abusive, land-hungry colonists were a more immediate threat than a distant king and Parliament?

While the commissioners discoursed on "the situation of our civil constitutions," the Iroquois in attendance had more practical items on their minds.[23] William Johnson was dead, his nephew was gone to Canada, and the flow of trade goods into Iroquoia had been disrupted. Kirkland was still allied with the Oneidas, but he did not command the political or material resources to replace Johnson's royal Indian agency. What evidence could the patriots provide that they were serious about taking up the slack that recent events had caused in the Covenant Chain?

In responding to the commissioners sent by Congress, the Iroquois in attendance reminded them of their obligations as hosts. They wanted to have their "kettles, axes, and hoes" mended gratis by local blacksmiths, as had been the practice in the past. They wanted a guarantee from the commissioners that the patriots would keep the fighting away from them: "You have just now made a good path; do not so soon defile it with blood." They also asked that John Johnson, the son of William, and John Stuart, the Anglican missionary still working among the Tiononderoge Mohawks, be left unmolested to "live in peace among them." Two other concerns weighed on their minds. They wanted to see the fur trade restored in Albany, "as it was in former times, when we had hold of the old covenant," and they wanted land that had been stolen from them in fraudulent transactions restored. To make sure that these issues were addressed, they appointed Schuyler, Albany's most prominent patriot, the keeper of the rekindled council fire.[24]

The Indians' requests and the commissioners' responses anticipated the difficulties that lay ahead on both sides of the

Covenant Chain. The Indians present—mostly eastern Iroquois accustomed to dealing with the growing colonial population in the Mohawk Valley—wanted something in return for their neutrality: diplomatic partnership and material support of the kind that William Johnson and the Albany magistrates before him had provided. With the fate of the fur trade at Oswego uncertain, they needed to have access to goods by way of Albany. Nor did they wish to see the colonial rebellion deprive them of valuable local patrons just because of their loyalist sympathies. They also wanted to have an agent who would help protect their lands from speculators and squatters. Iroquois neutrality, in other words, would not be costless for the patriots. They would have to take firm hold of the Covenant Chain and assume its reciprocal obligations.

Unfortunately, the commissioners did not comprehend the terms of this bargain. They expressed a condescending impatience with the Indians' appointment of Schuyler as the keeper of the Albany council fire, because "we have repeatedly told you that they [the Continental Congress] had appointed five persons, whose business it is to attend and preserve it bright and clear." Why were the Iroquois repeating work the Congress had already done for them? As for their land complaints, the commissioners offered a terse explanation that "we are not authorized to transact any business of that kind at present, but will represent the matter to the Grand Congress in Philadelphia." No doubt, the Indians had heard that one before. Outside of the formulaic professions of friendship that ended any treaty conference, there was nothing in the commissioners' response that indicated they had given serious consideration to any of the Indians' conditions for remaining neutral. Instead, they hoped to buy their cooperation with presents that they helped the Indians haul as far as Schenectady. From there, they were literally and figuratively on their own.[25]

Schuyler knew that Tory support in the Mohawk Valley would coalesce around the Johnson family. In January 1776, he marched an army of several hundred militia men from Albany to Johnstown to disarm John Johnson, William's son and heir, and the remaining tenants on Johnson family lands. The Mohawks at Tiononderoge protested Schuyler's move but lacked the numbers to stop it. The following spring, the patriots returned with another force intent on arresting Johnson. Warned by some Mohawk allies, Johnson and his supporters made haste to Canada.[26] The patriots had succeeded, at least temporarily, in securing the Mohawk Valley, but at the considerable cost of alienating the region's native inhabitants.

At the western end of the Longhouse, British agents recruited Iroquois warriors to help fight the colonial rebels. At Fort Niagara in May, John Butler, an associate of Joseph Brant and a longtime ally of the Johnson family, upbraided those Iroquois who preferred to stand aside when the Crown needed them. The patriots, he told them, were "born but yesterday" and had neither the "men, guns, cannon and ammunition or cloathing" to sustain their rebellion. The Crown, on the other hand, was in want of "neither men nor money" and could supply the Indians with their every need.[27] What Butler's speech lacked in subtlety it made up for in common sense. His boasts of the Crown's superior resources certainly made a stronger impression among the Iroquois than the "Chapter out of Locke" the patriots had read to them in Albany the previous year. Niagara had been an important point of trade and diplomacy for the western Iroquois since the early eighteenth century. So long as the British remained there, it would be hard to argue with Butler's logic.

Joseph Brant, who returned to America from London in July 1776, also recruited warriors for the British cause. Brant arrived in New York City just in time to participate in the British army's rout of George Washington's Continentals at the Battle of Long Island. The following fall, he left for Iroquoia, where he exploited the political divisions within the Confederacy to raise his own status and influence as a war chief. At Oquaga on the upper Susquehanna River, he found a sympathetic hearing among Mohawks who had relocated there as life in Canajoharie and Tiononderoge had become increasingly insecure. Although Oquaga was also home to many Oneidas and Tuscaroras inclined toward the patriots, Brant eventually raised a British flag there and used the town as a base for a force of loyalists and Iroquois warriors known as Brant's Volunteers. He also traveled west to Niagara, where he recruited among the western Iroquois who had been treating with Butler.[28]

The Longhouse Divided

By 1777, only the Onondagas appeared fully committed to the neutrality the Iroquois had staked out between the British and patriots a year earlier. The Senecas and Cayugas were leaning toward the British; the Mohawks, much more heavily so. The attachment of the Oneidas and Tuscaroras to the Americans' cause had been tightened by the patriots' occupation of Fort Stanwix and the renewal of trade there. It was at that post in January that the Oneidas relayed a bit of alarming news from the chiefs at Onondaga. An epidemic had recently swept through their largest town, carrying away ninety victims and several leading chiefs. "There is no longer a Council Fire at the Capitol of Six Nations," the Oneidas reported.[29]

To the patriots who received this news, its implication was clear enough: The Iroquois would not attempt to speak with a unified voice in their diplomacy. Every nation and every community would choose its own path. The significance of extinguishing the council fire at Onondaga for the Iroquois themselves is harder to measure. Since its inception, the Iroquois League had always lacked any powers other than persuasion when it came to influencing its member nations. The chief functions of the Grand Council were to raise up new sachems when old ones died and to keep the peace within Iroquoia by annually reenacting the League's founding. It was not the League's purpose to conduct war or diplomacy with outsiders. On one hand, then, extinguishing the council fire in Onondaga did little to alter Iroquois relations with the outside world. On the other, it suspended the rituals that had bonded the Iroquois together and provided a means for mediating their differences. It did not cause war among them, but it made it more possible than before.

The Iroquois had faced similar crises in previous colonial wars, when different communities had inclined toward different allies, yet the Grand Council had always remained in place. Several circumstances help explain why the "family quarrel" of the American Revolution became an internecine battle for the Iroquois as well. First, the authority and influence of the League's chiefs had been debilitated by the material dependence of the Iroquois on European goods. According to captive Mary Jemison, who spent her adult life among the Senecas, British agents made no headway against Iroquois neutrality until "they addressed their avarice, by telling our people [the Senecas] that the people of the states were few in number, and easily subdued . . . that the King was rich and powerful, both in money and subjects: That his rum was as plenty as the water in lake Ontario: that his men were as numerous as the sands on the lake shore: and that the Indians, if they would assist in the war, and persevere in their friendship to the King, till it was closed, should never want for money or goods."[30]

Young men drawn to the warpath because of the personal rewards it offered also received encouragement from their clan matrons. The Seneca chief Blacksnake, a contemporary of Jemison, recalled that "the female Sect . . . began to use their influence over the warriors" when they saw the material bounty offered by the British. Molly Brant was one such member of "the female Sect." In the Mohawk Valley and later at Niagara, she used her status as a clan matron and the widow of William Johnson to denigrate neutrality and urge warriors to take up the hatchet. Daniel Claus, who married into the Johnson family and worked as a British Indian agent, told his superiors that "one word" from Molly Brant "goes farther with them than a thousand from any white Man without Exception."[31]

Another factor contributing to the breakdown of Iroquois union was the invasion of Iroquois territory by the contending armies. Iroquois communities had not faced such serious threats to their security since the French military expeditions of the late seventeenth century. Schuyler arrived in the Mohawk Valley with a patriot army in spring 1776 to occupy Johnson Hall and Fort Stanwix. This move pleased some Oneidas and Tuscaroras but was rightfully interpreted as an act of war by Mohawks who thought they had negotiated neutrality in Albany the year before. In two successive campaigns in 1776 and 1777, the British pinned their hopes for quelling the American rebellion on marching armies from Montreal into the Hudson River Valley, where they intended to cut New England off from colonies farther south. Neither campaign met with success, and the second ended with Burgoyne's defeat at Saratoga.

Far more disastrous to the Iroquois was a bloody engagement that occurred near the Oneida town of Oriska on August 6, 1777. A British army led by General Barry St. Leger and supported by seven hundred Indians had marched from Oswego to lay siege to Fort Stanwix, the only patriot position blocking their path to Albany. General Nicholas Herkimer raised one thousand patriot militiamen and a small contingent of Oneida warriors to relieve the soldiers bottled up in the isolated post. As the patriots marched west through the Mohawk Valley, Molly Brant alerted St. Leger of Herkimer's advance.[32] St. Leger sent a detachment of loyalists and Indians, mostly Senecas recruited by Butler and Joseph Brant, to stop them. They ambushed Herkimer's force as it moved through a ravine near Oriska, and an intense battle ensued. The patriots suffered the brunt of the casualties, losing about half their number (including Herkimer, who was mortally wounded), but Iroquois on both sides died as well. The losses were especially shocking for the Senecas, who had been told at the start of St. Leger's campaign that the British "did not wish to have them fight, but wanted to have them just sit down, smoke their pipes, and look on." Rather than watching the Redcoats "whip the rebels," the Senecas had ended up in the middle of a fierce battle with fellow Iroquois.[33] To worsen matters, while the Senecas were engaged at Oriska, the patriots at Fort Stanwix sent out a sortie to plunder their camp, depriving the warriors of many of the supplies recently received from the British. Disgusted with this turn of events, St. Leger's Iroquois allies abandoned the siege in droves and went home. Initially so confident of rendezvousing with Burgoyne in Albany, St. Leger had no choice but to lift the siege and retreat to Oswego.[34]

What had once been the routes of peace in Iroquoia now became routes of war. Iroquois warriors who had accompanied St. Leger's army to Fort Stanwix attacked Oriska in retaliation for the aid its warriors had given to Herkimer's force, burning houses and fields and killing livestock. The Oneidas returned the favor by venting their rage on the Mohawk communities to the east. At Canajoharie, they looted the home and property of Molly Brant and her family, "robbing them of cash, cloaths, cattle, etc. and driving them from their home." From there, they went to Tiononderoge and "dealt in the same manner with the poor women and children whose husbands were in the King's service." Molly Brant made her way west to Niagara, where she resettled under British protection. The Mohawks of Tiononderoge moved north to join their kin and loyalists working with John Johnson, abandoning their homes and farms to the patriots.[35]

The pattern of raid and reprisal that unfolded in the Mohawk Valley repeated itself along other routes within Iroquoia in the years that followed. For the most part, Iroquois warriors avoided killing other Iroquois or taking them captive, directing such violence instead at European enemies.[36] They did, however, destroy each other's towns, burning homes and crops and looting property, which forced refugees to abandon their homes in search of security and sustenance. In 1778, Brant's Volunteers used Oquaga as their base, while Butler led Seneca and Cayuga warriors in a devastating attack on patriot militiamen in Pennsylvania's Wyoming Valley. The patriots responded by moving against Oquaga in October. Most of the town's population evacuated before the militiamen arrived, leaving their commander to find only an eerie stillness in "the finest Indians town I ever saw." He marveled at the houses, built as well as any on the colonial frontier, with shingled roofs, stone chimneys, and glass windows. The patriots burned them all except for the home of Good Peter, the Oneida convert who had led the patriot faction in Oquaga before Brant's arrival altered the town's political balance. They also destroyed the town's cornfields and murdered several small children they found hiding there "by running them through with bayonets and holding them up to see how they would twist and turn."[37]

A month after the destruction of Oquaga, a combined force of Iroquois warriors and British soldiers retaliated by attacking Cherry Valley, a settler community south of the Mohawk River. Joseph Brant and the Seneca war chief Cornplanter led the Indians. Unlike the Indians of Oquaga, the inhabitants of Cherry Valley did not get out of the way, and they suffered terribly as a consequence. Venting their rage over the destruction of Oquaga, the warriors killed and pillaged their way through the town and took approximately seventy captives. In the mayhem, they did not stop to inquire about political affiliation, and loyalists as well as patriots fell to their tomahawks. Brant, whose acculturation to British society had included the internalization of European rules of war, recoiled at the murder of women and children and interceded where he could to save lives and release loyalist captives, but he could not turn the tide of the violence around him.[38]

The destruction of Oquaga and Cherry Valley was repeated on a much grander scale in 1779, when George Washington ordered Continental troops to conduct a scorched-earth expedition against the Senecas and Cayugas. Marching west from Easton, Pennsylvania, an army led by Major General John Sullivan rendezvoused at the Indian town of Tioga (modern Athens, Pennsylvania) with General James Clinton's army marching south from the Mohawk Valley. Meanwhile, Colonel Daniel Brodhead led a smaller force from Fort Pitt into the Allegheny Valley, intending to join Sullivan and Clinton in Seneca country for an assault on Fort Niagara. Delays in all three expeditions prevented Brodhead from meeting the others, and neither force made it as far as Niagara.

That objective, however, was secondary to the work Washington charged each army with completing along the way: the systematic destruction of every Iroquois town they encountered, including homes, property, livestock, crops, and populations. Not far from Tioga, at Newtown on the Susquehanna River, British rangers and Iroquois warriors led by Butler, Brant, and Cornplanter tried to stop the advance of the Sullivan-Clinton army, but they were outnumbered ten to one, and when they lost the element of surprise, they chose to withdraw rather than face almost certain defeat. Thereafter, the Senecas and Cayugas pursued the same strategy they had used when facing French armies in the seventeenth century and vacated their towns as the troops advanced. Sullivan and Clinton found few humans to kill or capture, but they destroyed more than forty towns. After making it as far as the Genesee River, they turned around to visit the same destruction on any towns or isolated hamlets they had missed the first time. Brodhead blazed a similar trail through Seneca and Delaware towns along the Allegheny before returning to Fort Pitt.[39]

The Continentals left Iroquoia without bothering to build or garrison any posts along the way. Washington was not planning an expedition against Fort Niagara the following season. The Sullivan-Clinton campaign had been a punitive move against the Iroquois, plain and simple, and while it had failed to inflict Iroquois casualties on the field of battle, it had succeeded in uprooting a sizable population and depriving it of its sustenance for the coming winter. A refugee crisis ensued at Fort Niagara, where more than three thousand displaced Iroquois and affiliated Indians sought British protection. The casualties that the Continentals had failed to take during the campaign piled up from starvation, disease, and exposure during the bitterly cold winter of 1779–80.[40] As an old woman, Mary Jemison described that winter as "the most severe that I have witnessed in my remembrance," and recalled that it reduced the Senecas "to a state of starvation through that and three or four succeeding years."[41]

Clinton-Sullivan had changed the face of Iroquoia, erasing entire communities from a region they had occupied for generations. Brant, Cornplanter, and other war chiefs rallied their warriors in 1780 and 1781 to conduct reprisals, but raids on isolated frontier communities did not have the same impact. Settlers could be burned out of their homes, taken captive, or dispatched with the tomahawk, but there were too many patriots safely beyond Brant's and Cornplanter's reach. The only enemies upon whom Brant and Cornplanter could wreak the same kind of damage as the Sullivan-Clinton campaign were fellow Iroquois. In 1780, Brant convinced some wavering Oneidas, Tuscaroras, and Onondagas to declare themselves for the Crown and resettle at Niagara. He then raised a force of several hundred warriors to destroy the towns of the Oneida and Tuscarora holdouts, including the patriot stronghold of Kanowalohale, as well as Brant's old hometown of Canajoharie, which had been occupied by Oneidas after the Battle of Oriskany.[42]

Cornwallis's surrender at Yorktown in October 1781 ended the war's major military engagements, but it was no occasion for celebration among the Iroquois. No significant Iroquois community had managed to escape the war's violence, and many had been erased from the map, their populations dispersed to the margins of what had once been secure homelands. During the war, the population of the Six Nations had declined by approximately one-third.[43] Those Iroquois who had chosen to ally with the patriots were by war's end clustered around the Mohawk Valley town of Schenectady. Those who had chosen the British side had moved either north to Montreal or west to the Niagara region. Regardless of the side chosen, the futures of these refugee populations were as precarious as the peace that settled around them.

THE DIPLOMACY OF DISPOSSESSION

No Iroquois representatives participated in the negotiations that led to the Peace of Paris, the treaty that formally ended the American War for Independence in 1783. Nor had any of the commissioners at the treaty solicited the opinions of the Iroquois before signing it. If they had, they most certainly would have heard an earful about the boundaries the treaty established for the United States. Britain ceded to the United States its claim to all the territory between the Appalachian Mountains and the Mississippi River, roughly doubling the new nation's size and opening the door for its expansion into the Ohio River watershed, the heart of Indian country. The Americans interpreted this land cession as proof of their right of conquest to the trans-Appalachian West. Pleased with their good fortune, they did not bother asking what the region's native inhabitants thought about it. Likewise, the British ministers who ceded this territory did not concern themselves with its ramifications for the Indians. Prime Minister Lord Shelburne, when accused by his political opponents of having abandoned Britain's native allies, responded, "The Indian nations were not abandoned to their enemies; they were remitted to the care of neighbours, whose interest it was as much as ours to cultivate friendship with them, and who were certainly the best qualified for softening and humanizing their hearts."[44]

No one asked Shelburne who was going to "soften and humanize" the hearts of the Americans first. During the 1780s, the United States, still flush with victory over Britain, dictated rather than negotiated its peace terms with the Iroquois. The Americans regarded those Iroquois who had allied with the British as conquered peoples who had forfeited their lands by fighting for the wrong side. Even those Iroquois who had allied with the patriots felt the effects of this American hubris and quickly learned that they, too, were expected to cough up territory in exchange for vague promises of peaceful coexistence. If, as the old saying goes, war is a continuation of politics by other means, then in the decade following the Revolution, the Americans used diplomacy as a continuation of war against the Iroquois. Faced with this new challenge, the Six Nations resorted to the familiar strategies of the council fire to defend themselves, but met with mixed results.

In September 1784, a young Pennsylvanian named Griffith Evans journeyed to Fort Stanwix to take part in a treaty there with the Iroquois. Like Tilghman in 1775, Evans was struck by the strangeness of it all. He witnessed Indian dances and lacrosse games, heard native orators who rivaled ancient Romans for "force, eloquence, and accuracy," and was struck by Indians who exhibited "the greatest decorum and apparent impartiality" when conducting their councils. But Evans made other observations that revealed the profound changes the American Revolution had wrought in Iroquoia. He passed through former Indian and settler communities—places like Oquaga and Cherry Valley—that had been reduced to ashes by wartime raids. He met locals in the Mohawk Valley who held bitter grudges against former native and colonial neighbors and wondered "if their vengeance towards such should never subside."[45]

Another change Evans noticed was in the demeanor of the American treaty commissioners at the council fire. They dispensed with diplomatic niceties and immediately demanded hostages from their Indian guests to guarantee the return of wartime captives. When addressing the Indians in council, the commissioners "were very explicit of pointing in every matter," and this aggressive gesturing "made the Indians stare." The commissioners used language that was "by no means accommodating or flattering; quite unlike what they [the Indians] used to receive." Seasoned Iroquois orators responded to such haughtiness with evident displeasure. Captain Aaron Hill, a Mohawk chief, spoke "very audaciously" when he answered the commissioners' opening speech, "by no means agreeing with what was expected." Seneca chief Cornplanter "made a long and artful speech . . . couched in evasive and undecisive terms." The tensions so evident to Evans did not dissipate until the Oneida chief and longtime American ally Good Peter made a more conciliatory speech that restored a semblance of amity to the proceedings.[46]

The Americans' speeches were part of a purposeful effort to change the tone and character of their diplomacy with the Iroquois. Two months earlier, as New York governor George Clinton had been preparing for his own council with the Iroquois at Fort Stanwix, one of his advisers, attorney James Duane, captured the spirit of the times. He told Clinton that the days of treating the Iroquois as equals were over. "If we adopt the disgraceful system of pensioning, courting and flattering them as great and mighty nations," he warned, ". . . this Revolution in my Eyes will have lost more than half its Value." In order to disabuse the Iroquois of their inflated notions of importance, Duane recommended several unilateral changes in diplomatic protocol. First, Clinton should dispense with using wampum belts and strings to certify council proceedings and replace them instead with signed and sealed documents. Second, he should cease using words or phrases such as "nation, or Six Nations, or Confederates or Council Fire at Onondaga" that "would revive or seem to confirm their former Ideas of Independence." Conducting business on such terms in the past had only emboldened the Iroquois; now it was time to teach them humility. Duane thought it absurd to continue addressing them as "Brethren," which implied equality. The same logic applied to calling a few dozen Mohawks, Tuscaroras, and Onondagas "distinct nations." These people needed to recognize the extremity of their circumstances, to admit that by "entering into a wicked war, they had weakened and destroyed themselves and that the publick opinion of their importance had long since ceased."[47]

Duane was prescribing stiff medicine, but Clinton and his contemporaries were willing to force it down the throats of the Iroquois. Immediately after the war, an intense three-way competition developed between the federal government, the state governments, and private speculators for Iroquois land. A number of contending interests scrambled for access to chiefs to transact their business, but they all shared the fundamental assumption expressed by Duane: The Iroquois had been defeated and their territory rightfully belonged to Americans. Clinton led this effort on behalf of the state of New York. The Articles of Confederation had vested in Congress the power to conduct diplomacy and land purchases with Indians, but had also preserved to the individual states their power over Indians who were "members" of those states. Clinton and Duane regarded the Iroquois as "members" of New York and worked feverishly to cement their state's monopoly over the disposition of Iroquois lands. They met resistance from members of Congress who argued that the Iroquois were not dependents of New York and agents from Massachusetts and Pennsylvania, who had their own designs on Iroquoia.

Clinton lost the first round in this contest in 1784, when the Iroquois who gathered at Fort Stanwix preferred federal treaty commissioners to the New Yorkers. The Confederation Congress, however, lacked the political wherewithal to capitalize on this initial advantage. For most of the 1780s, Clinton cut his own deals to establish New York's claim to Iroquoia. To dispense with Massachusetts' claim (based on that state's seventeenth-century "sea-to-sea" charter from the English Crown), Clinton brokered a deal in which the New Englanders recognized New York's political jurisdiction over the disputed territory in exchange for a preemption right to the sale of the western half of it. Shortly thereafter, the Massachusetts government sold this preemption right to a group of private land speculators led by Oliver Phelps and Nathaniel Gorham, who then undertook a series of purchases to extract title to the land from the Senecas. With the New Englanders out of the way, Clinton focused his acquisition efforts on eastern Iroquoia. He dealt mostly with the Oneidas (many of the patriot-allied Tuscaroras migrated west into the Niagara region after the war), who because of their wartime alliance with the patriots had managed to retain more of their prewar territory and population than the Mohawks, Onondagas, or Cayugas. In a series of treaties undertaken independently of federal supervision, Clinton maneuvered around private speculators and reluctant chiefs to engross millions of acres in the heartland of the Longhouse. By 1790, the Oneidas, Onondagas, and Cayugas held only three small reservations, totaling a mere 4 percent of their prewar territory.[48]

Several factors contributed to the speed with which Clinton and other public and private interests dispossessed the Iroquois. The first was the privation many Iroquois faced after the war. As they had in the past, treaty conferences offered the chance to fill empty bellies, and the rum dispensed at such meetings promised a temporary respite from hard times. Seneca captive Mary Jemison noted how the drinking habits of her adopted kinsfolk changed after the Revolution. Before the war, Indian men had engaged in drinking "frolics," but the women had remained sober so as to minimize the damage to the community. After the war, however, "spirits became common in our tribe, and ha[ve] been used indiscriminately by both sexes," a change that no doubt made it easier for unscrupulous agents to influence native women as well as men when it came time to make land purchases.[49] Clinton and his peers lubricated this postwar diplomacy in other ways. They made liberal grants of land and cash to influential individuals who agreed to help them in their business. Chiefs long accustomed to receiving private presents at treaty conferences now found themselves tucking away cash, personal land grants, and private pensions in return for their cooperation. Agents that the Iroquois had trusted in the past to represent their interests realigned their loyalties after the war and used their skills as linguistic and cultural interpreters to abet rather than resist land cessions.[50]

In the postwar era, private and public agents also used annuities—guaranteed annual payments of cash or goods—to entice Indians into signing away their lands. Annuities promised a perpetual reward for surrendered land, but also perpetual dependence. Oftentimes, government agents and compliant chiefs invested the annuities with a higher purpose by stipulating that they be paid in the form of livestock, tools and technology, and religious and educational instruction to help their recipients make the transition to commercial farming on their reservations. This use of diplomacy to promote the cultural conversion of the Iroquois renewed and deepened divisions that had existed before the Revolution between those who promoted acculturation to white ways and those who argued that survival depended on revitalizing old customs and beliefs.

The generation of Iroquois leaders who had emerged during the Revolution illustrated these changes. Foremost among them was Joseph Brant, who remained firmly allied with the British. Not long after the Peace of Paris, he led the migration of a substantial number of Iroquois and affiliated Indians from Niagara into British Canada, where they settled on reservation lands granted to them on the Grand River in modern Ontario. Brant's political base had always been among the Canajoharie Mohawks, but at Grand River he welcomed Iroquois from throughout the Confederacy as well as non-Iroquois refugees dispossessed by the Revolution. Brant consciously imitated the model of intercultural leadership he had learned from his old patron William Johnson. Anxious to solidify Iroquois control over the new reservation, he invited colonial loyalists to lease lands there and developed an interdependent economy built around the fur trade and commercial farming with them. To strengthen the reservation's bond with the Crown, he made a second trip to London in 1785 to press for reimbursement of loyalist Mohawk claims, and he founded an Anglican chapel and schoolhouse at Grand River. His attachment to the British was evident in other ways as well. Patrick Campbell, a Scottish traveler who visited "Brant's Town" in 1792, marveled at the style in which Brant and his family lived. "Tea was on the table when we came in, served up in the handsomest China plate and every other furniture in proportion.... Supper was served up in the same genteel stile." The Indian inhabitants in Brant's new town did not live as regally, but Campbell thought them "more comfortably lodged than the generality of the poor farmers in my country," and he described their crops and cattle as among the best he had seen in America.[51]

Under Brant's leadership, the Indians at Grand River reestablished a council fire for the Iroquois Confederacy. While the Iroquois population at Grand River was substantial (about one thousand by 1790) and included a cross-section from all six nations, it did not speak for all Iroquois or even all those in Canada. The Mohawks from Tiononderoge had resettled at the Bay of Quinte along the northeastern shore of Lake Ontario and refused entreaties by British officials to remove to Grand River. The old *reserve* of Kahnawake remained in place near Montreal, and just south of it, the reservation of Akwesasne took root, straddling the new U.S.-Canada border along the St. Lawrence. These communities had predominantly Mohawk populations, but like Grand River, they offered refuge to other dispossessed Iroquois and non-Iroquois.

On the U.S. side of the border, three significant populations developed that challenged Grand River's preeminence among the postwar Iroquois. The Oneidas had replaced the Mohawks as the eastern door to the Longhouse, and they worked hard to cultivate alliances with agents who might help defend their lands from the grasping New Yorkers. Initially, they tried to capitalize on their historical ties to the French by welcoming French figures associated with the American Revolution into their councils. The Marquis de Lafayette, the most famous Frenchman to fight in the patriots' cause, attended the 1784 treaty at Fort Stanwix and shortly after sponsored the education of a young Oneida protégé named Peter Otsequette in France. Otsequette returned to his native country a few years later to serve as a liaison between the Oneidas and French. Pierre Penet, another Frenchman who had insinuated himself into the patriot leadership of the Revolution, picked up where Lafayette had left off, presenting himself to the Oneidas as an emissary of the French Crown. His arrival in Oneida country exacerbated a growing divide between warriors who favored Kirkland and his message of Christian conversion and a "pagan party" that rejected Christianity as a tool of dispossession. Penet briefly gained favor among a "French party" of Oneidas who were looking for a diplomatic alternative to Kirkland, a patron who could protect their lands without requiring them to abandon their traditional ways. Unfortunately, Penet's motives were as dubious as his credentials, and his service to the Oneidas consisted chiefly of exposing the land frauds of other speculators so that he could advance his own. The factionalism he and Kirkland inspired among the Oneidas stymied their ability to present a unified defense against the New Yorkers precisely when they needed it most.[52]

The primary center of Iroquois population at the western end of the Longhouse was at Buffalo Creek, near Lake Erie's outlet into the Niagara River. Its population, which numbered about two thousand in 1788, was mostly Seneca, but like other postwar Iroquois communities, it contained a hodgepodge of displaced native peoples.[53] Under the leadership of the Seneca chief Red Jacket, Buffalo Creek rivaled Grand River for population and prestige as the new center of the Iroquois Confederacy. Red Jacket's career as a warrior during the Revolution was not nearly as distinguished as Brant's. More than once, he avoided battle or deserted his comrades in crisis. His wartime conduct earned him the derogatory nickname "Cow-Killer," for an incident in which he allegedly smeared himself with the blood of slaughtered livestock and claimed it to be the blood of his enemies. Despite such an inauspicious start, Red Jacket's reputation rose after the war when he distinguished himself as an orator in treaty councils with the British and Americans. Unlike Brant, Red Jacket looked askance at efforts by missionaries and government agents to transform Iroquois farming, domestic economy, and religion. In negotiating with agents from New York and the federal government, he fought to preserve Iroquois sovereignty over their internal affairs, so that they might continue to govern themselves by traditional means.[54]

Brant encouraged the Indians at Buffalo Creek to remove to Canada with him and consolidate Iroquois power there. Some elected to follow him, but more decided to stay put with Red Jacket, heeding the advice of clan matrons who hedged their bets about where the Iroquois would be most secure. According to Seneca chief Blacksnake, the "feemal party" at Buffalo Creek thought it best that some of the Six Nations remain "on the South Side of the line Between America and Great Britain," so that if the Grand River Iroquois were ever "Drove off their lands," they might "have a share with us and if we Should be Droved off or Deprived of our lands we Shall have a Share with them." Taking that advice to heart, Red Jacket and his followers lighted their version of the Confederacy's council fire at Buffalo Creek and eventually moved it back to its traditional seat at Onondaga in the early nineteenth century.[55]

The last significant Iroquois population center in the United States stretched across the Pennsylvania–New York border in the northern Allegheny River Valley. In the early 1790s, about four hundred Senecas lived in this region, some of them returning to homes they had lost during the Revolution, others electing to live there over Grand River or Buffalo Creek. Their leader was Cornplanter, the son of a colonial fur trader and a Seneca woman who had first risen to prominence as a British-allied warrior during the Revolution. After the war, Cornplanter rivaled Red Jacket and Brant for influence among the western Iroquois, and he opted to move into the Allegheny Valley to consolidate his power. Like Brant, he advocated Iroquois acculturation and negotiated with missionaries and federal agents for material aid that would supposedly turn the Iroquois into prosperous citizen-farmers of the new nation. Cornplanter made such a transition necessary when he sold off Seneca claims to the Allegheny region to Pennsylvania. In return, he received land grants, some of which he resold to speculators but the rest of which became the Cornplanter Tract, a small, privately owned reservation that remained the sole self-governed Indian community in Pennsylvania until the Army Corps of Engineers flooded it in the 1960s to build a hydroelectric dam.[56]

Within a decade after the Revolution, the Iroquois found themselves confined to reservations and separated from each other by growing settler populations and an international border. They responded to the pressure on their lands and sovereignty by consolidating populations, assimilating non-Iroquois into their communities, and cultivating ties with outsiders who could help revive their economies and diplomatic prestige. But old strategies did not always achieve the same results in the postwar world. Private agents and public officials no longer felt compelled to treat the Iroquois as diplomatic equals, and in the frenzied land grabbing that followed the Peace of Paris, many dispensed with any pretense to fair dealing. Iroquois leadership also suffered. Chiefs such as Brant, Red Jacket, Cornplanter, and Good Peter were quite capable of holding their own in councils with their

European counterparts, but new geopolitical borders prevented them from exerting the kind of collective pressure on outsiders that their predecessors had during the heyday of Iroquois power in the mid-eighteenth century. The Six Nations had become by 1790 a collection of culturally related but politically isolated communities dotting the U.S.-Canada borderland, rather than a confederacy capable of unified deliberation and action.

New Nations

During the early 1790s, Iroquois diplomacy enjoyed a revival as the new federal government of the United States asserted itself in the nation's Indian affairs. Under the Articles of Confederation, federal involvement in Indian relations had shrunk to insignificance in the face of the assertive diplomacy practiced by states such as New York. The Constitution ratified in 1788, however, provided the opportunity for establishing federal supremacy in such matters, and in July 1790 Congress passed the Indian Trade and Intercourse Act, which established the framework for federal Indian policy for the next generation. In addition to regulating the Indian trade, this law stipulated that no purchase of Indian land would be valid unless it was conducted in a public treaty under authority of the United States. Henry Knox, the secretary of war in George Washington's first cabinet, oversaw the revitalization of federal Indian policy under this legislation. He rejected out of hand the right of conquest that the state or federal governments had asserted over Indian lands during the 1780s. Knox advised Washington that regardless of the British cession in the Peace of Paris, the Indians still possessed a right of property in that land, and the most cost-effective way to relieve them of it was through purchase at treaty conferences that followed precedents set during the colonial era.[57]

In describing the new government's Indian policy, Knox and Washington expressed a principled opposition to the land-grabbing diplomacy of the Confederation era, but neither acted out of conviction alone. They faced a growing crisis in the Ohio Country, where a powerful and militant confederacy of western nations led by the Shawnees had emerged to resist U.S. expansion beyond the 1768 boundary line set at Fort Stanwix. Federal power in this region was also compromised by the British refusal to evacuate military posts at Niagara, Detroit, and Michilimackinac that were now within U.S. territory. Federal officials feared that an alliance between the western confederacy and pro-British Iroquois would wreak havoc along the nation's poorly defended frontier. It became imperative, therefore, for Knox and Washington to convince the Iroquois that their interests lay in attaching themselves to the new federal government and not the western confederacy or British Canada.

Thus began a courtship that offered the Iroquois deliverance from the hands of state officials and private speculators. In his correspondence with New York's Governor Clinton, Knox asserted a federal primacy in Iroquois diplomacy by making clear that he considered them "independent nations" and not dependent "subjects of any particular State." Washington appointed Timothy Pickering, another fellow officer from the Continental Army, as his agent to the Iroquois, and Pickering brought a soldier's sense of order and decorum to a job that had been sadly lacking it. Pickering became a quick student of Iroquois diplomatic protocol and strove to conform to its rules. His efforts won over Red Jacket, but Brant and Cornplanter were harder to reach. Brant openly encouraged the western confederacy and hoped that an alliance with it might restore some prestige and muscle to the flagging Iroquois. But Brant also saw in the Americans a card he could play against the British and so allowed himself to be courted by American agents. In 1792, he agreed to visit Philadelphia, then the U.S. capital, where he met President Washington and received offers of a pension and land grants if he would resettle on the U.S. side of the border. Brant did not go that far, for his ties to the Iroquois and loyalists at Grand River were still strong, but the visit helped convince him that the western confederacy was too militant for its own good and that diplomacy offered the best means of dealing with the United States.[58]

Cornplanter was less concerned with the western confederacy and the British-American rivalry than either Brant or Red Jacket; he acted first and foremost to cement his hold on the Allegheny River lands that were his home. At Fort Harmar in the Ohio Country in 1789, he signed a controversial land cession that angered the western Indians but brought him a substantial personal reward. In late 1790, he traveled to Philadelphia to receive more favors. Federal officials received him warmly, assuring him that the new government would guarantee the security of his lands.[59] Cornplanter impressed his hosts with his charisma and sobriety, and he spoke eloquently about the injustices visited upon the Iroquois since the end of the war. He expressed his people's interest in learning to "till the ground with the plough, as the white people do," but stated that they must first know "whether you mean to leave us and our children any land to till." In his reply, Washington disavowed the fraudulent dealings of the past (although he pleaded an inability to "disannul treaties formed by the United States, before my administration"), promised the federal government's friendship in the future, and commended Cornplanter's willingness to learn how "the white people plow, and raise so much corn."[60]

In March 1792, another Iroquois delegation called upon Washington in Philadelphia. The Oneidas were heavily represented in this contingent of about fifty chiefs and warriors, but Red Jacket and several other prominent Senecas also attended. Once again, the conversation centered on federal guarantees of Iroquois sovereignty against the claims of New York and private speculators. Now familiar with the drill, Washington stepped into the role of "Father" to the visiting Indians, professing the federal government's desire to be their "friends and protectors" and promising substantial material and technological assistance to ease their transition to commercial agriculture.[61] While Red Jacket pressed for specific endorsements of Iroquois rights over the disposition of their lands, the mere presence of the aged patriot ally Good Peter made for public spectacle and brought an air of nostalgic amity to the proceedings.[62] By the time the delegation left for home, laden with presents and stories, the Washington administration's intensive bout of diplomacy with the Iroquois was already reaping dividends. The Iroquois chiefs had opened a new path to the federal government, which was at last powerful enough to act as a diplomatic "father" should. For the Americans, the payoff came in the refusal of the Iroquois to join in the Indian war in the Ohio Country. In November 1791, the western confederacy destroyed an army led by General Arthur St. Clair into the Wabash Valley. Despite this victory, the Iroquois who had been wined and dined in Philadelphia refused to take up arms and join forces with the western nations.

In a measure aimed at keeping the Iroquois out of the Ohio War, Pickering traveled to Iroquoia in fall 1794 to affirm the federal government's generosity and power. At Canandaigua, the site of a former Seneca town now on the edge of New York's settler frontier, Pickering met with sixteen hundred Iroquois men, women, and children, most of them Senecas from Buffalo Creek and Cornplanter Tract. Such a large assembly called to mind the great treaty conferences of old, when Sir William Johnson had won Iroquois favor by opening his home and storehouses to Indian guests.[63] Pennsylvanian James Emlen was one of four Quakers who attended the Canandaigua conference at the invitation of the federal government. The Quakers enjoyed a reputation for honesty and advocacy of Indian interests that dated back to the era of the Seven Years' War. Their presence at Canandaigua initiated a new era in Quaker-Iroquois relations, in which Quaker agents moved to Oneida and Seneca reservations to distribute private and federal aid and supervise the operation of model farms intended to convert the Iroquois into yeoman farmers.[64]

Emlen's journal from Canandaigua reveals how much the tenor of negotiations there differed from what had occurred at Fort Stanwix ten years earlier. Gone were the blustering and finger-pointing commissioners who considered engaging in native diplomatic rituals beneath the dignity of their office. Instead, Pickering waited patiently for his audience and treated them liberally to provisions when they arrived. He opened the conference with a traditional condolence ritual and mourned a recently murdered Indian with fifteen strings of black wampum. To ease the public negotiations around the council fire, he held private meetings with chiefs and clan matrons in his lodgings and listened attentively as they recited the traditional account of the founding of the Covenant Chain. Led by Cornplanter and Red Jacket, the Indians complained to Pickering of the "haughty and threatening Language" used by the U.S. treaty commissioners at Fort Stanwix in 1784 and at Fort Harmar in 1789, and they asked for the return of stolen land.[65] Pickering brokered a deal with them that for the first time restored some of the lost territory, but more important, he exhibited the kind of personal qualities that the Iroquois had not witnessed in a government official since William Johnson: patience, open-handedness, and a healthy respect for native customs. The treaty ended with Pickering distributing $10,000 worth of presents and promising an increase in the U.S. annuity to the Iroquois from $1,500 to $4,500, so that the two parties might "bury all former differences, and take hold of the chain of friendship."[66]

Pickering's revival of the customs and idioms that had governed Anglo-Iroquois relations in the colonial era was no accident. In conjunction with Henry Knox and George Washington, he had finally learned what previous federal, state, and private negotiators had forgotten in their postwar hubris: The Iroquois, regardless of the political realities surrounding them, insisted on treatment as equals in their diplomatic councils. They would never accord legitimacy to land cessions wrestled from them by intimidation and bribery. Reflecting on the proceedings he witnessed at Canandaigua, Emlen had the same epiphany. The Iroquois, he observed, had a different method of doing business than the Americans. They were "a people remarkably deliberate in all their proceedings," who refused to be hurried or bullied. In some notes at the end of his journal, Emlen expanded on this cultural difference:

> We often complain of their [the Iroquois] being tedious, not considering that they and we estimate time with very different judgments. We are apt to condemn any natural practices which differ from our own, but it requires a greater conquest over prejudices and more penetration than I am Master of clearly, to decide that we are the happier people.[67]

Pickering's patience, generosity, and horse-trading at Canandaigua helped keep the Iroquois out of the Ohio War and brighten the chain that now linked them to the federal government. For the Iroquois, the treaty also established precedent for their sovereign diplomatic relationship with the United States, independent of New York. Modern Iroquois living on reservations in New York trace their claim to political and legal sovereignty to the Canandaigua treaty, although the exact nature of their relationship to the state government of New York remains hotly contested to this day.[68]

That said, it is important to note that the treaty signed at Canandaigua did not end the post-Revolutionary plight of the Iroquois. After the Treaty of Greenville ended the Ohio War in 1795, the federal government turned its attention and largesse away from the Iroquois to focus on other Indian nations. The pacification of the western confederacy meant that it was no longer necessary to curry Iroquois favor, and the neglect of federal officials enabled New York to whittle away at Iroquois landholdings for another generation, until the Cayugas were entirely dispossessed, the Mohawks within the state limited to only the American side of the Akwesasne reservation on the St. Lawrence River, and the Oneidas and Onondagas left with only tiny footholds in their original homelands. The Senecas and Tuscaroras held on to comparatively larger reservations in western New York, but these, too, faced predation well into the nineteenth century. This renewed land-grabbing occurred at treaties without the federal supervision required by the Indian Trade and Intercourse Act, and thus remain at the center of Iroquois land claim cases in present-day New York.[69]

Canandaigua may have provided only a temporary respite for the Iroquois from the tide of dispossession that swept over them as the eighteenth century closed, but its symbolism was important then and remains so today. In 1784, Governor Clinton, James Duane, and other New Yorkers had wanted to see the Iroquois reduced to dependent "members" of their state. Ten years later, thanks to a timely alliance with the federal government, the Iroquois secured their status as nations within a nation.

EPILOGUE

JOHN NORTON'S AMERICAN FRONTIER

IN 1804, ALMOST a century after the visit of the four Indian kings, another Iroquois chief appeared in the streets and drawing rooms of London. Teyoninhokarawen, or John Norton as he was more commonly known, was a protégé of Joseph Brant, and he traveled to England to appeal directly to the Crown for its support in the political battles his mentor was then waging with colonial officials in Canada. Norton did not command the same degree of official attention that Brant had received during his visits to London in 1776 and 1785, nor did he generate as much public excitement as the four Indian kings had in 1710, but he was an exotic article in his own right, and the circumstances of his life up to that point illustrated the unique relationship the Iroquois had developed with Britain during the eighteenth century.

No one was quite sure if Norton was in fact an Indian. He claimed that his father was a Cherokee captured as a boy during the Seven Years' War and carried to Scotland by a British officer. According to Norton, he was born after his father married a Scottish woman, and he grew up working as a printer's apprentice in

Scotland. In 1784, Norton enlisted in the British army and shipped out for the Niagara frontier. After being discharged in 1788, he taught school among the Mohawks at the Bay of Quinte, engaged in some fur trading, and worked as an interpreter after gaining fluency in the Mohawk language. Ultimately, he settled at Grand River, where Joseph Brant adopted him as his nephew. Under Brant's tutelage, Norton became known as a Mohawk chief and intermediary with colonial officials.

Some officials in London doubted Norton's claim to Indian heritage. Back in North America, when Brant's enemies learned of Norton's mission, they sent word to Britain denouncing him as an impostor. Such reports were enough to sink Norton's political mission, but his time in Britain was not wasted. For nearly two years, he enjoyed the company of several prominent Quaker philanthropists, who were then involved in the antislavery movement and missionary work among Native Americans. Impressed by Norton's linguistic skills, familiarity with Indian culture, and refined manners, they became his patrons, and he traveled in their social circles in London and Bath. When not socializing with the well-to-do, Norton translated the Gospel of John into Mohawk, a project encouraged by friends who were benefactors of the Foreign Bible Society. Norton even posed for two portraits, each one showing a dark-complexioned figure dressed in the Indian fashion. He returned to Grand River in 1806 with five hundred copies of his translated Gospel to distribute among the Iroquois.

Norton's visit to Britain had an undeniably theatrical air about it. Questions arose about his background, but who he was did not seem to matter nearly as much as what he appeared to be: an exotic but faithful ally of the Crown from a distant land, a genteel and articulate example of Britain's civilizing mission among the indigenous peoples of its growing empire. As had been the case with the four Indian kings and Brant before him, Bibles figured prominently in the gifts Norton carried home from Britain.

No artifact better illustrated the moral justification upon which the British built their empire, and no Indian peoples in North America had used Christianity to form a stronger bond with the Crown than the Mohawks.

After returning to North America, Norton continued to move between Indian and European worlds. In 1809 he made a thousand-mile journey from Canada into Tennessee and Kentucky, where he claimed to find his kinsfolk among the Cherokees. He returned to Canada in time to participate in the War of 1812 and distinguished himself as a leader of British-allied Iroquois in several battles. After the war, Norton returned to Britain with his family, where he wrote his memoirs. By 1816, he was back at Grand River. Following in the footsteps of Joseph Brant, who had died in 1807, he assumed the life and airs of a country gentleman and continued his work as a translator of scripture and diplomatic broker between the Iroquois and British. In 1823, he killed a man in a duel and became entangled in some legal difficulties. Never one to stay put for long, he put his affairs in order and then set out for the Arkansas Territory. After 1826 he was not heard from again. Presumably, he died somewhere on the southern frontier of the United States.[1]

Norton combined many of the characteristics of the American folk heroes who were his contemporaries: Daniel Boone's wanderlust, Andrew Jackson's swagger, Davy Crockett's relentless self-invention. But Norton's story is not commonly told to American schoolchildren today, and for that matter, neither are those of the Flemish Bastard, Teganissorens, Canasatego, Hendrick, William Johnson, or Molly or Joseph Brant. Those figures, all of whom figured so prominently in the history of the colonial frontier, have been ignored or written out of our history because they did not fit the mold we have created for our frontier heroes. Boone, Jackson, and Crockett were Indian fighters. Their nineteenth-century Native American counterparts—Tecumseh, Black Hawk, Crazy Horse, Geronimo—have entered their own pantheon as Indian

folk heroes who fought back. We Americans prefer frontier stories in which the characters swing tomahawks, not wampum
belts. The sharp contrast those tales draw between red and white
leaves little room for the likes of John Norton.

Norton's life tells a different story, one of acculturation across
racial and geographic borders. The question of his Cherokee
parentage mattered little when compared to his conscious identifi-
cation with the Mohawks. Like William Johnson and Joseph
Brant, he found that by linking arms he could inhabit two worlds
at once and use each to his advantage. Not surprisingly, Norton's
legacy is most evident today in Brantford, Ontario, the town
founded by Joseph Brant at Grand River. There, visitors to Her
Majesty's Royal Chapel of the Mohawks, the church established by
Brant in 1785, can admire eight stained-glass windows depicting
scenes from the history of the Six Nations. One of these, installed
in 1962, portrays the distribution of the Bibles John Norton
brought back from Britain in 1806. It is a window onto another
world, one created when the four Indian kings visited Queen
Anne in 1710. Three centuries later, many people have forgotten
about that world and the partnership and obligations it entailed.
The Iroquois remember.

ACKNOWLEDGMENTS

I would like to thank Colin Calloway and Carolyn Carlson for inviting me to write this book and Ellen Garrison for guiding it through the editorial process. A research fellowship several years ago at the John Carter Brown Library in Providence, Rhode Island, gave me the opportunity to read their unparalleled collection of colonial-era Indian treaties. More recently, a sabbatical leave from Gettysburg College gave me the time to make good on all that research. Susan Roach and Karen Drickamer in the Gettysburg College library made sure I had access to the other materials I needed. Colin Calloway, Eric Hinderaker, and Bill Starna read an early draft of the manuscript, and their thoughtful criticism has helped me sharpen its content and argument. Every page gives evidence of the debt I owe to the community of Iroquois scholars, past and present.

As always, Colleen gave me something to look forward to when I stopped typing and rejoined the living. Caroline, Daniel, and Elizabeth arrived in our life together in alphabetical order and have lent joyful disorder to it ever since. This book is for them.

ABBREVIATIONS

AIA   Peter Wraxall, *An Abridgment of the Indian Affairs Contained in Four Folio Volumes, Transacted in the Colony of New York, from the Year 1678 to the Year 1751*, ed. Charles Howard McIlwain (1915; New York: Benjamin Blom, 1968).

BCC   Daniel K. Richter and James H. Merrell, eds., *Beyond the Covenant Chain: The Iroquois and Their Neighbors in Indian North America, 1600–1800* (Syracuse, N.Y.: Syracuse University Press, 1987).

BF Papers   *The Papers of Benjamin Franklin*, eds. Leonard W. Labaree, W. B. Willcox, Claude Lopez, Barbara B. Oberg, and Ellen R. Cohn, 38 volumes (New Haven, Conn.: Yale University Press, 1959–).

DCB   George W. Brown, David M. Hayne, and Francess Halpenny, eds., *Dictionary of Canadian Biography*, 4 volumes (Toronto: University of Toronto Press, 1966–1979).

DHNY   E. B. O'Callaghan, ed., *The Documentary History of the State of New-York*, 4 volumes (Albany, N.Y.: Weed, Parsons, and Company, 1849–51).

HNAI   Bruce G. Trigger, ed., *The Handbook of North American Indians: Volume 15: The Northeast* (Washington, D.C.: Smithsonian Institution Press, 1978).

MPCP   *Minutes of the Provincial Council of Pennsylvania*, 16 volumes (Harrisburg, 1852–53).

NIL   Robert S. Grumet, ed., *Northeastern Indian Lives, 1632–1816* (Amherst: University of Massachusetts Press, 1996).

NYCD   E. B. O'Callaghan and Berthold Fernow, eds., *Documents Relative to the Colonial History of the State of New-York*, 15 volumes (Albany, N.Y.: Weed, Parsons, and Company, 1853–57).

WJ Papers   *Papers of Sir William Johnson*, eds. James Sullivan, Alexander C. Flick, Milton W. Hamilton, Albert B. Corey, 14 volumes (Albany: University of the State of New York, 1921–62).

WMQ   *William and Mary Quarterly*, third series.

NOTES

PROLOGUE

1. The most detailed study of the four Indian kings' visit is Richmond P. Bond, *Queen Anne's American Kings* (Oxford, England: Clarendon Press, 1952). See also Eric Hinderaker, "The 'Four Indian Kings' and the Imaginative Construction of the First British Empire," *WMQ*, 53 (1996), 487–526.

2. The quotation is from Anglican missionary Reverend Thomas Barclay. See Hinderaker, "Four Indian Kings," 491, n. 8.

3. Hinderaker provides brief biographies of the kings in "Four Indian Kings," 490–91. This information should be supplemented with the additional material in Barbara J. Sivertsen, *Turtles, Wolves, and Bears: A Mohawk Family History* (Bowie, Md.: Heritage Books, 1996), 62–66. Sivertsen's work in Mohawk genealogy has uncovered material concerning the Indian kings' baptisms and has also helped straighten out confusion regarding Hendrick, or Tee Yee Neen Ho Ga Row, and another Mohawk named Hendrick (also known as Theyanoguin), who was prominent in the mid-eighteenth century. See ibid., 33. See also Dean Snow, "Theyanoguin," in *NIL*, 208–26. My thanks to Dean Snow for sharing with me some of his subsequent research that has helped to sort out the confusion about the two Hendricks.

4.   For literary works associated with the four Indian kings, see Bond, *Queen Anne's American Kings*, 66–91.

5.   After returning from England, Hendrick became embroiled in a controversy concerning claims to Mohawk land in the Schoharie Valley. See Sivertsen, *Turtles, Wolves, and Bears*, 72–74.

6.   For the text of the speech, see William Smith, Jr., *The History of the Province of New-York*, ed. Michael Kammen, 2 volumes (Cambridge, Mass.: Belknap Press of Harvard University Press, 1972), 1:136–37.

7.   See Bond, *Queen Anne's American Kings*, 56–65. For the SPG's mission among the Iroquois, see Daniel K. Richter, *Ordeal of the Longhouse: The Peoples of the Iroquois League in the Era of European Colonization* (Chapel Hill: University of North Carolina Press, 1992), 214–35, and John Wolfe Lydekker, *The Faithful Mohawks* (Cambridge, England: Cambridge University Press, 1938).

8.   For the queen's presents, see Hinderaker, "Four Indian Kings," 492.

9.   The classic version of this narrative of the Iroquois experience is Barbara Graymont, *The Iroquois in the American Revolution* (Syracuse, N.Y.: Syracuse University Press, 1972).

10. Francis Jennings discusses the origin and nature of the myth of Iroquois empire in *The Ambiguous Iroquois Empire: The Covenant Chain Confederation of Indian Tribes with English Colonies from its Beginnings to the Lancaster Treaty of 1744* (New York: W.W. Norton, 1984), 10–24. A modern edition of Parkman's history of colonial America is Francis Parkman, *France and England in North America*, 2 volumes (New York: Library of America, 1983). See also Lewis Henry Morgan's influential *League of the Iroquois* (1851; New York: Corinth Books, 1962).

11. For the U.S. Senate resolution, see Philip A. Levy, "Exemplars of Taking Liberties: The Iroquois Influence Thesis and the Problem of Evidence," *WMQ*, 53 (1996), 589. The so-called "Iroquois Influence Thesis"—the argument that Iroquois political ideas and forms left an unacknowledged imprint on modern American political ideas and institutions—has inspired a great deal of critical reaction from scholars. A good introduction to the topic and a source for the relevant citations in the literature is the forum "The 'Iroquois Influence Thesis'—Con and Pro" in *WMQ*, 53 (1996), 587–636. More recently, the two most prolific proponents of the thesis have pushed their claims to global dimensions in Bruce E. Johansen and Donald A. Grinde, Jr., "Reaching the Grassroots: The Worldwide Diffusion of Iroquois Democratic Traditions," *American Indian Culture and Research Journal* 27 (2003), 77–91.

12. On the reception of Indian "kings" in London, see Nancy Shoemaker, *A Strange Likeness: Becoming Red and White in Eighteenth-Century North America* (New York: Oxford University Press, 2004), 35–60.

CHAPTER 1

1. Whitfield J. Bell, Jr., ed., *A Journey from Pennsylvania to Onondaga in 1743, by John Bartram, Lewis Evans, and Conrad Weiser* (Barre, Mass.: Imprint Society, 1973), 56–60. This book contains the separate journals Bartram, Evans, and Weiser kept of their visit to Onondaga. Evans's is the briefest of the three and limits itself mostly to observations concerning his interests in geography.

2. Ibid., 116, 131–32.

3. *HNAI*, 322–23, and Dean R. Snow, *The Iroquois* (Malden, Mass.: Blackwell Publishers, 1994), 10–33.

4. References to the Iroquois creation story can be found in colonial-era sources, but the most complete versions were not recorded until the late nineteenth century. No single version is considered authoritative. The version presented here is condensed from the one found in Hazel Hertzberg, *The Great Tree and the Longhouse: The Culture of the Iroquois* (New York: Macmillan, 1966). For analysis of the creation story and its continuing relevance to the Iroquois, see William N. Fenton, *The Great Law and the Longhouse: A Political History of the Iroquois Confederacy* (Norman: University of Oklahoma Press, 1998), 34–50.

5. For early descriptions of Iroquois towns and longhouses, see Harmen Meyndertsz van den Bogaert, *A Journey into Mohawk and Oneida Country, 1634–1635: The Journal of Harmen Meyndertsz van den Bogaert*, transl. and ed. by Charles T. Gehring and William A. Starna (Syracuse, N.Y.: Syracuse University Press, 1988), 3–5, 7–9, 12–13, and Adriaen Cornelissen van der Donck, "Description of New Netherland, 1653," in *In Mohawk Country: Early Narratives about a Native People*, eds. Dean R. Snow, Charles T. Gehring, and William A. Starna (Syracuse, N.Y.: Syracuse University Press, 1996), 110–13.

6. Daniel K. Richter, *Ordeal of the Longhouse: The Peoples of the Iroquois League in the Era of European Colonization* (Chapel Hill: University of North Carolina Press, 1992), 15–24, and Snow, *The Iroquois*, 39–54.

7. Francis Jennings, *The Ambiguous Iroquois Empire: The Covenant Chain Confederation of Indian Tribes with English Colonies, from Its Beginnings to the Lancaster Treaty of 1744* (New York: W.W. Norton, 1984), 36–39.

8. Fenton provides an in-depth discussion of Iroquois clans and moieties in *The Great Law and the Longhouse*, 24–31. For briefer but also valuable treatments see Snow, *The Iroquois*, 55–57, and Richter, *Ordeal of the Longhouse*, 20–22.

9. José António Brandão, ed., *Nation Iroquoise: A Seventeenth-Century Ethnography of the Iroquois* (Lincoln: University of Nebraska Press, 2003), 63–65.

10. The eighteenth-century French missionary Joseph François Lafitau explained the connection between diplomacy and trade in *Customs of the American Indians Compared with the Customs of Primitive Times*, 2 volumes, ed. and transl. by William N. Fenton and Elizabeth L. Moore (Toronto: Champlain Society, 1974), 2: 173–85. The treaty council quotation is from *AIA*, 195.

11. Richter, *Ordeal of the Longhouse*, 28–29.

12. Bogaert, *Journey into Mohawk and Oneida Country*, 13.

13. *HNAI*, 418.

14. Jennings traces the evolution of myths surrounding Iroquois power in colonial America in *The Ambiguous Iroquois Empire*, 10–24. For the relevant literature on the Iroquois Influence Thesis, see "The 'Iroquois Influence Thesis'—Con and Pro," in *WMQ*, 53 (1996), 587–636. Particularly useful for exposing erroneous ideas about the Iroquois imprint on the Constitution is Elisabeth Tooker, "The United States Constitution and the Iroquois League," *Ethnohistory* 35 (1988), 305–36.

15. Snow, *The Iroquois*, 57–66.

16. Fenton traces the history of the Deganawidah Epic from oral tradition to written accounts in *The Great Law and the Longhouse*, 51–103. See also Anthony F. C. Wallace, "The Dekanawideh Myth Analyzed as the Record of a Revitalization Movement," *Ethnohistory* 5 (1958), 118–30.

17. On the role of women in Iroquois politics, see Elisabeth Tooker, "Women in Iroquois Society," in *Extending the Rafters: Interdisciplinary Approaches to Iroquoian Studies*, eds. Michael K. Foster, Jack Campisi, and Marianne Mithun (Albany: State University of New York Press, 1984), 109–23.

18. See Richter, *Ordeal of the Longhouse*, 39–44, and Snow, *The Iroquois*, 60–66.

19. The condolence and requickening ceremonies and their significance within the Iroquois League's operation are succinctly described in *HNAI*, 437–40. See also Fenton, *Great Law and the Longhouse*, 135–40, 180–90.

20. Bell, *A Journey from Pennsylvania to Onondaga in 1743*, 73–74, 121–22.

21. Fenton examined the names of chiefs recorded in the Bartram and Weiser journals and found no evidence of the traditional titles associated with the sachems of the Grand Council, suggesting that the chiefs who conducted business with Weiser were not acting in that capacity. See Fenton, *Great Law and the Longhouse*, 418–19. It is certainly possible that some of the chiefs who gathered for this meeting were also members of the Grand Council.

22. Bell, *A Journey from Pennsylvania to Onondaga in 1743*, 91.

23. For analysis of the archaeological evidence of the effects of the fur trade on Iroquois material culture, see James W. Bradley, *Evolution of the Onondaga Iroquois: Accommodating Change, 1500–1655* (Syracuse, N.Y.: Syracuse University Press, 1987), 120–65.

24. See Bogaert, *Journey into Mohawk and Oneida Country*, 4, 7, 9, 62.

25. Richter, *Ordeal of the Longhouse*, 75–104.

26. For a critical re-evaluation of the "Beaver Wars," see José António Brandão, *Your Fyre Shall Burn No More: Iroquois Policy toward New France and Its Native Allies to 1701* (Lincoln: University of Nebraska Press, 1997).

27. For analysis of the cultural imperatives behind Iroquois warfare and captivity, see Daniel K. Richter, "War and Culture: The Iroquois Experience," *WMQ*, 40 (1983), 528–59, and Brandão, *Your Fyre Shall Burn No More*, 31–61.

28. Several eyewitness accounts from the seventeenth century provide detailed descriptions of the Iroquois' treatment of captives. The most important source in this regard is the *Jesuit Relations*, the annual reports written and compiled by Jesuit missionaries in North America. See Reuben Gold Thwaites, ed., *The Jesuit Relations and Allied Documents: Travels and Explorations of the Jesuit Missionaries in New France, 1610–1791*, 73 volumes (1896–1901; New York: Pageant Books, 1959). These and other eyewitness accounts are included in the narratives of Isaac Jogues, Francesco Giuseppe Bressani, Pierre Esprit Radisson, and Wentworth Greenhalgh in Snow, Gehring, and Starna, *In Mohawk Country*, 14–37, 47–55, 62–92, 188–92. Also see Lafitau, *Customs of the American Indians*, 2:148–64.

29. The impact of colonial-era epidemics on the Iroquois is summarized in Snow, *The Iroquois*, 80–89, 94–111.

30. For the Huron experience with the French and Iroquois, see Bruce G. Trigger, *The Children of Aataentsic: A History of the Huron People to 1660*, 2 volumes (1976; Kingston and Montreal: McGill-Queen's University Press, 1987).

31. Brandão, *Your Fyre Shall Burn No More*, 62–91.

32. Ibid., 53.

33. See Jérôme Lalemant, "Of the Condition of the Country of the Iroquois, and of Their Cruelties, 1659–1660," in Snow, Gehring, and Starna, *In Mohawk Country*, 133.

34. Brandão, *Your Fyre Shall Burn No More*, 78.

35. Ibid., 92–116.

36. Richter, *Ordeal of the Longhouse*, 105–32, and Allan Greer, *Mohawk Saint: Catherine Tekakwitha and the Jesuits* (New York: Oxford University Press, 2005), 89–110.

37. For biographical details on the Flemish Bastard, see *DCB*, 1:307–8.

38. *Jesuit Relations*, 41:87.

39. *NYCD*, 3:435.

40. On the economic nature of the Dutch relationship with the Iroquois, see Allen Trelease, *Indian Affairs in Colonial New York: The Seventeenth Century* (1960; Lincoln: University of Nebraska Press, 1997), 112–37.

41. See Narrative of Pierre Esprit Radisson in Snow, Gehring, and Starna, *In Mohawk Country*, 89.

42. I have paraphrased this rendition of the Covenant Chain story, and taken the direct quotations therein from the version told by the Onondaga chief Canasatego at the Lancaster Treaty of 1744. See *A Treaty, Held at the Town of Lancaster, in Pennsylvania . . . with the Indians of the Six Nations, in June, 1744* (Philadelphia: B. Franklin, 1744), 11–13. See also Jennings, *The Ambiguous Iroquois Empire*, 47–57, 145–71.

43. William N. Fenton provides a detailed analysis of how the Iroquois used the condolence ritual as a framework for their treaty-making in "Structure, Continuity, and Change in the Process of Iroquois Treaty-Making," in *The History and Culture of Iroquois Diplomacy: An Interdisciplinary Guide to the Treaties of the Six Nations and Their League*, eds. Francis Jennings et al. (Syracuse, N.Y.: Syracuse University Press, 1985), 3–36.

44. On the significance of wampum in Iroquois League ceremonies, see *HNAI*, 422–24.

45. See Richter, *Ordeal of the Longhouse*, 140, 165.

46. See Snow, *The Iroquois*, 125, and Mary A. Druke, "Linking Arms: The Structure of Iroquois Intertribal Diplomacy," in *BCC*, 29–40.

47. See Jennings, *The Ambiguous Iroquois Empire*, 191–94, and *NYCD*, 3:418.

48. See Cadwallader Colden, *The History of the Five Indian Nations Depending on the Province of New York* (1727, 1747; Ithaca, N.Y.: Cornell University Press, 1958), 159.

49. Richard White provides a cogent explanation of the meaning of "father" in French-Indian diplomacy in *The Middle Ground: Indians, Empires, and Republics in the Great Lakes Region, 1650–1815* (Cambridge, England: Cambridge University Press, 1991), 36–40.

50. Richter, *Ordeal of the Longhouse*, 131.

51. Ibid., 133–61.

52. See the report on this expedition by Jean Bochart de Champigny, Sieur de Noroy et de Verneuil, in Snow, Gehring, and Starna, *In Mohawk Country*, 231–37.

53. Richter, *Ordeal of the Longhouse*, 162–89, and Jennings, *The Ambiguous Iroquois Empire*, 194–210.

54. See Snow, *The Iroquois*, 110, and Brandão, *Your Fyre Shall Burn No More*, 126.

CHAPTER 2

1. For Montour's background and career as a trader and diplomat, see *NYCD*, 5:65, and Daniel K. Richter, *Ordeal of the Longhouse: The Peoples of the Iroquois League in the Era of European Colonization* (Chapel Hill: University of North Carolina Press, 1992), 223–25. For a geographic and cultural description of the *pays d'en haut*, see Richard White, *The Middle Ground: Indians, Empires, and Republics in the Great Lakes Region, 1650–1815* (Cambridge, England: Cambridge University Press, 1991), x–xv.

2. For biographical details on Joncaire, see *DCB*, 2:125–27. For Vaudreuil's orders to Joncaire, see *NYCD*, 9:902.

3. The details of Montour's murder, as reported by three Onondaga messengers to Albany, are found in *AIA*, 64–65.

4. See Richter, *Ordeal of the Longhouse*, 105–61.

5. Richter, *Ordeal of the Longhouse*, 180–85. For the diplomatic career of Teganissorens, see *DCB*, 2:619–23.

6. *NYCD*, 4:79–80.

7. Ibid., 9:578.

8. Ibid., 9:577–84.

9. Cadwallader Colden, *The History of the Five Indian Nations Depending on the Province of New York* (1727,1747; Ithaca, N.Y.: Cornell University Press, 1958), 140.

10. Ibid., 151.

11. *NYCD*, 9:582, 584.

12. Colden, *History of the Five Indian Nations*, 152–60.

13. *NYCD*, 4:122.

14.   See Richter, *Ordeal of the Longhouse*, 195–206.

15.   *NYCD*, 9:708–11.

16.   *AIA*, 33–34; *NYCD*, 4:727–46.

17.   *NYCD*, 4:893.

18.   On the character of seventeenth-century Albany, see Janny Venema, *Beverwijck: A Dutch Village on the American Frontier, 1652–1664* (Albany: State University of New York Press, 2003), and Donna Merwick, *Possessing Albany, 1630–1710: The Dutch and English Experiences* (Cambridge, England: Cambridge University Press, 1990). For Montreal, see W. J. Eccles, *The Canadian Frontier, 1534–1760* (New York: Holt, Rinehart, and Winston, 1969), 111–15.

19.   On the Albany fur market, see Merwick, *Possessing Albany*, 77–101; for Montreal's annual trading fair, see White, *The Middle Ground*, 24–25, 105–8.

20.   *Propositions made by the Five Nations of Indians, viz. The Mohaques, Oneydes, Onnondages, Cayouges & Sinnekes, to his Excellency Richard Earl of Bellomont, Capt General and Governour in chief his Majesties Province of New-York, &c. in Albany, the 20th of July, Anno Dom. 1698* (New York: William Bradford, 1698), 2.

21.   *NYCD*, 4:714.

22.   Ibid., 7:362.

23.   For the history of these *reserves*, see *HNAI*, 469–73; for their relations with their colonial French neighbors, see Evan Haefeli and Kevin Sweeney, *Captors and Captives: The 1704 French and Indian Raid on Deerfield* (Amherst: University of Massachusetts Press, 2003), 63–73.

24.   See Daniel K. Richter, "'Some of Them . . . Would Always Have a Minister With Them': Mohawk Protestantism, 1683–1719," *American Indian Quarterly* 16 (1992), 471–84.

25.   For a retelling of the 1701 Montreal treaty, see Gilles Havard, *The Great Peace of Montreal of 1701*, trans. Phyllis Aronoff and Howard Scott (McGill-Queen's University Press, 2001), 111–59.

26.   Pierre F. X. Charlevoix, *History and General Description of New France*, transl. John Gilmary Shea, 6 volumes (1744; Chicago: Loyola University Press, 1962), 5:145–48.

27.   Ibid., 5:149–51.

28.   *NYCD*, 9:722–25.

29.   Ibid., 4:905.

30.   Ibid., 4:908–11. For the significance of the deed and map to British imperial pretensions in North America, see José António Brandão and William A. Starna, "'Some things may slip out of your memory and be forgott': The 1701 Deed and Map of Iroquois Hunting Territory Revisited," *New*

York History 86 (2005), 417–33. For a modern map and description of the region in question, see José António Brandão and William A. Starna, "The Treaties of 1701: A Triumph of Iroquois Diplomacy," *Ethnohistory* 43 (1996), 210, 226–27.

31. The classic statement of this view is Anthony F. C. Wallace, "Origins of Iroquois Neutrality: The Grand Settlement of 1701," *Pennsylvania History* 24 (1957), 223–35. For thoughtful re-evaluations of Wallace's thesis, see Richard Haan, "The Problem of Iroquois Neutrality: Suggestions for Revision," *Ethnohistory* 27 (1980), 317–30, and Brandão and Starna, "The Treaties of 1701," 229–32.

32. On the Tree of Peace metaphor, see William N. Fenton, *The Great Law and the Longhouse: A Political History of the Iroquois Confederacy* (Norman: University of Oklahoma Press, 1998), 185–86.

33. For Indian paths traveled by the Iroquois, see Paul A. W. Wallace, *Indian Paths of Pennsylvania* (Harrisburg: Pennsylvania Historical and Museum Commission, 1971). On the perils and difficulties faced by Indian and colonial diplomats on these paths, see James H. Merrell, *Into the American Woods: Negotiators on the Pennsylvania Frontier* (New York: Norton, 1999), 128–40.

34. Historians have debated the exact nature of the Iroquois role as middle-men in the western fur trade. Allen W. Trelease dismantled earlier pre-sentations of the Iroquois as economic middlemen in this trade in "The Iroquois and the Western Fur Trade: A Problem of Interpretation," *Mississippi Valley Historical Review* 49 (1962), 32–51. Richard Haan described the role of diplomatic middlemen sought by the Iroquois in the western fur trade in "The Problem of Iroquois Neutrality," 317–30. Richard Aquila convincingly describes the diplomatic role of the Iroquois in open-ing Albany's trade to the western Algonquians in *The Iroquois Restoration: Iroquois Diplomacy on the Colonial Frontier, 1701–1754* (Detroit: Wayne State University Press, 1983), 129–45.

35. See *AIA*, 66–68.

36. See Cadwallader Colden, "History of the Five Nations, Continuation, 1707–1720," in *Collections of the New-York Historical Society* 68 (1935), 385–86.

37. Colden, "History of the Five Nations, Continuation," 418.

38. For the Niagara and Oswego trade, see Thomas Elliot Norton, *The Fur Trade in Colonial New York, 1686–1776* (Madison: University of Wiscon-sin Press, 1974), 152–73, and Richter, *Ordeal of the Longhouse*, 262–68.

39. The story of the repatriated Oneida adoptee is related in Colden, "History of the Five Nations, Continuation," 360. On Iroquois relations with

Kahnawake, see Haefeli and Sweeney, *Captors and Captives*, 68–73, and John Demos, *The Unredeemed Captive: A Family Story from Early America* (New York: Vintage Books, 1994), 120–39.

40. *AIA*, 145–48.

41. For episodes of diplomacy involving the Kahnawake Indians in Albany, see *AIA*, 44, 53, 58–59, 80–81.

42. On the Albany-Montreal trade, see Norton, *Fur Trade in Colonial New York*, 121–51, and David Arthur Armour, *The Merchants of Albany, New York, 1686–1760* (New York: Garland Publishing, 1986), 126–55. For its role in the wider Anglo-French competition for the western fur trade, see White, *The Middle Ground*, 119–28.

43. For a study of the Susquehannocks in the precontact and colonial eras, see Barry C. Kent, *Susquehanna's Indians* (1984; Harrisburg: Pennsylvania Historical and Museum Commission, 2001).

44. See Aquila, *Iroquois Restoration*, 156–59.

45. On the River Indians, see Neal Salisbury, "Toward the Covenant Chain: Iroquois and Southern New England Algonquians, 1637–1684," in *BCC*, 69–71.

46. See Francis Jennings, "William Penn: Good Lord!" in *World of William Penn*, eds. Richard S. Dunn and Mary Maple Dunn (Philadelphia: University of Pennsylvania Press, 1986), 195–214, and Francis Jennings, "'Pennsylvania Indians' and the Iroquois," *BCC*, 80–84.

47. See Jennings, "Pennsylvania's Indians and the Iroquois," 83–84, and Aquila, *Iroquois Restoration*, 158–59.

48. See Fenton, *Great Law and the Longhouse*, 382–97, and Douglas W. Boyce, "'As the Wind Scatters the Smoke': The Tuscaroras in the Eighteenth Century," in *BCC*, 151–63. According to Peter Wraxall, New Yorkers were informed of the Tuscaroras' adoption as the sixth nation in May 1723; see *AIA*, 144.

49. Colden described the Tuscarora migration as consisting of "600 fighting men and 400 old men and boys." See Colden, "History of the Five Nations, Continuation," 414. A conservative estimate to include women is this total would yield at least another one thousand emigrants.

50. *NYCD*, 5:387. The minutes do not identify the Indian who delivered this speech, but they do identify Teganissorens as the Indians' spokesman in the previous exchange of speeches. A year earlier, Teganissorens had made a similar comment in a speech to New York agents visiting Onondaga, calling the Tuscaroras "Indians [who] went out heretofore from us." See *NYCD*, 5:376.

51. See David Landy, "Tuscarora Among the Iroquois," *HNAI*, 15:519–20.

52. Daniel K. Richter offers a useful model for distinguishing between the Iroquois League and the Confederacy in "Ordeals of the Longhouse: The Five Nations in Early American History," in *BCC*, 11–27.

53. See Fenton, *Great Law and the Longhouse*, 396, 493–94.

54. The minutes of this conference do not identify the speakers of the Indians' speeches. Teganissorens's name, however, appears on one of the documents brought home by the Virginia delegation. See Fenton, *Great Law and the Longhouse*, 395. Cadwallader Colden attended this meeting as a member of Governor Burnet's council. It may have been here that he witnessed Teganissorens speak, an occasion he described in his book on the Iroquois ("He was grown old when I saw him, and heard him speak: he had a great Fluency in speaking, and a graceful Elocution"). See Colden, *History of the Five Indian Nations*, 140.

55. *NYCD*, 5:657–61.

56. Ibid., 5:665.

57. Ibid., 5:677–81. For further discussion of the incident that prompted this diplomacy, see John Smolenski, "The Death of Sawantaeny and the Problem of Justice on the Frontier," in *Friends and Enemies in Penn's Woods: Indians, Colonists, and the Racial Construction of Pennsylvania*, eds. William A. Pencak and Daniel K. Richter (University Park: Penn State University Press, 2004), 104–28.

58. On Catawba relations with the Iroquois, see James H. Merrell, "'Their Very Bones Shall Fight': The Catawba-Iroquois Wars," in *BCC*, 115–33.

59. *NYCD*, 5:669–75.

60. Ibid., 5:666.

CHAPTER 3

1. Witham Marshe, "Journal of the Treaty Held with the Six Nations by the Commissioners of Maryland, and other Provinces, at Lancaster, In Pennsylvania, June, 1744," in Massachusetts Historical Society, *Collections*, first series, 7:178–79. Hereinafter cited as Marshe, "Journal of the Treaty."

2. *A Treaty, Held at the Town of Lancaster, in Pennsylvania, by the Honourable the Lieutenant-Governor of the Province, and the Honourable the Commissioners for the Provinces of Virginia and Maryland, with the Indians of the Six Nations, in June, 1744* (Philadelphia: B. Franklin, 1744); Benjamin Franklin to William Strahan, July 4, 1744, *The Papers of Benjamin Franklin*, eds. Leonard W. Labaree et al., 38 volumes (New Haven, Conn.: Yale University Press, 1959–), 2:411.

3. *The Treaty Held with the Indians of the Six Nations, at Lancaster, in Pennsylvania, in June, 1744. To which is prefix'd, An Account of the first Confederacy of the Six Nations, their present Tributaries, Dependents, and Allies, and their Religion, and Form of Government* (Williamsburg, Va.: William Parks, 1744), iii–xii.

4. William N. Fenton, *Great Law and the Longhouse: A Political History of the Iroquois Confederacy* (Norman: University of Oklahoma Press, 1998), 434–35.

5. James H. Merrell, "Some Thoughts on Colonial Historians and American Indians," *WMQ* 46 (1989), 94–119.

6. Richard White, *The Middle Ground: Indians, Empires, and Republics in the Great Lakes Region, 1650–1815* (Cambridge, England: Cambridge University Press, 1991).

7. *Treaty Held with the Indians of the Six Nations, at Lancaster*, 20. On the similarities and differences between Indian and European views of treaties, see Francis Jennings, *The Invasion of America: Indians, Colonialism, and the Cant of Conquest* (New York: W.W. Norton, 1975), 120–24, and Nancy Shoemaker, *A Strange Likeness: Becoming Red and White in Eighteenth-Century North America* (New York: Oxford University Press, 2004), 61–81.

8. Fenton, *Great Law and the Longhouse*, 294–95, 411.

9. For the roots of Iroquois treaty-making in Iroquois condolence rituals, see the essays in Part I of Francis Jennings, William N. Fenton, Mary A. Druke, and David R. Miller, eds., *The History and Culture of Iroquois Diplomacy: An Interdisciplinary Guide to the Treaties of the Six Nations and Their League* (Syracuse, N.Y.: Syracuse University Press, 1985), 3–124.

10. James H. Merrell, *Into the American Woods: Negotiators on the Pennsylvania Frontier* (New York: W.W. Norton, 1999), 253. For attendance figures at other intercolonial treaty conferences in the mid-eighteenth century, see Timothy J. Shannon, *Indians and Colonists at the Crossroads of Empire: The Albany Congress of 1754* (Ithaca, N.Y.: Cornell University Press, 2000), 127–28.

11. Merrell, *Into the American Woods*, 129–36.

12. See "Conrad Weiser's Report of his Journey to Onondaga on the Affairs of Virginia," in Whitfield J. Bell, Jr., ed., *A Journey from Pennsylvania to Onondaga in 1743, by John Bartram, Lewis Evans, and Conrad Weiser* (Barre, Mass.: Imprint Society, 1973), 116.

13. See Michael K. Foster, "On Who Spoke First at Iroquois-White Councils: An Exercise in the Method of Upstreaming," in *Extending the Rafters: Interdisciplinary Approaches to Iroquoian Studies*, eds. Michael K. Foster, Jack

Campisi, and Marianne Mithun (Albany: State University of New York Press, 1984), 183–207.

14. In 1736, the governor of Pennsylvania warned a party of Iroquois approaching Philadelphia for a treaty conference to delay their arrival because of a recent outbreak of smallpox. See *A Treaty of Friendship held with the Chiefs of the Six Nations, at Philadelphia, in September and October, 1736* (Philadelphia: B. Franklin, 1737), 4–9. In 1757, Iroquois visiting Pennsylvania refused to come to Philadelphia because they were "afraid of Sickness" and instead recommended Lancaster as a treaty site. See *Minutes of Conferences, held with Indians, at Harris's Ferry, and at Lancaster, in March, April, and May, 1757* (Philadelphia: B. Franklin and D. Hall, 1757), 6.

15. Helga Doblin and William A. Starna, transl. and ed., *The Journals of Christian Daniel Claus and Conrad Weiser: A Journey to Onondaga, 1750* (Philadelphia: American Philosophical Society, 1994), 19.

16. See *A Treaty, between his Excellency The Honourable George Clinton . . . and The Six United Indian Nations, and other Indian Nations, depending on the Province of New-York. Held at Albany in the Months of August and September, 1746* (New York: James Parker, 1746), 18–20.

17. See Shannon, *Indians and Colonists at the Crossroads of Empire*, 120–24.

18. Marshe, "Journal of the Treaty," 177, 184, 192, 201.

19. William N. Fenton, "Structure, Continuity, and Change in the Process of Iroquois Treaty Making," in Jennings et al., *History and Culture of Iroquois Diplomacy*, 21–30.

20. Marshe, "Journal of the Treaty," 181.

21. For the woods' edge greetings involved in Weiser's 1743 journey to Onondaga, see Bell, ed., *Journey from Pennsylvania to Onondaga*, 49, 56–59. Also see the description of Weiser's arrival in Onondaga with a group of Moravian missionaries in 1745 in William M. Beauchamp, ed., *Moravian Journals Relating to Central New York, 1745–1766* (1916; Bowie, Md.: Heritage Books, 1999), 12.

22. Marshe, "Journal of the Treaty," 194.

23. See Beverly McAnear, ed., "Personal Accounts of the Albany Congress of 1754," *Mississippi Valley Historical Review* 39 (1953): 738, n. 50.

24. On the use of the "one-dish" metaphor in Indian diplomacy, see Jennings et al., *History and Culture of Iroquois Diplomacy*, 117.

25. Marshe, "Journal of the Treaty," 185, 195.

26. McAnear, "Personal Accounts of the Albany Congress," 738–39.

27. See Shannon, *Indians and Colonists at the Crossroads of Empire*, 43–44.

28. *A Treaty held with the Ohio Indians at Carlisle, in October, 1753* (Philadelphia: B. Franklin and D. Hall, 1753), 3.

29.   *Minutes of Conferences held with the Indians, at Easton, in the Months of July and November, 1756* (Philadelphia: B. Franklin and D. Hall, 1757), 16.

30.   "Journal of Isaac Norris, during a Trip to Albany in 1745, and an Account of a Treaty Held There in October of that Year," *Pennsylvania Magazine of History and Biography* 27 (1903), 25–27, and *An Account of the Treaty Held at the City of Albany, in the Province of New-York . . . with the Indians of the Six Nations, in October, 1745* (Philadelphia: B. Franklin, 1746), 14–15.

31.   Marshe, "Journal of the Treaty," 179, 200.

32.   *NYCD*, 6:293.

33.   Carl Bridenbaugh, ed., *Gentleman's Progress: The Itinerarium of Dr. Alexander Hamilton 1744* (Chapel Hill: University of North Carolina Press, 1948), 112, 141. See also Timothy J. Shannon, "Dressing for Success on the Mohawk Frontier: Hendrick, William Johnson, and the Indian Fashion," *WMQ* 53 (1996), 13–42.

34.   Marshe, "Journal of the Treaty," 180.

35.   Marshe, "Journal of the Treaty," 179–80, 187. For the role of Africans in Anglo-Iroquois relations, see William B. Hart, "Black 'Go-Betweens' and the Mutability of 'Race,' Status, and Identity on New York's Pre-Revolutionary Frontier," in *Contact Points: American Frontiers from the Mohawk Valley to the Mississippi, 1750–1830*, eds. Andrew R. L. Cayton and Fredrika J. Teute (Chapel Hill: University of North Carolina Press, 1998), 88–113.

36.   On women's participation in treaty conferences, see Merrell, *Into the American Woods*, 68–71, and Alison Duncan Hirsch, "Indian, *Métis*, and Euro-American Women on Multiple Frontiers," in *Friends and Enemies in Penn's Woods: Indians, Colonists, and the Racial Construction of Pennsylvania*, eds. William A. Pencak and Daniel K. Richter (University Park: Penn State University Press, 2004), 69–72. For a reference to their work in making wampum belts, see *Minutes of Conferences held with the Indians, at Easton, in the Months of July and November, 1756* (Philadelphia: B. Franklin and D. Hall, 1757), 13–14.

37.   *WJ Papers*, 3:707–8.

38.   See William N. Fenton, ed., "The Journal of James Emlen Kept on a Trip to Canandaigua, New York," *Ethnohistory* 12 (1965), 306.

39.   On the career of Madame Montour, see Alison Duncan Hirsch, "'The Celebrated Madame Montour': 'Interpretess' across Early American Frontiers," *Explorations in Early American Culture* 4 (2000), 81–112.

40.   For the career of Andrew Montour, see James H. Merrell, "'The Cast of his Countenance': Reading Andrew Montour," in *Through a Glass Darkly: Reflections on Personal Identity in Early America*, eds. Ronald Hoffman,

Mechal Sobel, and Fredrika J. Teute (Chapel Hill: University of North
Carolina Press, 1997), 13–39, and Nancy L. Hagedorn, " 'Faithful, Knowing, and Prudent': Andrew Montour as Interpreter and Cultural Broker,
1740–1772," in *Between Indian and White Worlds: The Cultural Broker*, ed.
Margaret Connell Szasz (Norman: University of Oklahoma Press, 1994),
44–60.

41. Marshe, "Journal of the Treaty," 189–90.

42. Marshe, "Journal of the Treaty," 180, 193.

43. For Joncaire's career, see Frank A. Severance, "The Story of Joncaire: His
Life and Times on the Niagara," *Publications of the Buffalo Historical Society* IX (1906), 81–219; for Claessen's, see Nancy L. Hagedorn, "Brokers
of Understanding: Interpreters as Agents of Cultural Exchange in
Colonial New York," *New York History* 76 (1995), 382–85.

44. On interpreters as cultural brokers, see Nancy L. Hagedorn, " 'A Friend
to Go Between Them': The Interpreter as Cultural Broker During
Anglo-Iroquois Councils, 1740–1770," *Ethnohistory* 35 (1988), 60–80, and
Merrell, *Into the American Woods*, 54–105.

45. *The Treaty Held with the Indians of the Six Nations at Philadelphia in July
1742, To which is Prefix'd An Account of the first Confederacy of the Six Nations, their present Tributaries, Dependents, and Allies* (London: Reprinted
and sold by T. Sowle Raylton and Luke Hinde, n.d. [1744?]), 34.

46. Hagedorn, "A Friend to Go Between Them," 62.

47. Merrell, *Into the American Woods*, 71–95.

48. Cadwallader Colden, *The History of the Five Indian Nations Depending on
the Province of New York* (1727, 1747; Ithaca, N.Y.: Cornell University
Press, 1958), xi.

49. On the use of kinship terms in treaty conferences, see Jennings et al.,
History and Culture of Iroquois Diplomacy, 119–20.

50. See Marshe, "Journal of the Treaty," 188–89, 191–92, 196–97, and
Shannon, *Indians and Colonists at the Crossroads of Empire*, 165–69.

51. See *Treaty Held with the Indians of the Six Nations at Philadelphia in July
1742*, 33, and *Minutes of Conferences, held with Indians, at Harris's Ferry, and
at Lancaster, in March, April, and May, 1757*, 20.

52. Benjamin Franklin, *The Autobiography and Other Writings*, ed. Kenneth
Silverman (New York: Penguin Classics, 1986), 135–36.

53. Peter C. Mancall, *Deadly Medicine: Indians and Alcohol in Early America*
(Ithaca, N.Y.: Cornell University Press, 1995), 63–84.

54. Theodore Atkinson's journal from the Albany treaty conference in 1754
describes getting "very merry" with his fellow colonial delegations; see
McAnear, "Personal Accounts of the Albany Congress," 730, 733, 737–39.

Likewise, Witham Marshe got "extremely merry" in Lancaster in 1744. See Marshe, "Journal of the Treaty," 185.

55. Marshe, "Journal of the Treaty," 183, 185–86.

56. See Journal of Conrad Weiser at the Albany Treaty of 1745, in Julian P. Boyd, ed., *Indian Treaties Printed by Benjamin Franklin, 1736–1762* (Philadelphia: Historical Society of Pennsylvania, 1938), 311.

57. See *Treaty Held with the Indians of the Six Nations, at Lancaster, in Pennsylvania, in June, 1744*, 59, 73.

58. See, for example, *The Treaty Held with the Indians of the Six Nations at Philadelphia in July 1742*, 28.

59. Ibid., 16–17, 19.

CHAPTER 4

1. *NYCD*, 6:781–82.

2. See *HNAI*, 213–24, and Anthony F. C. Wallace, *King of the Delawares: Teedyuscung, 1700–1763* (1949; Syracuse, N.Y.: Syracuse University Press, 1990), 1–17.

3. See James H. Merrell, "Shamokin, 'the very seat of the Prince of darkness': Unsettling the Early American Frontier," in *Contact Points: American Frontiers from the Mohawk Valley to the Mississippi, 1750–1830*, eds. Andrew R. L. Cayton and Fredrika J. Teute (Chapel Hill: University of North Carolina Press, 1998), 16–59, and James H. Merrell, "Shickellamy, 'A Person of Consequence,' " in *NIL*, 227–57.

4. *Two Indian Treaties The One held at Conestogoe in May 1728. And the other at Philadelphia in June following* (Philadelphia: Andrew Bradford, n.d.), 7–16, and Richard Aquila, *The Iroquois Restoration: Iroquois Diplomacy on the Colonial Frontier, 1701–1754* (Detroit: Wayne State University Press, 1983), 169–71.

5. Francis Jennings, "'Pennsylvania Indians' and the Iroquois," in *BCC*, 86–90.

6. *A Treaty of Friendship held with the Chiefs of the Six Nations, at Philadelphia, in September and October, 1736* (Philadelphia: B. Franklin, 1737).

7. See Francis Jennings, *The Ambiguous Iroquois Empire: The Covenant Chain Confederation of Indian Tribes with the English Colonies from its Beginnings to the Lancaster Treaty of 1744* (New York: Norton, 1984), 320–24, 330–40.

8. *MPCP*, 4:579–80.

9. Jennings, "Pennsylvania Indians and the Iroquois," 79–80, and Nancy Shoemaker, *A Strange Likeness: Becoming Red and White in*

Eighteenth-Century North America (New York: Oxford University Press, 2004), 107–14.

10. Paul A. W. Wallace, *Conrad Weiser, 1696–1760: Friend of Colonist and Mohawk* (Philadelphia: University of Pennsylvania Press, 1945), 153–70, 217–28.

11. See William A. Starna, "The Diplomatic Career of Canasatego," in *Friends and Enemies in Penn's Woods: Indians, Colonists, and the Racial Construction of Pennsylvania*, eds. William Pencak and Daniel K. Richter (University Park: Penn State University Press, 2004), 144–63.

12. *The Treaty Held with the Indians of the Six Nations, at Lancaster, in Pennsylvania, in June, 1744. To which is prefix'd, An Account of the first Confederacy of the Six Nations, their present Tributaries, Dependents, and Allies, and their Religion, and Form of Government* (Williamsburg, Va.: William Parks, 1744), 13–14.

13. Ibid., 16–17.

14. Ibid., 18–19.

15. Ibid., 42.

16. Ibid., 58, 68.

17. For a good case study of the Canajoharie Mohawks' tense relations with their colonial neighbors, see David L. Preston, "George Klock, the Canajoharie Mohawks, and the Good Ship *Sir William Johnson*," *New York History* 86 (2005), 473–99.

18. On the SPG mission to the Mohawks, see John Wolfe Lydekker, *The Faithful Mohawks* (Cambridge, England: Cambridge University Press, 1938). For its impact on the Mohawks of Tiononderoge, see Daniel K. Richter, *Ordeal of the Longhouse: The Peoples of the Iroquois League in the Era of European Colonization* (Chapel Hill: University of North Carolina Press, 1992), 229–35.

19. Helga Doblin and William A. Starna, transl. and ed., *The Journals of Christian Daniel Claus and Conrad Weiser: A Journey to Onondaga, 1750* (Philadelphia: American Philosophical Society, 1994), 35.

20. Georgiana C. Nammack, *Fraud, Politics, and the Dispossession of the Indians: The Iroquois Land Frontier in the Colonial Period* (Norman: University of Oklahoma Press, 1969), 22–69.

21. See Thomas Elliot Norton, *The Fur Trade in Colonial New York, 1686–1776* (Madison: University of Wisconsin Press, 1974), 121–51.

22. Timothy J. Shannon, *Indians and Colonists at the Crossroads of Empire: The Albany Congress of 1754* (Ithaca, N.Y.: Cornell University Press, 2000), 34.

23. *AIA*, 193.

24. See, for example, Cadwallader Colden's indictment of the Albany-Montreal trade in his 1724 "Memoir on the Fur Trade," *NYCD*, 7:726–33.

25. *NYCD*, 6:296–300.

26. Shannon, *Indians and Colonists at the Crossroads of Empire*, 32–34.

27. The quoted description of Hendrick comes from Dr. Alexander Hamilton in Carl Bridenbaugh, ed., *Gentleman's Progress: The Itinerarium of Dr. Alexander Hamilton 1744* (Chapel Hill: University of North Carolina Press, 1948), 112. The fullest biography of Hendrick is Dean R. Snow, "Theyanoguin," in *NIL*, 208–26. Since its publication, however, Snow and other scholars have concluded that Theyanoguin/Hendrick was not the same person as Tee Yee Neen Ho Ga Row/Hendrick, the Mohawk chief who was one of the "four Indian kings" earlier in the eighteenth century. See Shannon, *Indians and Colonists at the Crossroads of Empire*, 30, n. 40.

28. Wallace, *Conrad Weiser*, 226–27.

29. *NYCD*, 6:294.

30. On Johnson's Irish background and early life, see Fintan O'Toole, *White Savage: William Johnson and the Invention of America* (New York: Farrar, Straus and Giroux, 2005), 16–69.

31. [New York], *A Treaty between his Excellency . . . George Clinton . . . and the Six . . . Nations* (New York: J. Parker, 1746), 7–8.

32. *WJ Papers*, 1:59–61.

33. Shannon, *Indians and Colonists at the Crossroads of Empire*, 36–45.

34. *WJ Papers*, 1:342.

35. *NYCD*, 6:437–52. On the Mohawks' participation in King George's War, see Ian K. Steele, *Betrayals: Fort William Henry and the "Massacre"* (New York: Oxford University Press, 1990), 18–27.

36. *WJ Papers*, 1:342–44.

37. Wallace, *Conrad Weiser*, 329–30.

38. *NYCD*, 6:781–88.

39. William N. Fenton, *Great Law and the Longhouse: A Political History of the Iroquois Confederacy* (Norman: University of Oklahoma Press, 1998), 452, 459.

40. Michael N. McConnell, *A Country Between: The Upper Ohio Valley and Its Peoples, 1724–1774* (Lincoln: University of Nebraska Press, 1992), 5–46.

41. On the Anglo-French competition for the Ohio Country's fur trade, see Eric Hinderaker, *Elusive Empires: Constructing Colonialism in the Ohio Valley, 1673–1800* (Cambridge, England: Cambridge University Press, 1997), 3–45.

42.   See Frank A. Severance, "The Story of Joncaire: His Life and Times on the Niagara," *Publications of the Buffalo Historical Society* IX (1906), 214–19.

43.   *NYCD*, 9:1065.

44.   Aquila, *Iroquois Restoration*, 166–93.

45.   *MPCP*, 5:146–47.

46.   Ibid., 5:148–49.

47.   On Croghan's background and early career, see Nicholas B. Wainwright, *George Croghan: Wilderness Diplomat* (Chapel Hill: University of North Carolina Press, 1959), 3–46.

48.   *MPCP*, 5:307–10, 312–15.

49.   Ibid., 5:348–58.

50.   Richard White, *The Middle Ground: Indians, Empires, and Republics in the Great Lakes Region, 1650–1815* (Cambridge, England: Cambridge University Press, 1991), 206–8.

51.   *MPCP*, 5:530–32, 536.

52.   Ibid., 5:398–400, and Wallace, *Conrad Weiser*, 277–85.

53.   *MPCP*, 5:478.

54.   Ibid., 5:474–76, and Starna, "Diplomatic Career of Canasatego," 146–47.

55.   See Merrell, "Shickellamy, 'A Person of Consequence,' " 247–53, and Starna, "Diplomatic Career of Canasatego," 160–63.

CHAPTER 5

1.   John Shebbeare, *Lydia, or Filial Piety. A Novel*, 4 volumes (London: J. Scott, 1755), 1:3–10; 2:1–13; 3:257–83; 4:9–17; 111–17.

2.   Troy Bickam, *Savages within the Empire: Representations of American Indians in Eighteenth-Century Britain* (Oxford, England: Clarendon Press, 2005), 65–109.

3.   For Iroquois perspectives on the Seven Years' War, see Francis Jennings, *Empire of Fortune: Crowns, Colonies, and Tribes in the Seven Years' War in America* (New York: W.W. Norton, 1988); Jon Parmenter, "After the Mourning Wars: The Iroquois as Allies in Colonial North American Campaigns, 1676–1760," *WMQ* 64 (2007), 39–82; and Timothy J. Shannon, "War, Diplomacy, and Culture: The Iroquois Experience in the Seven Years' War," in *Cultures in Conflict: The Seven Years' War in North America*, ed. Warren Hofstra (Lanham, Md.: Rowman and Littlefield, 2007), 79–103.

4.   For the 1726 treaty, see *NYCD*, 5:799–801.

5. See Timothy J. Shannon, *Indians and Colonists at the Crossroads of Empire: The Albany Congress of 1754* (Ithaca, N.Y.: Cornell University Press, 2000), 141–201.

6. *NYCD*, 6:862–63, 870.

7. The Pennsylvanians' land purchase negotiations are detailed in the report made by Richard Peters and John Penn to James Hamilton, August 5, 1754, in *Pennsylvania Archives*, 9 series (Harrisburg, Pa.: J. Severns and Company, 1852–1935), series 4, 2:697–724.

8. Penn Papers, Indian Affairs, 4:7, Historical Society of Pennsylvania, Philadelphia.

9. On the Susquehannah Company's and Lydius's actions at the Albany Congress, see *Pennsylvania Archives*, series 4, 2:697–98, 723–24, and *The Susquehannah Company Papers*, eds. Julian P. Boyd and R. J. Taylor, 11 volumes (Ithaca, N.Y.: Cornell University Press, 1962–71), 1:101–21.

10. *NYCD*, 6:884, and Beverly McAnear, ed. "Personal Accounts of the Albany Congress of 1754," *Mississippi Valley Historical Review* 39 (1953), 738.

11. Shannon, *Indians and Colonists at the Crossroads of Empire*, 208–20.

12. *BF Papers*, 5:392–93.

13. *NYCD*, 6:917–18, and *WJ Papers*, 1:465–66. See also John R. Alden, "The Albany Congress and the Creation of the Indian Superintendencies," *Mississippi Valley Historical Review* 27 (1940), 193–210.

14. *NYCD*, 6:964.

15. The suspicions of other Iroquois about Johnson's partnership with the Mohawks had first been expressed at a conference in Onondaga in the fall of 1753. See *WJ Papers*, 9:110–20, and *NYCD*, 6:866–68.

16. *NYCD*, 6:978, 980, 983, 986, 988.

17. Hendrick's appearance at the battle was also described in *A Prospective View of the Battle fought near Lake George, on the 8th of Sept. 1755, between 2000 English, with 250 Mohawks, under the Command of General Johnson and 2500 French and Indians* . . ., T. Jefferys, sculp., and Samuel Blodget, delin. (London, 1756).

18. Society of Colonial Wars in the State of New York, *Daniel Claus' Narrative of His Relations with Sir William Johnson and Experiences in the Lake George Fight* (New York, 1904), 13–14.

19. Ian K. Steele, *Betrayals: Fort William Henry and the "Massacre"* (New York: Oxford University Press, 1990), 28–56.

20. *NYCD*, 6:1020, and *WJ Papers*, 2:434–35, 448–51, 508–10.

21. *NYCD*, 6:1010.

22. *WJ Papers* 2:80, and Steele, *Betrayals*, 54.

23. *NYCD*, 6:965.
24. Ibid., 10:265–69.
25. Ibid., 10:345–47.
26. Picquet's work with the Iroquois is described in *Adventure in the Wilderness: The American Journals of Louis Antoine de Bougainville, 1765–1760*, transl. and ed. Edward P. Hamilton (1964; Norman: University of Oklahoma Press, 1990), 16–17, 30, 103.
27. Ibid., 103.
28. *NYCD*, 10:448.
29. On the Fort William Henry campaign, see Steele, *Betrayals*, 57–128. On Franco-Iroquois relations during the war, see Jon Parmenter, "*L'Arbre de Paix*: Eighteenth-Century Franco-Iroquois Relations," *French Colonial History* 4 (2003), 63–80.
30. *A Treaty held with the Ohio Indians at Carlisle, in October, 1753* (Philadelphia: B. Franklin and D. Hall, 1753), 3–4.
31. *MPCP*, 6:148–50, 156–58.
32. See Beverly Bond, ed., "The Captivity of Charles Stuart, 1755–57," *The Mississippi Historical Review* 13 (1926), 63–64.
33. *MPCP*, 6:685–87.
34. Matthew C. Ward, *Breaking the Backcountry: The Seven Years' War in Virginia and Pennsylvania, 1754–1765* (Pittsburgh, Pa.: University of Pittsburgh Press, 2003), 36–58.
35. Anthony F. C. Wallace, *King of the Delawares: Teedyuscung, 1700–1763* (1949; Syracuse, N.Y.: Syracuse University Press, 1990), 1–56.
36. William N. Fenton, *Great Law and the Longhouse: A Political History of the Iroquois Confederacy* (Norman: University of Oklahoma Press, 1998), 485–89.
37. *Minutes of Conferences held with the Indians, at Easton, in the Months of July and November, 1756* (Philadelphia: B. Franklin and D. Hall, 1757), 8, 10–11. For a discussion of Teedyuscung's speeches at Easton in 1756 and the difficulties inherent in deciphering their meaning, see James H. Merrell, "'I Desire All That I Have Said . . . May Be Taken Down Aright': Revisiting Teedyuscung's 1756 Treaty Council Speeches," *WMQ* 63 (2006), 777–826.
38. For an astute analysis of Teedyuscung's behavior and personality, see Wallace, *King of the Delawares*, 181–82, 192–207.
39. Ibid., 113, and *Minutes of Conferences held with the Indians, at Easton, 1756*, 13–14.
40. *Minutes of Conferences held with the Indians, at Easton, 1756*, 23, and Ward, *Breaking the Backcountry*, 137–41.

41. Francis Jennings, *Empire of Fortune: Crowns, Colonies, and Tribes in the Seven Years' War in America* (New York: W.W. Norton, 1988), 371–72.

42. *Minutes of Conferences, held with the Indians, at Harris's Ferry, and at Lancaster, in March, April, and May, 1757* (Philadelphia: B. Franklin and D. Hall, 1757), 3–6, 12.

43. *Minutes of Conferences, held with the Indians, at Easton, 1757*, 3, 9.

44. *The Minutes of a Treaty held at Easton, in Pennsylvania, in October, 1758* (Woodbridge, N.J.: James Parker, 1758), 4.

45. "Benjamin Chew's Journal of a Journey to Easton, 1758," in Julian P. Boyd, ed., *Indian Treaties Printed by Benjamin Franklin, 1736–1762* (Philadelphia: Historical Society of Pennsylvania, 1938), 312, 314.

46. *Minutes of a Treaty held at Easton, 1758*, 12–13, 18–19.

47. Ibid., 20.

48. Wallace, *King of the Delawares*, 239–66.

49. Fred Anderson, *Crucible of War: The Seven Years' War and the Fate of Empire in British North America, 1754–1766* (New York: Alfred A. Knopf, 2000), 50–66.

50. See Michael N. McConnell, "Pisquetomen and Tamaqua: Mediating Peace in the Ohio Country," *NIL*, 273–94.

51. *NYCD*, 7:388–92.

52. Ibid., 10:981–90, and Anderson, *Crucible of War*, 330–39.

53. For the Indians' disgust with Amherst's orders, see *WJ Papers*, 13:190, and for the total numbers involved at the start and end of the campaign, see *WJ Papers*, 10:180–85.

54. On the meaning of Johnson's Indian name, see *WJ Papers*, 13:192. On Johnson Hall, see Fintan O'Toole, *White Savage: William Johnson and the Invention of America* (New York: Farrar, Straus and Giroux, 2005), 280–82.

55. Johnson detailed his disbursements in his accounts; see, for example, the detailed account for the period between November 1756 and March 1757 in *WJ Papers*, 9:644–58, during which he spent £5,142 on his Indian agency.

56. Ibid., 13:223–25.

57. Ibid., 3:492. On the western Indians' admission into the Covenant Chain, see Jon Parmenter, "Pontiac's War: Forging New Links in the Anglo-Iroquois Covenant Chain, 1758–1766," *Ethnohistory* 44 (1997), 617–54.

58. *WJ Papers*, 3:476.

59. See Gregory Evans Dowd, *A Spirited Resistance: The North American Indian Struggle for Unity, 1745–1815* (Baltimore: Johns Hopkins University Press, 1992), 27–35.

60. See Gregory Evans Dowd, *War under Heaven: Pontiac, The Indian Nations, and the British Empire* (Baltimore: Johns Hopkins University Press, 2002), 54–147.

61. *NYCD*, 7:557–59.

62. Anderson, *Crucible of Empire*, 565–71. See also Dorothy V. Jones, *License for Empire: Colonialism by Treaty in Early America* (Chicago: University of Chicago Press, 1982), 58–92.

63. Peter Marshall, "Colonial Protest and Imperial Retrenchment: Indian Policy, 1764–1768," *Journal of American Studies* 5 (1971), 1–17.

64. *NYCD*, 7:726–35, and Jones, *License for Empire*, 75–87.

65. Jack M. Sosin, *Whitehall and the Wilderness: The Middle West in British Colonial Policy, 1760–1775* (Lincoln: University of Nebraska Press, 1961), 165–80.

66. For the treaty proceedings and a map of the boundary line, see *NYCD*, 8:111–37. For a clear explication of the public and private interests involved, see Peter Marshall, "Sir William Johnson and the Treaty of Fort Stanwix, 1768," *Journal of American Studies* 1 (1967), 149–79. The reference to the cash piled on the table is from *NYCD*, 8:134.

67. See Colin G. Calloway, *The Shawnees and the War for America* (New York: Viking, 2007).

CHAPTER 6

1. For the details of Brant's visit, see Isabel Thompson Kelsay, *Joseph Brant, 1743–1807: Man of Two Worlds* (Syracuse, N.Y.: Syracuse University Press, 1984), 161–74. The *London Chronicle* reports may be found in the issues of February 29, March 2, and March 19, 1776. Boswell's piece on Brant appeared in the July 1776 issue of the *London Magazine*.

2. *London Magazine*, July 1776, 339. An engraving of the portrait of Brant commissioned by Boswell also appeared in this issue.

3. For Johnson's estimate of Iroquois populations in 1763, see *NYCD*, 7:582.

4. Ibid., 7:471–79.

5. Ibid., 8:361–62.

6. See Samuel Kirkland, *The Journals of Samuel Kirkland: Eighteenth-Century Missionary to the Iroquois, Government Agent, Father of Hamilton College*, ed. Walter Pilkington (Clinton, New York: Hamilton College, 1980), 98.

7. See Lois M. Feister and Bonnie Pulis, "Molly Brant: Her Domestic and Political Roles in Eighteenth-Century New York," in *NIL*, 295–320.

8. See Alan Taylor, *The Divided Ground: Indians, Settlers, and the Northern Borderland of the American Revolution* (New York: Alfred A. Knopf, 2006), 46–52.

9. Pilkington, *Journals of Kirkland*, 3.

10. Ibid., 23–24.

11. Taylor, *Divided Ground*, 52–61, and William N. Fenton, *Great Law and the Longhouse: A Political History of the Iroquois Confederacy* (Norman: University of Oklahoma Press, 1998), 548–56. On the relocation of the Stockbridge community to Oneida country in the post-Revolutionary period, see Patrick Frazier, *The Mohicans of Stockbridge* (Lincoln: University of Nebraska Press, 1992), 238–45.

12. Taylor, *Divided Ground*, 43–44, and Fenton, *Great Law and the Longhouse*, 539–40.

13. Pilkington, *Journals of Kirkland*, 67, 82–83, 93–94, and Taylor, *Divided Ground*, 58–68.

14. The patriots described the conflict as a "family quarrel" to the Iroquois in a speech delivered in August 1775. See *NYCD*, 8:619.

15. Ibid., 8:635–36. See also Barbara Graymont, *Iroquois in the American Revolution* (Syracuse, N.Y.: Syracuse University Press, 1972), 64–69.

16. *NYCD*, 8:605–8.

17. Graymont, *Iroquois and the American Revolution*, 71.

18. Samuel Harrison, ed., *Memoir of Lieut. Col. Tench Tilghman* (Albany, N.Y.: J. Munsell, 1876), 79–101.

19. Ibid., 83–84, 92–93.

20. Ibid., 82, 86.

21. Ibid., 91–96.

22. Ibid., 94.

23. *NYCD*, 8:615.

24. Ibid., 8:610, 621–24.

25. Ibid., 8:625–26.

26. Graymont, *Iroquois in the American Revolution*, 82–84, 92–94.

27. *NYCD*, 8:689.

28. Graymont, *Iroquois in the American Revolution*, 108–16.

29. Ibid., 113.

30. See James Seaver, ed., *A Narrative of the Life of Mrs. Mary Jemison* (1824; Syracuse, N.Y.: Syracuse University Press, 1990), 50–51.

31. Thomas S. Abler, ed., *Chainbreaker: The Revolutionary War Memoirs of Governor Blacksnake, as told to Benjamin Williams* (Lincoln: University of Nebraska Press, 2005), 76–77. Claus's description of Brant's influence is cited in Graymont, *Iroquois in the American Revolution*, 159.

32. *NYCD*, 8:720–21.

33. *Narrative of Mary Jemison*, 52–53. Graymont describes the Battle of Oriskany in detail in *Iroquois in the American Revolution*, 129–43.

34. Graymont, *Iroquois in the American Revolution*, 142–45.

35. *NYCD*, 8:725, and Graymont, *Iroquois in the American Revolution*, 145–49, 157–62.

36. See Karim M. Tiro, "A 'Civil' War? Rethinking Iroquois Participation in the American Revolution," *Explorations in Early American Culture* 4 (2000), 148–65.

37. The reports on Oquaga's destruction are cited in Colin G. Calloway, *The American Revolution in Indian Country: Crisis and Diversity in Native American Communities* (Cambridge, England: Cambridge University Press, 1995), 124–25.

38. Graymont, *Iroquois in the American Revolution*, 183–89.

39. For the Iroquois perspective on the Sullivan-Clinton Campaign, see ibid., 192–222; for the Continental Army's perspective, see Joseph R. Fischer, *A Well-Executed Failure: The Sullivan Campaign Against the Iroquois, July–September 1779* (Columbia: University of South Carolina Press, 1997).

40. On the Niagara refugees, see Calloway, *American Revolution in Indian Country*, 135–40.

41. *Narrative of Mary Jemison*, 60.

42. Graymont, *Iroquois in the American Revolution*, 234–36.

43. Taylor, *Divided Ground*, 108.

44. Quoted in Graymont, *Iroquois in the American Revolution*, 262.

45. Hallock F. Raup, "Journal of Griffith Evans, 1784–1785," *Pennsylvania Magazine of History and Biography* 65 (1941), 206, 209, 213, 215, 218, 221.

46. Ibid., 211–14.

47. *Early American Indian Documents: Treaties and Laws, 1607–1789*, ed. Alden T. Vaughan, 10 volumes (Bethesda, Md.: University Publications of America, 1979–94), 10:299–301.

48. Taylor, *Divided Ground*, 142–202.

49. Seaver, *Narrative of Mrs. Mary Jemison*, 126–27.

50. See, for example, Karim Tiro's discussion of the postwar loyalties of interpreter James Dean in "James Dean in Iroquoia," *New York History* 80 (1999), 391–422, and Taylor's discussion of the postwar career of Samuel Kirkland in *Divided Ground*, 208–14.

51. Patrick Campbell, *Travels in the Interior Inhabited Parts of North America in the Years 1791 and 1792*, ed. H. H. Langton (Toronto: The Champlain Society, 1937), 165–67. See also Taylor, *Divided Ground*, 119–28.

52. See Laurence M. Hauptman, *A Conspiracy of Interests: Iroquois Dispossession and the Rise of New York State* (Syracuse, N.Y.: Syracuse University Press, 1999), 35–55; Anthony Wonderley, "'Good Peter's Narrative of Several Transactions Respecting Indian Lands': An Oneida View of

Dispossession, 1785–1788," *New York History* 84 (2003), 237–73; and J. David Lehman, "The End of the Iroquois Mystique: The Oneida Land Cession Treaties of the 1780s," *WMQ*, 47 (1990), 523–47.

53. Taylor, *Divided Ground*, 177.

54. Christopher Densmore, *Red Jacket: Iroquois Diplomat and Orator* (Syracuse, N.Y.: Syracuse University Press, 1999), 11–22, 60–75.

55. Abler, *Chainbreaker*, 168. See also Anthony F. C. Wallace, *Death and Rebirth of the Seneca* (New York: Random House, 1969), 162–68.

56. Wallace, *Death and Rebirth of the Seneca*, 168–72, 337. On the forced relocation of the Senecas living on the Cornplanter Tract, see Joy A. Bilharz, *The Allegany Senecas and Kinzua Dam: Forced Relocation Through Two Generations* (Lincoln: University of Nebraska Press, 1998).

57. For Knox's role in shaping federal Indian policy, see Francis Paul Prucha, *American Indian Policy in the Formative Years: The Indian Trade and Inter-course Acts, 1790–1834* (Cambridge, Mass.: Harvard University Press, 1962), 43–49. For the impact of this policy on the Iroquois, see Jack Campisi, "National Policy, States' Rights, and Indian Sovereignty: The Case of the New York Iroquois," in *Extending the Rafters: Interdisciplinary Approaches to Iroquoian Studies*, eds. Michael K. Foster, Jack Campisi, and Marianne Mithun (Albany: State University of New York Press, 1984), 95–108, and William A. Starna, "'The United States will protect you': The Iroquois, New York, and the 1790 Nonintercourse Act," *New York History* 83 (2002), 4–33.

58. Taylor, *Divided Ground*, 242–60, 275–77.

59. Ibid., 246–49.

60. Abler, *Chainbreaker*, 245, 256. Cornplanter's speeches and Washington's responses to them are reproduced in their entirety ibid., 238–59.

61. Ibid., 262–63.

62. Taylor, *Divided Ground*, 270–73.

63. Ibid., 288–93.

64. On the Quaker missions among the Oneidas, Senecas, and other Indians in the early national era, see Karim M. Tiro, "'We Wish to Do You Good': The Quaker Mission to the Oneida Nation, 1790–1840," *Journal of the Early Republic* 26 (2006), 353–76; Robert S. Cox, "Supper and Celibacy: Quaker-Seneca Reflexive Missions," in *The Sixty Years' War for the Great Lakes, 1754–1814*, eds. David Curtis Skaggs and Larry L. Nelson (East Lansing: Michigan State University Press, 2001), 243–74; and Daniel K. Richter, "'Believing That Many of the Red People Suffer Much for Want of Food': Hunting, Agriculture, and a Quaker Construction of Indianness in the Early Republic," *Journal of the Early Republic* 19 (1999), 601–28.

65. William N. Fenton, ed., "The Journal of James Emlen Kept on a Trip to Canandaigua, New York," *Ethnohistory* 12 (1965), 302–16.

66. Ibid., 316.

67. Ibid., 291, 333.

68. William A. Starna and Jack Campisi, "On the Road to Canandaigua: The Treaty of 1794," *American Indian Quarterly* 19 (1995), 467–90.

69. On post-Canandaigua land treaties in New York, see Hauptman, *Conspiracy of Interests*, 101–220, and George C. Shattuck, *The Oneida Land Claims: A Legal History* (Syracuse, N.Y.: Syracuse University Press, 1991).

EPILOGUE

1. This account of Norton's life is based on Carl F. Klinck and James J. Talman, eds., *The Journal of Major John Norton, 1816* (Toronto: Champlain Society, 1970), xiii–xcvii.

INDEX